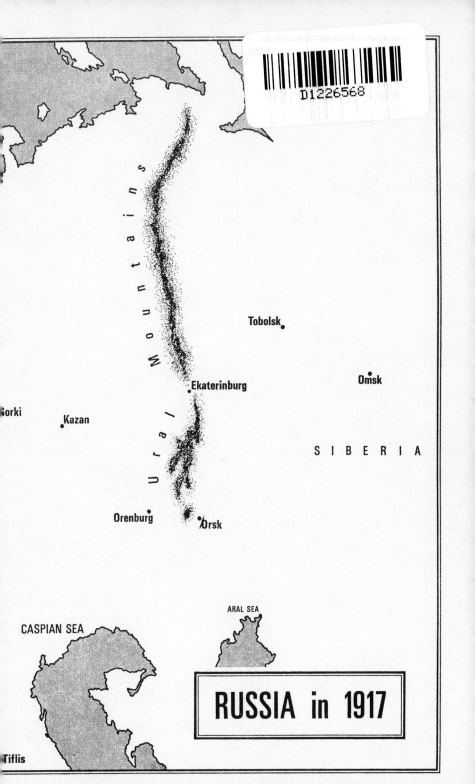

Tobolsk

Omsk

Ekaterinburg

Gorki

Kazan

Ural Mountains

S I B E R I A

Orenburg

Orsk

ARAL SEA

CASPIAN SEA

RUSSIA in 1917

Tiflis

THE DIARY OF A DIPLOMAT
IN RUSSIA, 1917–1918

THE DIARY OF A DIPLOMAT
IN RUSSIA, 1917–1918

Louis de Robien

Translated from the French by
CAMILLA SYKES

PRAEGER PUBLISHERS

New York · Washington

BOOKS THAT MATTER

Published in the United States of America in 1970
by Praeger Publishers, Inc., 111 Fourth Avenue,
New York, N.Y. 10003

Library of Congress Catalog Card Number: 73-109483

Printed in Great Britain

Comte Louis de Robien was twenty-six when he was appointed to the French Embassy in Tsarist St. Petersburg. Three years later, in 1917, he began his diary in which he set down the events which grew into the Menshevik and Bolshevik revolutions of March and October and swept away the Old Order in Russia.

The book is a unique document, being first and foremost an eye-witness account of the violent and terrible day-to-day happenings in St. Petersburg at the outbreak of the revolution: the burning of the Law Courts, the murder of General Stackelbarg and wholesale slaughter of officers, the abdication of the Tsar and his removal with his family to prison leading to their murder in Ekaterinburg, the imprisonment of the Grand Dukes, and the cholera epidemic. As such it is an important historical document; and later, when the French Mission had removed to Archangel under the protection of the American troops, it is the outspoken and intimate journal of a diplomat in direct contact with events in the capital and the anti-Red government. We read, for instance, of the sacking of the British Embassy and the killing of the Naval attaché, and of the first hand reports from Czech soldiers about the murders at Ekatrienburg.

The diary also records the young diplomats frank opinion of the leading personalities of the revolution: Kerensky, the Tsar, Tereschenko, the Grand Duke Michael, Lenin and Trotsky. Opinions which are of special fascination as showing the impact of the revolution on the mind of the old school.

This book is a document of inestimable value for the student of the 1917 revolutions.

ILLUSTRATIONS

Petrograd, Thursday 8th March 1917

During the last few days the discontent of the populace, weary of queueing outside every shop for the necessities of life, has greatly increased. It is certain that ever since the winter of 1914 the poor have suffered from bad food supplies, but the situation does not seem to have worsened recently in this respect.

It is to be feared that revolutionary agitators and German agents are profiting by the conditions. It is said that there is a certain amount of unrest in the suburbs. I went out at about four o'clock to take Friquet for a walk, and went as far as the Nevsky Prospekt. I met a small group of demonstrators who were, however, quite quiet and surrounded by police. Everything is perfectly calm and the passers-by watch them with amused sympathy.

In Sadovaya Street the trams have stopped. . . . I don't know whether it is because of other demonstrations, or simply because of a power breakdown. On my way back to the Embassy I meet Etienne de Beaumont,[1] with whom I walk a few yards and who tells me that there is talk of popular movements in the outskirts.

That evening, a big dinner at the Embassy:

Robien

Etienne de Beaumont	Chambrun
Katargy	Nani Mocenigo
Nicolas de Bezak	Vicomtesse du Halgouet
Mme Miklachevsky	Savinsky
M. Polovtsov	Mme Olive
Princess Gorchakov	Marquis of Villasinda
The Ambassador[2]	Mme Polovtsov
Countess Kleinmichel	M. Trepov
Count Tolstoy	Princess Dolgoruky
Mme Benois	M. Alexandre Benois
Prince Gorchakov	Comtesse de Robien
Stopford	M. Olive
Guazzone	Gentil

[1] A well-known member of fashionable French society.
[2] The French Ambassador, M. Maurice Paléologue.

7

After dinner, Alexandre Benois confirms that there have been some incidents in the outskirts. They say that at one place a tram was overturned.

Friday 9th March 1917

On arrival at the Embassy I notice a certain amount of agitation. At the corner of Gagarinskaya Street and the French Quay, a group is forming. They are people from the Vyborg[1] district who have had to walk across the frozen Neva, as the Liteiny Bridge is guarded and traffic across it has been stopped. . . . People are coming in Indian file, crossing the river diagonally from the hospital on the right bank to the beginning of Gagarinskaya Street. They walk one behind the other, as the paths through the conglomerated blocks of ice and thick snow is difficult. . . . The Cossacks are therefore not venturing on to the river. . . . But they gallop along the Quay, and I amuse myself by watching their little game from the Chancery windows. . . . They are very picturesque on their little horses, with a truss of hay tied to the saddle in a net. They have both lances and carbines.

Towards eleven o'clock the movement across the river had, in fact, completely stopped. Probably measures have been taken on the other bank. The Cossacks have stopped patrolling, and on going home to lunch I notice some of them standing dismounted at the corner of Gagarinskaya Street, lined up in front of the Serebriakov house, with their little shaggy horses and their long lances. . . . They make a picturesque group.

In the afternoon I go with Shubin to pay a visit to Mme de Mouy at the Hôtel de l'Europe. Having been detained, he sends his motor-car to fetch me, and I drive to his office in the Nevsky Prospekt and wait for him. The security forces are out in considerable numbers.

Shubin tells me that this morning there were some scuffles in the suburbs: bakeries were pillaged and there are said to have been some wounded. The movement appears to be more serious than had been thought and people are rather worried.

In the Nevsky Prospekt there is a certain effervescence, but everything is still orderly. . . . It's true that there is a deployment of police which makes any attempt at violence impossible. Nevertheless, as we were leaving we could see in the distance, in the direction of the

[1] An industrial suburb to the North of Petrograd.

Gostiny Dvor,[1] a crowd of demonstrators which seemed to me of a considerable size.

Lotte, who went shopping with Mme de Scavenius,[2] didn't see anything worrying either. She went by *izvoztchik*,[3] as the Danish Legation carriage was at the station waiting for Scavenius who went this afternoon, together with Buisseret[4] and other ministers, to be received in audience by the Empress at Tsarskoye Selo. I learnt through the Belgians that the Empress was very calm. But she did speak of the danger there is "when the people are hungry", and she said "the army is loyal and we can rely on it".

Saturday 10th March 1917

The movement has taken on a political character, and this morning numerous factories are on strike.

At eleven o'clock I go to the office of the Wagons-lits company in the Nevsky Prospekt, passing through Kanyuchennaya Street.

The security force is bigger than ever: police and *gardavoys*, both on foot and mounted. On the way I meet several patrols of about ten of the latter, looking very smart on their beautiful horses, dressed in their very plain black cloaks slashed with red cord, and their flat black astrakhan caps surmounted with black aigrettes.

In the square in front of the Kazan cathedral there are reserves of infantry.

At midday a large crowd of demonstrators arrives from the direction of the Nicholas station and assembles in front of the Town Hall. I can distinctly see a red flag. At this moment the police officers announce that there is going to be a charge—and they move back the passers-by without jostling them. I go back inside the Wagons-lits office.

The charge is made with a great deal of *brio* by horsemen at the gallop, who come swinging out of Kazan Square down the Nevsky Prospekt to meet the demonstrators with drawn swords. The demonstrators are caught at the same time from the rear by another charge

---

[1] The *Gostiny Dvor*, or 'merchants' bazaar', was the covered market of Petrograd.
[2] Wife of the Danish Minister.
[3] The term strictly means 'cab-driver', but is more often used here instead of the word 'cab'.
[4] The Belgian Minister.

of mounted *gardavoys*, whose aigrettes I can see over the people's heads. . . . The crowd disperses as if by magic.

With great trouble I find an *izvoztchik* and go home to lunch. On my return along Kanyuchennaya Street I meet two armoured cars carrying machine-guns driving at full speed, with their headlights blazing and making a continuous whistling noise. . . . It made a bad impression on me.

At five o'clock I want to go back to the Nevsky with Binet, but Gentil and Dulong, who have just come back from there, tell us that there is no point: all is quiet. I go and pay a visit to Bezak.

Going along Mokhovaya Street I meet Shubin walking home from a concert organized by the little Micha orchestra, which plays at the house of the Grand Duke Boris, and in other places where people dance.

That evening, to the Michel Theatre with Charlier and Countess Kleinmichel. They are doing *L'Idée de Françoise*. The theatre is practically empty. The troops opened fire in the Nevsky Prospekt at about six o'clock. Armour and Yanin, who were there, told me that most of the rounds were blank, and that they didn't fire at the demonstrators, but in front of them in the snow. All the same, there were some killed and wounded. Mme du Halgouet, who arrived at the Hôtel de l'Europe at the time of the shooting, helped to pick up a woman who was thought to be wounded, but who in fact had only had a heart attack. . . .

Charlier doesn't believe in the seriousness of the present crisis, and thinks that work will be resumed on Monday. Countess Kleinmichel is less optimistic. She thinks that there will be defections among the troops and says that the Preobrajensky[1] regiment in particular is not reliable.

Sunday 11th March 1917

There are no cabs and I walk to Mass at the French church, leaving Lotte at home as she is very tired. But in the afternoon she comes for a walk with me in Sergevskaya Street. The weather is splendid. All the streets are guarded by armed soldiers moving about in small groups of twos and threes.

[1] One of the oldest regiments, formed by Peter the Great as a royal bodyguard, roughly equivalent to the Household Cavalry.

Notices signed by the Governor of Petrograd are posted up, forbidding all meetings and promising bread.

In the evening Charlier sends his motorcar to take us to Princess Radziwill's party at the Fontanka Palace. Entry to the Nevsky Prospekt is forbidden, and we have to go round by the quays, the Palace Square, Morskaya and Gorokhovaya Streets.

On arriving at the party we hear that there has been serious trouble in the Nevsky Prospekt during the course of the afternoon which was so peaceful in our own part of the town. The troops fired several volleys and there were many victims. It appears that five dead and thirty-two wounded were taken into the English hospital nearby.

The party is lugubrious at first. . . . The musicians arrived very late, and separately. But people try to dance in spite of it. Grand Duke Boris is very worried, but he dances too.

In spite of everything we actually ended by enjoying ourselves, and it was with difficulty that I got Lotte to leave early, in order to take advantage of Charlier's offer of a drive home in his motorcar.

Our return is ominous . . . all the streets are filled with troops, and we are stopped at several points by soldiers mounting guard round huge fires. There are so many that one has the impression of passing through a camp. The Nevsky Prospekt is barricaded, completely evacuated, and only lit by a naval searchlight on top of the spire of the Admiralty.

There is not a cab anywhere and Gentil and Dulong, who had been to the ballet, had to walk home.

Charlier, who yesterday was so reassured, is very worried today. . . . Chambrun still hopes that everything will be settled, but he too is very worried.

When we get back to our house, a *sotnia*[1] of Cossacks passes along the street. . . . The snow deadens the sound of the horses' hooves. One can only hear the clink of weapons. . . .

Monday 12th March 1917

The impression I had on arriving at the Embassy this morning was a better one: people were saying that work had been resumed in

[1] A company of one hundred men.

most of the factories. We had also just received news of the capture of Baghdad by the English, and Chambrun was calculating the good effect of this success on public opinion.

But little by little less reassuring news was arriving: in certain factories the workers are still on strike. There is even talk of the possibility of a general strike, and a rumour of fights between troops and police in the suburbs is spreading.

We were arguing about yesterday's events and the number of victims in the Nevsky Prospekt. Chambrun and I thought that the incidents had been greatly exaggerated and that blank rounds were being fired. . . . The rest of our colleagues, on the other hand, were taking sides against the repressive action and sympathizing with the victims, when Leonid came in to say that someone had started shooting in Liteiny Street, near the Arsenal. As the Ambassador wanted to find out for himself, I went out with him and Colonel Lavergne. And indeed, one hears explosions in every direction, but they make so little noise that I get the impression that they are using blanks, which confirms what I thought before. Nevertheless, volleys can be heard in the distance.

From Zakharevskaya Street, where we are sheltered from the crowd's movements (which seem more dangerous than the bullets), we contemplate the scene in Liteiny Street, which is filled with quantities of soldiers swarming about in utter confusion. Several motor lorries, also filled with soldiers, plough their way through the crowd, and we are struck by the small red flags which they carry, and which at first we mistake for pennons. At this moment, there is a big movement near the bridge, where it would seem that a charge is being made, but it is impossible to make head or tail of the disorderly ebb and flow of all these panic-stricken people running in every direction. The soldiers we interrogate know nothing: they are clearly only interested in running away. One gets an impression of indescribable confusion.

We return to the Embassy, where news has been received over the telephone, which is working normally. Serious mutiny has broken out among the troops, and all the men we saw belong to regiments sent to restore order who, after firing a few volleys, made common cause with the mutineers. All the units sent to fight the mutiny are defecting one after the other.

From the big bay window of the Chancery we follow events while carrying on with our work at the same time. A compact column advances towards the bridge: they are fresh troops who are to re-establish order: but they are immediately won over. There is a great surge forward, the shooting redoubles in intensity, and the fleeing crowd overflows on to the quay. All one can see is soldiers running madly, with panic-stricken faces. . . . They throw away their arms in order to run faster. Underneath Halgouet's motorcar, which is standing outside the Embassy, there is a whole pile of guns, which have been flung there to hide them. Chambrun picks one up: it is all rusty, the sights are bent, and the mechanism is in bad condition. It is not surprising that men who look after their arms as badly as that should mutiny in the streets. . . . In fact, it is not even mutiny, it is panic. The mutineers are fleeing for fear of repressive action, and already regret what they have done. . . . Luckily for them, the troops ordered out against them are running away in their direction. . . . It's like the battle in *Candide*! Even the police, who are outflanked, have vanished. . . .

I go back to my house for lunch, where I find Lotte, very calm. She had driven Mme Halgouet, who had come to give her an injection, as far as Liteiny Street. She also saw the soldiers firing and then running away. Others were stopping motorcars and getting into them, and arresting officers in order to remove their arms . . . and their pocket-books.

Lorries flying the red flag are rattling and clanging all over this part of the town. Mutineers are piled inside them, the tips of their bayonets bristling above the drab mass of cloaks and caps. The people, although not daring to take sides openly, approve and make gestures of encouragement.

After lunch I return to the Embassy by way of Panteleevskaya Street and the Fontanka,[1] as it is impossible to get along Liteiny Street, where the shooting has started again, worse than before. On the way, I call in for a moment on Shubin, who is very worried. The situation has become much more serious since this morning, and I distinctly get the impression that the uprising is gaining ground hourly. People are shooting here, there and everywhere. . . . I meet groups of men running, but they look less panic-stricken than this morning. The mutineers hold all this part of the town, and they have realized that they have got to win if they are to escape reprisals. Some reserve officers are trying to organize them. . . . Others are panic-stricken. One of them is galloping about at full speed on a

---

[1] The Fontanka Canal, made by Peter the Great, about four miles long.

shaggy horse, firing his revolver in the air. There is an atmosphere of indescribable confusion.

At the Embassy, all reports confirm that the uprising is rapidly winning over all the troops who were sent to maintain order throughout the town yesterday: this concentration of troops only encouraged the flame to spread by degrees, like the flame of a taper which lights the candles on an altar. At one o'clock the middle of the town was still quiet, and Gentil was able to get without any trouble to the Yacht Club, where he lunched. But this evening it is very difficult to get about. Chambrun came to dine with us at home, but Beaumont was unable to join us. Riggs remained stuck in his apartment in Liteiny Street for the whole afternoon. From his windows, he watched the fighting between the insurgents and loyal troops. They all shot as badly as each other, and there are hardly any wounded ... but what a noise, and what distracted rushing about! In the end, they all made common cause.

At five o'clock someone came to the Chancery to say that the mutineers have set fire to the Law Courts. I went there with Chambrun. It was a ghastly sight, with huge flames coming out of all the gaping windows. However, the firemen are there fighting the fire and are being allowed to get on with their work. Shots can be heard on all sides: the firing sounds particularly heavy on the other side of the Neva, in the Vyborg district, and spent bullets fall all round us on the quay. On our return we find the Ambassador, who managed to get back to the Foreign Ministry, where he had been this morning. He was with Sir George Buchanan[1] in his car, when it was followed by a lorry and stopped by a gang of soldiers. Luckily he was able to make himself known and the crowd of mutineers, which had become threatening, now acclaimed the two ambassadors. The government, on its own initiative, has dismissed Protopopov, hoping thereby to give satisfaction to the people.

During the evening the mutiny spread to all the troops of the garrison. Certain regiments have, however, kept up an appearance of discipline, and the Paul regiment marched in good order, led by its band, to occupy the Winter Palace.

The mutineers hold all the important points. They have put up barricades to prevent all attempts by troops which may be sent against them. . . . In fact, it is being said that an Army Corps is coming from Tsarskoye Selo, and the mutineers are visibly

[1] British Ambassador in Petrograd from 1910 to January 1918.

frightened of repressive action. In Liteiny Street a pile of crates, round two old cannon, blocks the road as far up as Sergevskaya Street.

All the prisons have been flung open and the prisoners set free. Some German officer prisoners who were liberated in this way went to the Swedish Legation for sanctuary.

Tuesday 13th March 1917

Shots were being fired all through the night. In the middle of the town the firing was so heavy that Halgouet, who had gone to the Chamber of Commerce, couldn't get away and had to spend the night there.

But this morning, at any rate in our part of the town, no gunfire can be heard. The mutineers seem to be confining their activities to travelling in all directions in private motorcars which they have seized, whose chauffeurs are forced to drive them all over the town.

There is a constant stream of motorcars along the quay, many of which I recognize as they go past, crammed with soldiers, with their guns sticking out of the windows. Other soldiers stand on the running-boards, or are perched on the roofs. On the front part of almost every car there are two men stretched out on the mudguards on either side, aiming their guns ahead of them with fixed bayonets. There are also lorries armed with machine-guns piled full of soldiers: many of them have strapped cartridge-belts full of machine-gun ammunition round their bodies. Open army cars which have fallen into the hands of the mutineers bowl across the snow, their occupants throwing out proclamations which flutter in the wind and are seized in mid-air by the outstretched hands of passers-by, anxious for news.

In the Duma, a committee of twelve members has been set up, which is trying to canalize the revolutionary torrent. This committee has telegraphed to the Emperor and the army commanders informing them of the situation. The Tsar has invested General Ivanov with full powers—but what can he do, as he is at Mohilev!

M. Pokrovsky[1] is still at his post at the Foreign Ministry, and the Ambassador was able to see him this morning at about eleven o'clock. While walking to the Ministry, M. Paléologue was recog-

[1] M. N. Pokrovsky, Foreign Minister from November 1915 to March 1917.

nized by a gang of soldiers and students who gave him an ovation and wanted to drive him to the Duma in a red-flagged lorry. Meanwhile, other soldiers came to demonstrate outside the Embassy, demanding that the red flag be hoisted. Chambrun had to go out and speak to them. An officer made a speech to him in French, promising that revolutionary Russia would be loyal to the alliance. A military band played the *Marseillaise*.

These fine promises made a strong impression in the Chancery. Only Chambrun and I refuse to expect anything from these people who have started a revolution by running away. One thing alone can still save the cause of the war and the Allies: drastic repression, and we are hoping for it whole-heartedly.

In the afternoon the rifle fire began again with such intensity that at first I took it to mean the arrival of troops to restore order. But it is only the soldiers who, believing the police (who are now called 'pharaohs') to be hidden on the roofs of churches and houses, are possessed by real terror. Lorries are stationed at every street corner, their machine-guns aimed in the air and emptying round upon round of ammunition. The bullets fall back on the assailants or on soldiers of other units, making them believe that their fire is being returned. But people are shooting in all directions. The rifle-fire is particularly heavy at the corner of Sergevskaya and Liteiny Streets, where several machine-guns cover the bestarred dome of St. Simeon's church with cross-fire.

Meanwhile the populace, realizing that the revolutionaries are now masters, take advantage of the situation to give free vent to their hatred of the police. Police stations are being burned down and looted. I walk past the one in Mokhovaya Street at the moment when they hurl a grand piano out of the window, and it lands on the pavement with a crash, with all its strings vibrating. In the snow nearby they are making a bonfire of bursting files out of which fall cascades of papers. . . . Half-blackened pages blow away and scatter on the snow.

At four o'clock, with Lotte, a visit to Shubin and then to Princess Dolly Radziwill's, where we find Galitzin and Princess Sophie Dolgoruky.

We return to the Embassy while grape-shot firing is going on in Sergevskaya Street. Lotte goes home, accompanied by Colonel Lavergne, whilst I remain in the Chancery.

The crowd has also pillaged and set fire to Count Fredericks' house and he has been arrested and taken to the fortress,[1] together with Stürmer,[2] Protopopov, the Metropolitan Pitirin, and so on. The latter was taken away in Shubin's Delaunay-Belleville and, in order not to lose sight of his beautiful limousine and to be kept supplied with news, Shubin had the bright idea of serving a meal to the soldiers who seized his motorcar, so that now they come back whenever they are hungry.

The mutineers are searching houses for 'pharaohs' and arms. They went to Mme Halgouet's, where they were fairly polite. But in other houses there have been scenes of savagery. One of my close friends, General Stackelberg (in whose veins French blood is mixed with that of Teutonic knights) refused to give in to the demands of the soldiery as did most of the other Russian officers, and was massacred in front of his wife. The soldiers, having insulted his corpse and robbed him of everything he had on him, then threw his body into the Neva.

Wednesday 14th March 1917

My first impression on leaving the house this morning was a better one. There seem to be fewer shots, and there is even some attempt at organization: in fact, I met a convoy of sledges carrying food supplies, escorted by soldiers.

The revolution appears to have definitely triumphed. The troops are going to the Duma to take the oath, and on returning from the Embassy I stopped at the corner of Liteiny and Sergevskaya Streets to watch a regiment go past, which was making for the Taurid Palace. The men were in marching order, led by their band, which was playing the march from the ballet of 'The Little Hunch-backed Horse'. Only the red flags, the men's red arm-bands, and the red rags decorating the bayonets remind one of the sad reality.

In Gagarinskaya Street, on our way to luncheon at the Embassy, we met eight old generals who were also making their way towards the Duma to take the oath. Four of them were wearing the Cross of

[1] 'the fortress', or 'Peter-Paul', refers to the Fortress of SS. Peter and Paul, containing the State prison.
[2] B. Stürmer. Master of Ceremonies at the Court. Foreign Minister July–November 1915; Prime Minister 2nd February 1916–23rd November 1916; Minister of the Interior March–September 1916. A puppet of Rasputin.

St. George. They all wore red arm-bands. The last one was quite helpless, held up by a woman.

All officers, in fact, have to make their submission and take the oath in the Duma. As well as this, they have to register with an organization installed in the Army and Navy Club, on the corner of Liteiny Street and Kirochnaya Street. Beaumont, who managed to get inside the hall, told me that it was a scene of humiliation. Officers have to appear before a committee composed of students and private soldiers sitting at a big table, towards which they are roughly pushed by the crowd of soldiers filling the hall. They are issued with three different kinds of certificate: an identity card; a permit of free circulation; and lastly, for those who have given surety, a kind of 'civic card' inviting them to contribute to the re-establishment of order and confirming them in their employment.

In the afternoon many regiments went to the Taurid Palace to take the oath.

The Grand Duke Cyril went there at the head of the mounted units of the guards. The Finland Regiment, which I saw passing, was in relatively good order, but I met some marines who were in a lamentable state of confusion. Nevertheless, in spite of everything, these troops who have submitted to the authority of the Duma are the only elements of relative order in the face of the gangs of the extremist committee of the Finland Station[1] and the soldiers' committee of the Peter-Paul Fortress, who continue to snipe in the streets and to search houses on the pretext of looking for police or arms.

The Committee of the Finland Station is particularly dangerous.

It consists of revolutionaries and notorious anarchists around whom all the violent elements are grouped. Following the example of the 1905 Revolution, it has invited factories and army units to elect worker and soldier representatives to replace the members of the Duma who, according to the Committee, are not the true representatives of the people, and whose authority it refuses to recognize.

It is a Jacobin club in opposition to the Assembly.

It is said that the Emperor has left Headquarters, but that his train has been stopped by the revolutionaries while he was on his way to Tsarskoye Selo.

[1] On the North side of the town, across the Neva.

Thursday 15th March 1917

The night has been quiet. The snow which started to fall during yesterday evening has somewhat curbed the zeal of the 'pharaoh' hunters.

After lunching at the Embassy, Lotte, Chambrun and I went for a little walk. There are a lot of people in the streets. At last the people are no longer afraid, and they have come out to celebrate their liberty. As a *dvornik*[1] says to me, "It's a country where everyone is rich and where one parades about all the time . . ." Today all the new citizens saunter about in the streets . . . they watch the red flags flying on many of the houses. . . . Especially on the houses where one least expected to see them. . . . Certainly people are not very brave here. . . . Motorcars are driving round scattering proclamations by the Finland Station Committee, which is demanding the abdication of the Emperor and the establishment of universal suffrage. Patrols composed of ill-assorted soldiers commanded by students armed with sabres and revolvers are taking arrested policemen to the Duma. Many of these are wounded and have their heads bound up in bandages. Their hands are tied behind their backs.

We walk past the burned-out Law Courts, where long stalactites of ice hang down, and in front of the Liteiny Street barricade, which is made of cases piled up around two cannon.

In Sergevskaya Street, a red flag flies on Countess Kleinmichel's palace, and a placard fixed to the door indicates that the proprietress has been arrested. The coats-of-arms on the Grand Duchess Olga's[2] palace are veiled in a red material.

We stop at Mme Halgouet's and at Mme Olive's, where we find the Gorchakovs and Bezak, who has had his epaulettes torn off by the military.

On leaving the Olives' house, we met a whole headquarters staff of about a hundred officers going in a body to the Duma, without their arms and accompanied by their secretaries.

During the evening we hear that the executive committee of the Duma and the committee of the Finland Station have been able to reach agreement. The Committee of the Duma has bowed to the

[1] A house-porter, hall-porter, or *concierge*.
[2] Sister of the Tsar.

demands of the extremists and promised to admit one of their representatives—Kerensky[1] or Chkeidze[2]—to the new government. The Committee of the Finland Station, which consists of workers' and soldiers' delegates, grows in importance every day and seems as though it must overwhelm the men of the Duma, of whom even the most liberal are terrified at the turn of events.

It is reported that the Emperor has arrived at Pskov, where he is said to have abdicated in favour of his son. People still hope that it will be possible to save the monarchic principle and establish a constitutional empire . . . in spite of the extremist committee, which wants a republic.

Friday 16th March 1917

The Emperor abdicated tonight. But, contrary to what everyone thought, he renounced his son's right to the throne, and designated his brother, the Grand Duke Michael, as his successor.

The Grand Duke this morning received the delegates of the Duma and the Finland Station committee, who insisted that he too should renounce the crown. While awaiting the Constituent Assembly, a provisional dictatorship will be formed under the presidency of Prince Lvov,[3] with Guchkov,[4] Milyukov,[5] Tereschenko,[6] Kerensky, etc.

After lunching at the Embassy, to which the Ambassador invites us every day since the revolution started, we went to see Princess Radziwill, where we found several of our friends. They are very pessimistic. Prince Galitzin says: "All is over".

Shubin, whom we call on afterwards, is hardly more reassuring. He knows most of the men who are coming into power quite well, and he has few illusions about their energy, their courage and their capabilities.

And yet some attempt at organization seems to have started. They have sent a guard of about thirty officer-cadets from the *Corps des*

---

[1] A. F. Kerensky, Minister of Justice, March–May 1917; War Minister, May–September 1917; Prime Minister, 21st July–November 1917. (Still alive)

[2] Georgian Menshevik politician.

[3] Prime Minister and Minister of Interior, March–July 1917.

[4] War Minister, March–May 1917.

[5] Foreign Minister, March–May 1917.

[6] Finance Minister, March–May 1917; Foreign Minister, May–November 1917.

Pages[1] to the Embassy. Also, the Prefecture of Police has made out safe-conducts for the members of the Diplomatic Corps. It is high time measures were taken. In fact, this very afternoon Mme Binet was arrested and taken to the police station, although she was accompanied by a French non-commissioned officer in uniform.

The gangs of soldiers, tired of hunting policemen, are now busy removing eagles and other imperial emblems. They pull down and smash the name-boards and escutcheons of the tradesmen appointed to the Court. An immense red flag floats over the Winter Palace.

Monday 19th March 1917

A decree has come out, abolishing *tchine*[2] and decorations: officers have hastened to remove their crosses . . . they only keep the red cockades.

People continue to bring jewellery, silver and objects of value to the Embassy, begging us to put them in a safe place.

In the evening, after dinner with Chambrun and Beaumont, we went to see Shubin, who has just been released from having been shut up in Peter-and-Paul for two days. In fact, nobody knows why he was arrested, as he has always been a liberal and it is precisely his friends who are in power. On the same day that a gang of soldiers came to take him away, the people in the provisional government offered him an important post!—What confusion!

He was put in a cell where there was an Austrian officer prisoner-of-war, and an ex-policeman whose stories helped to pass the time for him.

After his liberation, instead of giving his order of release back to the guard, he gave him a three-rouble note, which the man greatly preferred.

This document enabled Shubin to prove that he had actually been incarcerated, contrary to the conclusions of the enquiry conducted by his friends, which naturally proved that he had never been arrested. . . .

People say that the Emperor is asking to be taken to Tsarskoye Selo, to be near the Grand Duchesses, who are ill. From there he would go to England by way of Murmansk.

[1] *Pajsky Korpus*, a military school.
[2] Rank.

Tuesday 20th March 1917

This morning I went with Lotte and Beaumont to the Duma, which is open to everyone. The Palace looks like an immense guardroom. Soldiers are everywhere, all unbuttoned and eating at dirty wooden tables or sprawling on the floor round a samovar. Others, still carrying arms, are asleep on top of piled-up sacks of flour, brought there as food supplies for the town, and which cover everything with white dust. The floor is filthy, covered with bits of paper, cigarette ends, and litter of all kinds. Unshaved students with long mops of hair, wearing green caps, and typists with short hair and *pince-nez* glasses, typical Russian Nihilists, move about among the soldiers. A lot of Jews. It makes a lamentable impression in this Empire interior with its classical columns. The portrait of the Emperor has been removed, but they have left a bust of Alexander and given it a red cravat. Outside the entrance is one of the Court motorcars, from which the coronets have been roughly scratched off and on top of which a red cloth has been hoisted.

On our return, we walk past Countess Kleinmichel's palace, which has been turned into a 'supply centre', that is to say a canteen for the military, and afterwards we stop at the Nostitzes' house. The general has removed his shoulder-knots and his decorations. He fulfils the function of delegate of the General Staff to the President of the Council.

The government has published a manifesto, which consists entirely of *razgavors*[1] against Tsarism and for liberty! . . . Nothing practical. A brief reference to 'honouring our alliances'.

Wednesday 21st March 1917

At the insistence of the *Soviet*,[2] the Minister of Justice has published a *prikase*[3] decreeing that the Emperor has been arrested, accused, and handed over to justice for having plotted *with the Duma* (!) against the revolution. Some commissioners of the Soviet have left to secure the person of the Emperor, who returned to Mohilev

[1] *Razgavor:* a discourse.
[2] *Soviet:* a committee.
[3] *Prikase:* an order, or writ.

after his abdication. They are to take him to Tsarskoye Selo, where he will be kept prisoner in his palace.

In the Champ de Mars, where the victims are to be solemnly buried and a monument erected, they have started digging the graves of these 'heroes'. I went there. When walking through the Palace Square, I saw a gang of soldiers hustling a Cossack, who was wearing three Crosses of St. George and refusing to remove them: "I won them by my bravery in the war, and it is right that I should be distinguished from those who have never left Petrograd." The crowd was somewhat hostile towards the Cossack.

Saturday 24th March 1917

The Allied ambassadors today proceeded to recognize the provisional government. They went alone, without taking their staff, and did not wear uniform. I am very glad to have been excused this ceremony.

They were received in the Mariinsky Palace in a room with a dirty floor and broken windows. It really is the setting which best suits this government, which is the outcome of revolt, treachery and cowardice.

This government has, moreover, thought of a reward for the soldiers to whom it owes its power, the only kind of reward of which these men are worthy, and which dishonours the government which confers it as much as it does the one hundred and sixty thousand soldiers of the Petrograd garrison to whom it is given: the promise that they will never be sent to the front.

This fact throws much light on the real implications of the last few days' events, and the heroism of the people who, if we are to believe the extracts from the French press received by telegraph, rose against the rule of the Tsar in order to fight the war better until an Allied victory is achieved!!! People who write this, and those who believe it, are a lot of simpletons and are letting themselves in for bitter disappointments!

Monday 26th March 1917

The decisions taken a few days ago by the workers' and soldiers' deputies confirm my fears concerning Russia's participation in the war. The 'Soviet', in fact, insists on the immediate opening of

23

negotiations with the proletarians of the enemy countries, and on the renunciation of all plans for conquest or annexation. It proclaims the necessity of 'democratizing' the army, which comes to the same thing as suppressing all discipline. Lastly, it enjoins the soldiers of the revolution to prepare for general peace by fraternizing with enemy soldiers at the front.

That is how the Russian revolution means to pursue the war to victory.

To think that these are the men who reproached the Empress with being German, and who have accused Count Fredericks and many other worthy people of being traitors to the country!

The people are only half satisfied, and we are a long way from the enthusiasm of a week ago.

One hears people saying this kind of thing: "We have neither Tsar nor President . . . there is nothing. . . ." Or else: "We want the Republic . . . but with a good Tsar."

A coachman who mistook the picture of the Republic for the portrait of an Empress did not hide his displeasure from me: "Why do they turn out the Tsar, in order to have the Tsarina . . . as the Tsarina is the one who was bad!"

Tuesday 27th March 1917

Major Gallaud met an officer from Kronstadt[1] who had been given forty-eight hours leave in Petrograd by his men. The leave permit was signed by his former ship's cook.

Most of the officers are still at the mercy of the crews and are forced by them to undertake the hardest and most humiliating work. Nevertheless, they are thankful to have escaped death. In fact, the sailors have shown unbelievable brutality and have massacred a large number of officers. Many of them suffered real martyrdom before being put to death; they were mutilated and soaked in icy water or petrol. Admiral Wirren was burnt to death in a barrel near the Makharov monument, and his eighteen-year-old daughter was raped before his eyes and then had her throat cut.

I can hardly believe in such scenes of savagery, although those brutes are capable of anything.

[1] The fortress built by Peter the Great on an island at the mouth of the Neva, the naval base of Petrograd.

Thursday 29th March 1917

Food supplies, which had improved during the days following the revolution, because reserves had been indiscriminately drawn on, have now become even more difficult than under the old régime.

The queues outside bakeries and other food shops are longer than ever. Endless lines of people stand shivering outside closed doors, on which are painted naïve pictures of every kind of victual although the shops themselves are empty, and while walking past them this morning Chambrun said to me: "To think that these people have overthrown the old régime just to get rid of Rasputin![1] What are they going to do with all these equally troublesome queues?"[2]

He is right. The people are dissatisfied. They have overthrown the Tsar in order to eat their fill. Now that they see that that was not enough, they will pillage the houses of the bourgeois. The awakening of these people who are so peaceful and so apathetic will be terrible.

Sunday 1st April 1917

This morning, the provisional government organized a military parade in the square in front of the Winter Palace. The regiments of the 'heroic' Petrograd garrison, more or less in disorder, filed past the members of the government carrying red banners. . . . The bands played the *Marseillaise*, every word of which sounds bitterly ironical in the present circumstances: "*Allons, enfants de la Patrie . . . le jour de gloire est arrivé*"!!

And to think that there are people who still have illusions about the Russian army, and who have swallowed this gigantic April Fool's Day hoax. . . .

Thursday 5th April 1917

Lotte's departure.

[1] Assassinated 30th December 1916. See pages 28–32.
[2] The pun contained in this sentence is untranslatable: ". . . pour être débarrassés de la seule queue de Rasputin! . . . ces queues autrement gênantes!"

I accompany her as far as Byelo-Ostrov.

All circulation is forbidden because of the funeral of the victims of the revolution. The Ambassador had lent us his motorcar to go to the station at seven o'clock this morning but, in spite of the flag and the protests of the footmen, they stop us on the bridge and try to make us get out.

After lengthy negotiations and after having examined our papers, they end by letting us go to the station under escort of four civilians with hang-dog faces, their bayonets at the ready, who sit on the front seat and on the running-boards of the car.

I went in the train with Lotte as far as the frontier, which she crossed without any trouble this time. While waiting for a train to take me back to Petrograd, I talked to the station-master. He told me that the station had been occupied by workmen who, after burning all the official papers, thought they could take over control! . . . Everyone who knows how to run the service, the police etc., are all in prison. What a windfall for the spies!

After arriving at the Finland Station, I had to make the rest of the journey on foot, and circulation was very difficult. . . . In every street there were processions taking part in the ceremony in honour of the 'heroes' of the revolution.

Choirs were singing revolutionary hymns, the *Marseillaise* in particular. . . . There were prodigious quantities of standards, banners, and red streamers. . . .

Order was being kept by groups of men holding hands or forming a chain with handkerchiefs to surround the funeral procession. Commissioners wearing red arm-bands, or long red ribbons round their necks, like the grand cordon of Alexander Nevsky! It's enough to make Monsieur Doumergue jealous.

On the emblems there are inscriptions: 'Eight-hour days'—'Social Republic'—'Votes for Women' and, above all, '*Zemlya i volya*'—land and liberty—which apparently was the battle cry of the peasants who revolted against Catherine the Great under the leadership of Pougachev. . . . In Russia, nothing changes.

I saw no inscriptions bearing any relation to the war.

The number of demonstrators is estimated at nearly a million, divided up into six enormous processions which succeeded each other in the Champ de Mars from ten o'clock in the morning until ten o'clock at night. As each procession arrived at the Champ de Mars from a different quarter, it was saluted by cannon firing from the fortress. They brought their dead . . . or at any rate their coffins, draped in red cloth, with the traditional cutlet-paper frills. Altogether, there were a hundred and eighty. . . . For overthrowing a régime, it was cheap!

The members of the provisional government arrived at the common grave at two o'clock. But it was at night that the scene became the most interesting. The Champ de Mars was lit by six big naval searchlights. The countless red banners, pennants and flags were lit up by the crude light of the projectors.

Saturday 7th April 1917

The declaration of war by the United States has had no effect whatsoever on the Russian people.

In spite of Chambrun's enthusiasm, I myself am sceptical. In losing Russia, we lose one of the jaws of the pincer in which we could try to seize the central Empires. . . . The Americans will perhaps reinforce the other jaw, but it is no longer a pincer.

In spite of their lofty principles, the United States are only coming into the war to get their money back. . . . Besides, they are on the other side of the Atlantic. When one thinks about it all, one wonders what use their alliance can be to us at the moment, except by way of moral support! . . .

Monday 9th April 1917

Shubin is still very worried. The apparent orderliness of the demonstration in honour of the victims of the revolution does not reassure him.

He analysed the psychology of Russian crowds to us with great shrewdness—he understands them better than we do, their mentality is so far removed from ours.

"I saw," he told us, "a troop of a thousand demonstrators in a small side-street, waiting their turn to take up their position in one of the processions. There they stood, each one in his place, from ten o'clock in the morning until eight o'clock at night, marking time in the melting snow without the slightest sign of impatience, with nothing to eat and nothing to drink, without asking for anything from the neighbouring houses. The bearers laid five or six red coffins down on the bare earth, and none of this great crowd gave any sign of impatience. And yet, on the banners which they carried, the most extreme and violent demands were inscribed. From time to time a leader raised his baton, giving the note, and they began to sing: 'We will pillage!—we will kill!—we will cut throats!—to the gallows with the Tsar!—the bourgeois are vampires!' etc. . . . The tenors cried out for the heads of the aristocrats, the sopranos for that of the Tsar, the basses wanted no one spared. Then, when the verse was over they rested for ten minutes and then, at a new signal, they started again. It wasn't until that night that the procession could start marching, the bearers lifted the coffins on to their shoulders, and the crowd left in an orderly fashion, singing: 'We will pillage!— We will murder!' etc. . . ."

Fat Shubin mimed the scene all the while he described it, rolling his pale blue eyes, beating time, singing first in a tenor voice, then in a bass . . . and then marching across the drawing-room with superb calm.

He was most amusing. But his observation is very exact. In no other country could people confine themselves to words like this, without breaking into action. But how dangerous it all is! Because, once let loose, these brutes are terrifying. In 1905 there were atrocious scenes and the *moujiks*, so mild in appearance, pillaged everywhere with sadistic cruelty. Someone told me about one 'estate', where the peasants cut three legs off all the sheep. In other places they tore out the cattles' tongues and put out their eyes. Let us hope that we do not see horrors like these!

Wednesday 11th April 1917

Chambrun had lunch with Prince Yusupov, who described to him in detail what had happened.[1]

I took notes, bit by bit, of his account, which Chambrun gave us immediately afterwards.

Yusupov had already known Rasputin for some time. He had been put in touch with him by Mme Golovin, in order to discuss some aspects of occultism and magic which interested him.

[1] Prince Yusupov's conversation with Chambrun was a 'flash-back' to an event which took place some three months previously, the date of Rasputin's assassination being 30th December 1916.

He only saw Rasputin at his house in Gorokhovaya Street, and without the knowledge of his parents. The Prince even claims that the liver complaint from which he suffers has been relieved by the mysterious practices of the miracle-worker. . . . But in the Chancery we think that, strange and vicious man that he is, he must have profited by these meetings to get himself treated a little lower down. . . .

Be that as it may, the Prince maintains that, as a result of these conversations, he became convinced that Rasputin was a danger to Russia, and he conceived the idea of ridding the country of him. The Grand Duke Dmitry, on being consulted, warmly approved of the plan, in these words: "Yes, we must kill the dog!"

The difficulty was how to entice Rasputin to a place where they could get rid of him. He was, in fact, thoroughly supervised by the police and besides, he himself was very much on his guard and used the pretext that the police, who were responsible for protecting him, prevented him from going out. However, his parents having gone away, Yusupov decided to take advantage of this fact to entice Rasputin to the Yusupov Palace on the Moïka,[1] where he lived alone, and there to put his plan into execution.

To this effect he ordered the preparation of a dozen cakes poisoned with cyanide, and a bottle of Crimean wine also containing poison.

And yet, when the moment came for action, the Prince still hesitated. He went to Rasputin's house late in the evening and walked up the back stairs. . . . He was very frightened. The electric light was switched off and, as he had never used these stairs before, he did not know for certain which floor Rasputin's apartment was on, nor which was the right door.

He therefore decided to consign 'the old man's' fate to chance. He would open the first door, at random, and if it was Rasputin's then his fate would be sealed. . . . He lit his cigarette lighter: there are two doors facing him. He rings one of the bells, on the chance: the door half opens—it is Rasputin himself.

Yusupov proposed that he should go with him to the Moïka Palace, where they can talk freely. He flatters him and makes a show of great friendship. But notwithstanding, Rasputin hesitates and it is only with great difficulty that Yusupov finally induces him to accompany him in the car which is waiting outside: they drive away in it, at full speed to outwit the police attached to Rasputin.

[1] The Moïka Canal.

Meanwhile, those friends of Yusupov who were in the plot had met at the Yusupov Palace: the Grand Duke Dmitry, M. Purishkevich, M. Sukhotin (brother of the Horse Guards officer), and a doctor called Lazovert. Some women may have been there right at the beginning, while Yusupov was away fetching Rasputin, but Yusupov had no knowledge of it.

Besides, the accomplices had to stay in a room over the one in which the Prince had had prepared to receive Rasputin. They were not to appear at all. Indeed, Rasputin had insisted that he would only make the visit on the strict understanding that he was alone with Prince Yusupov. Only a trusted servant was to be there, to serve them.

Prince Yusupov's apartment is on a raised ground floor. From several steps giving access to the courtyard of the palace, you go into a vestibule out of which a staircase rises to the floor above, where the Grand Duke was waiting; this staircase also goes down to another room. It is to this room that Yusupov takes his guest.

In this room with its low ceiling there is a table with a samovar, cigarettes, the poisoned cakes, the bottle of Crimean wine prepared beforehand, and another bottle containing wine which was not poisoned. After having got Rasputin to sit down and having engaged him in conversation, the Prince offered him some cakes and suggested a little wine. Rasputin obstinately refuses. Yusupov begins to get worried, but puts this refusal down to a habit of the peasant, who will never eat straight away the first time he enters a house.

After an hour's time, Rasputin has still taken nothing. (He is therefore not the glutton and drunkard, always ready to fling himself on the food and wine, which people told us he was.)

So now Yusupov complains of feeling thirsty, and pours himself out a glass from the unpoisoned bottle. Rasputin gives in and follows his example, drinking a glass and declaring "it's good!", which gives Yusupov an excuse to fill up the glass again.

As Rasputin has relaxed a little, Yusupov manages to get him to take a cake, then he pours out some more wine, this time from the poisoned bottle. Rasputin was now beginning to take to it, he became animated, talked about his gift of divination, and so on. All the while he is talking, he takes the cakes which Yusupov hands him and eats them quite automatically, and he drinks three glasses of the poisoned wine with which Yusupov fills up his glass as soon as it becomes empty.

30

And yet he shows no sign of discomfort and Yusupov already feels alarmed, fearing some supernatural power. Seeking for consolation, he thinks of an excuse to go up to the floor above, where he finds his friends seething with impatience. Rasputin has been there for over three hours, and nothing has been achieved. He will leave, and it will not be easy to find another such chance of having him at their mercy. They talk Yusupov into using more certain methods, and they go and look for arms. The Grand Duke Dmitry then hands a revolver to Yusupov, who goes downstairs again, holding the weapon in his left hand, which is hidden behind his back. When he arrives in the other room, trembling all over, he sees that Rasputin has got up and is walking up and down the room, hiccuping and belching.

Yusupov is still trembling and does not dare shoot because, small and weak as he is, he is frightened of this robust, strapping fellow, even though he is unarmed. He does not want to shoot until he is sure of a direct hit, so he tries to find an excuse to get quite close to him:

"As you have got up, let us go into the next room. I have a beautiful Italian crucifix in there—would you like to see it?"

"Let's go."

It is there, as they stand side by side leaning over and examining the ivory crucifix, that Yusupov slips the revolver into his right hand and, point blank, lets it off into Rasputin's left side, in the region of the heart.

He falls in a heap, with a cry of: "A-a-a-ah! . . . "

Yusupov bends over the body, feels his pulse: he is motionless. There is no doubt; he is dead.

He runs to the floor above, and they all come down to see the corpse. They prod it, and turn it over. The doctor lifts the eyelid and turns back the lips to ascertain that death has occurred.

They go upstairs again, to discuss how to dispose of the body. They drink, and the discussion goes on for some time. Finally, the Grand Duke Dmitry says: "I will take him in my car and we will chuck him into the water," and he goes downstairs with Sukhotin to fetch his car and bring it into the courtyard. Purishkevich also leaves the room for a moment.

Meanwhile Yusupov, seized with the desire to see the corpse of his victim again, goes back to the room in which the drama took place, and bends over the body. . . . It seems to him that one eye is half open. Seized with horror, he bends lower when, all at once the

31

corpse rises up and Rasputin's hand clutches hold of him, tearing off one of his epaulettes. And Yusupov, rooted to the spot with horror, watches Rasputin drag himself along on his stomach and pull himself up by the staircase leading to the vestibule. His voice sticks in his throat, and it is only after several seconds that he is able to shout: "Purishkevich! He's moving! He's alive!"

Purishkevich rushes in, seizes the revolver which had been put down on a table, and they both run out together. Rasputin has managed to get down the stairs leading to the courtyard and he is dragging himself on all fours through the snow: he is going to reach the carriage gates which have been opened to let the car in. The murderers follow him, with Purishkevich emptying his revolver and Yusupov hitting him with a log seized from the pile of wood. He collapses. . . . They wrap him in his fur-lined coat and hurriedly put his galoshes on his feet, to do away with any incriminating evidence. They put him into the car, which disappears in the direction of the islands. A dog which happened to be in the courtyard is killed with a final revolver shot and, to explain away the bloodstains in the snow, it is shown to the police, who have come running at the sound of firing.

In spite of everything, Rasputin was still not quite dead, because at the inquest it was proved by the state of his lungs that he was still breathing when he was thrown into the Neva. . . . When they found him, one arm was raised as though to make the sign of the cross.

Chambrun and I feel that this account must be accurate . . . there are details in it which could not have been invented. Besides, the characteristics of each person are found here: the Grand Duke, who does nothing, but makes the decision and lends his revolver: Prince Yusupov, superstitious, nervous, a mystic even at the moment when he kills his victim while contemplating a crucifix. And then the sadism which drives him to go back and gaze at the corpse. . . .

Thursday 12th April 1917

French, English and Belgian socialist deputies are expected to arrive on Saturday to bring messages of goodwill to the *tovariches*.—What ambassadors!

Soon, the rabble will rule everywhere. It is fair punishment for the so-called 'orderly people', who used their power solely in order to make war. They will learn, at the expense of their pocket-books, that it would have been better to agree with their equals, even on the other side of the frontier, than to all be devoured by the internal enemy.

Saturday 14th April 1917

The famous Allied socialist deputies arrived yesterday at the Finland Station.

Representing France: Cachin, Lafont, and Moutet—two professors of philosophy and a lawyer. Representing England: O'Grady and Thorne, a cabinet-maker and a plumber. . . . I decidedly prefer the English socialists!

There was a crowd at the station—not to honour the Allies, but to welcome the Russian socialist, Plekhanov . . . there were people up on the wooden beams of the platform roof, and on the roofs of the trains. Three bands played the *Marseillaise*. . . .

Our parliamentarians seem bewildered by this disorder. They had lunch today at the Embassy, and made a good impression on M. Paléologue. Afterwards, they went to the Champ de Mars, to the grave of the 'heroes'.

Sunday 15th April 1917

Easter!

I did not go to midnight Mass, which was celebrated in the customary way, as I had work to do in the Embassy. But towards one o'clock in the morning I went with Chambrun to have supper with the Gorchakovs. It was a fine night, and there were crowds in the streets. There certainly seems to have been trouble in some parts of the town, as shots could be heard in the distance. . . . But perhaps they were a sign of rejoicing.

The whole town was lit up. The great onion domes of the Church of the Resurrection, all gold in the reflection of the light from the stained-glass windows below, glowed in the sky. Behind, all the windows of the Preobrajensky barracks were lit up. All the bells were ringing. The cannon of the Fortress were firing salvos. . . . The events of the last few days seemed like a bad dream. It was the Russia of old, rising again with Christ.

The supper party at the Gorchakovs accentuated this impression. The women, who had just come from the Easter services, were in pure white evening dresses. Some of them wore long necklaces of miniature enamelled Easter eggs. The Olives, the Polovtsovs, Bezak, Muraviev, Petr Raievsky, Chambrun and many others were there.... The table was loaded with food, not forgetting the *Paskha*[1] and the little pig with the woe-begone expression.... Gorchakov had fetched the best bottles from his cellar.

This morning an incident brought me back to reality. While I was alone in the Chancery, everyone having gone to Mass, they telephoned from the French hospital to say that M. Lévi, a member of the French colony, had had his car shot at and that the mob had broken into the chapel.

I telephone to the Prefecture where, after several attempts, I manage to speak to the chief of police, who answers that he doesn't know what it's all about and that he can't do anything about it.... Besides, it's a *prazdnik*[2] ... there are no officers, and no one on guard.

Nevertheless I manage to find out what has happened. M. Lévi arrived at the hospital for Mass with his wife and daughter, who were to sing at the ceremony. On arrival, a tyre burst. On hearing the noise, the militiamen who were in the street, believing that they were being attacked, fired on the car which immediately stopped. A crowd rapidly collected at the sound of firing, and as M. Lévi and his family had gone into the chapel, the crowd rushed after them to give them a rough handling. Free fight inside the church. They arrest our compatriots and take them to the police station. The angry crowd throws frozen snow at them and insults them: the militia, however, protect them.

At the police station, which is fortunately close at hand, everything went off in more or less orderly fashion; but our compatriots had to be kept there for several hours, as the crowd was waiting to lynch them on their reappearance. All that, because of a burst tyre!

Monday 16th April 1917

Gentil met the Grand Duke Nicholas Michael, who knew that the

---

[1] Traditional Easter dish made of curds and eggs.
[2] A holiday.

Ambassador had forbidden us to go to his house, and was very hurt by it. He maintains that he said to M. Paléologue to his face, when he met him one day on the quay: "I would be pleased to see you: if you are afraid, use the back stairs."

The Grand Duke talked a great deal about the Emperor. He seems to be unconscious of what is happening. He plays patience, walks in the park which is for his private use, and gives himself up to gardening. Apparently he saw the pit which was being dug in front of the palace for the Tsarskoye victims of the revolution and he approved the choice of site and took an interest in the work. He asked good-naturedly which priests would be taking the service. On being told that there wouldn't be any, he at first criticized this omission. Then the soldiers told him that they would sing all right without the priests. "In that case," he replied, "it will do very well like that!"

Apparently he said that he appreciated Kerensky and regretted not having known him earlier, but he is angry with Guchkov because the revolution, when all's said and done, is only "just a piece of his personal chicanery".

What is one to make of all this talk? Each bit of gossip one hears about the Emperor is different. According to some people, he is an intelligent man, cunning, false, crafty and wicked. According to others, he seems a worthy man but somewhat simple-minded. Some of his actions, for example his abdication manifesto, are sublime. At other times they are disconcerting in their naïvety and lack of discretion. Is he a mystic, and did he believe in Rasputin? Or did he just tolerate him, like a good fellow who allows a concession for the sake of peace in the household?

Tuesday 17th April 1917

The situation remains the same but is hardly reassuring. The French socialist deputies were not received in the way they expected, and show that they are disillusioned. They weakly gave in and approved the demands of the extremists—and Milyukov complained of their action to the Ambassador, asking him to take steps to see that they showed more firmness.

This morning, Kerensky came to lunch at the Embassy. This is a success for Paléologue because up to the present time no member of the government has consented to come. He was dressed in a kind of coat buttoned up to the neck, without hard collar or tie: neither bourgeois, nor workman, nor soldier. On arrival he shook hands with the footmen.

Everyone agrees that they can detect rather a humbug side to him, and a certain falseness. Shubin, who has known him for a long time, says that before the revolution he dressed like everyone else and did not treat the servants as comrades.

He noticeably makes an exhibition of himself. People say, however, that he is intelligent and they think that, without having any great sense of political reality, he is not just a mystical madman living in a dream like most of the Russian socialists. And yet his emaciated face, his glance, his sickly aspect, give him the appearance of a hysteric. He does not inspire me with any confidence.

However that may be, and whatever he is, he seems to be the only man capable of uniting people.

Thursday 19th April 1917

Our socialist missionaries are brightening up a bit. They were able to get a hearing with the Soviet, which seems to be rallying to Plekhanov, who had been exiled and has come with them from France and is in complete agreement with them. The French socialists think that this has lessened the effect made by the speeches of Lenin, the Russian socialist, who has arrived from Switzerland with forty Nihilists. They travelled through Germany, who gave every facility to these people who are so useful to her cause.

Milyukov, however, told Paléologue that he did not think that this extremist would succeed in leading the people, and that he was booed at his first contact with the Soviet.

Friday 20th April 1917

There is beginning to be trouble in country districts. The Petrograd socialists have sent nearly thirty thousand of their people to preach the word to the peasants. The effect is beginning to be felt, and Princess Obolensky has had a telegram from her peasants, asking her to be at her estate "on such-and-such a day, at a certain hour, to discuss the question of partition".

The committee is also making strenuous propaganda for peace. It undertakes to make the government approach the Allies with proposals for a general peace without annexations or indemnities. And yet there can be no question of Russia making a separate peace. But she will inevitably be brought to it, as she is disintegrating from day to day; everything is being frittered away: the lands collected together by the Romanovs are being dispersed. Following Poland and Finland, Siberia wants to separate and have a Constituent Assembly *of its own* and establish an entirely independent government at Irkutsk. Lithuania, the country of the Letts, Little Russia and the Caucasus also want their independence. Someone from Kiev told me that they can only just talk Russian there now. An *officer* said, in front of Chambrun and our deputies: "What do these countries matter to us? Let them go. We prefer a Russia of twenty million free men to an empire of two hundred million serfs." The idea of the Russian state has disappeared with the old régime . . . and now one can see why the Tsars always had to govern with Balts and Germans, because they alone had the idea of the state. The real Russians, they only know how to destroy. In ten minutes they have struck down the régime and dispersed the heritage which the foreign dynasty had amassed for the Russian people. It's a record. But they are quite incapable of remaking what they have destroyed . . . even more incapable of realizing the hopes of the world.

Saturday 21st April 1917

Chambrun saw the Grand Duke Nicholas Michael yesterday and, wishing to get to the bottom of the story about the Grand Dukes' plot of last December, he put the question to him frankly: "Sir, do you recollect seeing me one day when you were shutting the door of the big ground-floor drawing-room behind you, in the Grand Duchess Maria Pavlovna's palace?"—"Yes."—"Were you there, Sir, solely for the purpose of writing the letter about the Grand Duke Dmitry to the Tsar, which was published? . . . Was there not something else?"—"That letter was just a pretext."—"Was there, how shall I put it, a 'reminiscence' of Paul I?"—"Yes," said the Grand Duke again, "but our courage failed us at the last minute. . . ."

There can therefore be no doubt as to what happened that day.

We lunched with the Gorchakovs, who are leaving tomorrow for Moscow. Old Prince Savinsky was there, and Muraviev. The various wines had been particularly carefully treated, for Chambrun, and for me there were the famous little pots of chocolate cream! Naturally, people talked about the events and their repercussion on the war. Chambrun, in a very lively way, upheld the official Embassy view. "If the Russians make peace, *so much the worse for them*. We will be victorious without them, and when peace comes they will get nothing." Muraviev argued against this thesis very cleverly. He said: "Above all, do not say that . . . because people will answer: 'If you can be victorious without us, then carry on alone . . . our only worry is leaving you in the soup. If we are not indispensable to you (since, by the way, we do not want any annexations), we are free and we can leave without any remorse.' On the contrary, you must flatter the Russians and say to them: 'We *need* you. . . . You have just established liberty in Russia: help us to establish it throughout the whole world and let us be more united than ever, to prevent there being a German victory, which would give you back the old régime. . . .' "

Perhaps Muraviev is right. One mustn't try and catch flies with vinegar. . . .

Sunday 22nd April 1917

The whole day has been spent in demonstrations and speeches: "Walk and talk", as an English journalist says.

When I was walking back from Mass, at the corner of Basseinaya Street I ran into an enormous column coming from the Nevsky Prospekt. It was a women's demonstration. I walked alongside the interminable procession as far as Zakharevskaya Street, but I could not reach the head of it, which had turned to the right, towards the Duma. There were several thousand women arm-in-arm, marching ten to a row, singing revolutionary songs. Many of them carried children, or provisions for the day. There were a certain number of them with arm-bands and white flags who directed the progress of the procession, which advanced in the greatest orderliness, with banners and red placards proclaiming their demands. They want the vote for women, higher allowances for the families of those on active service, but above all the end of the war and the return of the soldiers. A big banner displayed the picture of a soldier leaving for the front, with his wife and children trying to hold him back.

The crowd of inquisitive people was on the whole sympathetic towards the demonstrators, and when signs of approval came from a window, the whole procession was covered with a moving forest of waving handkerchiefs.

After lunching at the Embassy, where M. Paléologue had asked me to go with the new attaché Pingaud, I went out with Chambrun and we walked along the quay.

A group of about five hundred women was returning from this morning's demonstration, which had broken up at the Taurid Palace.

As on the day of the 'heroes' funeral, they were singing blood-thirsty songs to the tune of a hymn. The shape of the banners, the good order of the procession, and these tearful women's voices made us think of a pilgrimage. Besides, when they passed the little chapel of the *Jardin d'Eté*, built on the site of the attempted murder of the Emperor Alexander I, nearly all of them crossed themselves while still continuing to sing: "We will pillage! We will cut their throats! We will disembowel them!"

The worst part of all this are the leaders: students in greenish-blue caps and long hair, and fanatical girl students. Just a few of them are enough to lead this flock of sheep, and that is where the danger lies.

We got as far as the Champ de Mars, where a meeting was being held beside the grave of the *tovariches*. Mixing with the crowd of ragged soldiers and *dvorniks* on the spree, we listened to speeches of incredible violence, all of which were applauded and interrupted by pieces of music played by a brass band from a circus.

Our socialist deputies and their English colleagues took the platform, and everything they said was translated sentence by sentence. Although they never mentioned the word war, and although they praised the "heroes who lie facing those palaces which bear witness to an age of shame and abjection", the audience visibly showed its distrust of them. The hurrahs were half-hearted, and no enthusiasm was shown until a man in glasses got up on the wooden case which served as a platform: his coat was buttoned up to the neck, his hair was red and bushy, and he was the real *Herr Professor* type, known popularly as Hansi.

Further away, on the other side of the bridge, on the balcony of Kchessinskaya's[1] house, now the headquarters of the extremists,

[1] Mathilde Kchessinskaya, prima ballerina.

Lenin was rousing the crowd against the "brigand governments of France and England". He added: "You want to get rich: there is money in the banks. . . . You want palaces: go where you please. . . . You don't want to walk in the mud: stop those cars! . . . All this belongs to you—it's your turn—you are the power now!"

In any other country incitement of this kind would lead to the worst excesses. . . . Here, people listen and applaud and everyone throws a few *kopeks* into big, open tanks which stand, unguarded, near the graves on the Champ de Mars. Paper money is piled up inside them and is perfectly safe in the midst of these poor wretches, to whom everyone talks of pillaging and plundering!

I went to the Finland Station to meet M. Albert Thomas.

I arrived there a little too early and I saw groups of *tovariches* with red flags and rusty rifles, who were massing on the quay. I asked one of them if they were waiting for the socialist minister who was due to arrive from France. My question was received with a pitying smile: they were there because of comrades arriving from Germany!

I did not press the point. Anyhow, the scene at the station was well worth watching. On the one hand, the Ambassador in a top-hat, with General Janin and all the officers in military uniform. Opposite, there were militiamen with hang-dog faces, carrying banners and wearing red cockades. There were soldiers who had been given officer rank, dressed in ragged cloaks, epaulettes pinned on with safety-pins, red cloths across their chests, shouting loudly and behaving like rioters. Of course the waiting-room was closed but Leonid, with his usual dignity, managed by negotiating to get it opened for us, so we took refuge in there to wait, as the train was already an hour late and the *tovariches* were getting restive.

At this moment the members of the government arrived: Mil-yukov, Konovalov, and the handsome Tereschenko. Their arrival made no impression on the *tovariches*. And yet they realized that the personage who was expected must be more important than any old murderer of a grand Duke and, at a warning from a few of the leaders, all these sheep changed their minds. Forgetting that they had come there to acclaim international anarchists, they got into line with really astonishing orderliness, with their rifles and their red flags. The train drew into the station. We walked towards Albert Thomas, who stepped down from the carriage and walked to the exit between two rows of armed and orderly thugs, shouting thunderous hurrahs which were primarily intended for international pacifists from

Germany, in honour of the most out-and-out pro-war man, come from France in order to score a triumph for the cause of war.

But in spite of this welcome, I could see that M. Albert Thomas was somewhat taken aback by the appearance of his guard of honour. As for Saint-Sauveur, who returned to Petrograd in his party, he followed like a faithful dog. . . . His nose was even sharper than usual and, to me, he looked quite green.

Tuesday 24th April 1917

This morning we had an interesting lunch. The Ambassador had M. Albert Thomas opposite him, between Sir George and Carlotti. Next to the Ambassador were M. Petit (who is attached to M. Thomas) and Chambrun. At the ends of the table, Dulong and myself.

M. Thomas is hirsute, with shaggy hair and beard, and a carelessly knotted loose tie, and tries in vain to act the fierce socialist by eating his wing of pullet from the end of his knife, and by talking of how he "will make them sweat for it" at the afternoon's meetings. . . . None of this makes the slightest effect and he is completely ignored. The newspapers call him a 'bourgeois' come to represent 'pro-war capitalism'. He is reproached with having already come here last year and been received by the Tsar. They even go so far as to say that he was "the delight of the Countesses of the old régime Rasputinian *salons*".

The workers' and soldiers' committee has decided not to have any relations with this envoy of a bourgeois régime. So for the moment he can only meet the members of the provisional government, that is to say, the people who no longer count. . . . Anyhow, he has not many illusions now.

He is, moreover, a good fellow, with some wit, perhaps a bit too much the French commercial traveller. He likes good food and good wine, and appreciated the excellent bottle of Burgundy which Paléo was keeping for an Imperial dinner-party, and which he resigned himself to uncorking for lack of a better occasion. He is intelligent and forceful, full of ideas which he must know how to put into practice. He has to stay here for a certain time in order to try and get something done, and I am looking forward to having to work with him.

Unfortunately, I fear that he will find himself faced with insurmountable difficulties.

The situation is still the same, and the power for action of the committee seems to take increasing precedence over that of the government. This power has now spread to the whole of Russia. In each administration and in every town there are sub-committees constituted in the same way and which counteract the efforts of the government. In the country districts, propaganda is beginning to bear fruit: this morning's newspapers contain a fairly long recital of estates which have been pillaged, notably under the administrations of Tambov, of Saratov, and in Bessarabia. Naturally these internal disorders react on the army. The soldier thinks about the partition of land and cannot resist the urge to go to his village in order to see what is happening, and to be there and be sure of getting the bit that he covets. Consequently, the number of deserters for last month exceeded seven hundred thousand. Many of them take their rifles with them, and even machine-guns, which *may be useful* to them in their villages.

The officers, too, have second thoughts. They are discouraged by what they see, and are obsessed by the thought of their families whom they have had to leave in the country, exposed to the demands and the acts of violence of the peasants. The war is no longer the most important thing for anyone, not even for those at the front. It is an accessory factor which is added to the internal situation to make it more tragic. Really patriotic officers, seeing that there is nothing to do, are all asking to go to France, and we get some every day begging us to do them this favour. Needless to say, we cannot intervene. Only yesterday I saw one who roused my pity, a Knight of St. George and of the Legion of Honour who, in an awful jargon and with tears in his eyes, implored me to send him to fight in France. I had to tell him that I could do nothing for him.

Wednesday 25th April 1917

I went last night, with Chambrun, Shubin and Colebrook, to a charity concert for which Marianne Derfelden touched each of us for a twenty-rouble note.

It was in a reception-room of the Fontanka Palace, next to the

Tomato's[1] house. It was very old régime: the eagles were still there, and there was a portrait of Peter the Great at the end of the room. All the familiar faces in the audience: Vladimir Paley, the Radziwills, Sophie Dolgoruky, General Knorring, the two Derfeldens (the husband and the brother-in-law), Nicholas Zarnikau, Duchène, Stopford, etc.

The officers had almost all put back their shoulder-knots, as there was no danger in showing them in this place and one could hide them under an overcoat when going outside. The women were in low-cut dresses . . . one could have believed it was before the revolution, and this *entr'acte* amused me. . . .

The concert itself was worse than mediocre. The great attraction was a tango danced by Marianne with Nicholas Zarnikau's brother. All these people have seen her dance like this every night—and it wasn't even a new dress: it's the one she wore one night at the Embassy and which was considered rather daring—but they stood on chairs so as to miss nothing of the spectacle, and gave her a terrific ovation.

I talked to Stopford, who was able to get to Kislovodsk, where he saw the Grand Duchess Maria Pavlovna. The poor woman has had a stroke, and all one side of her face is out of line with the other.

People were talking a lot about an article in the *Russkaya Volya*, attacking Countess Nostitz.

Thursday 26th April 1917

It is very cold again, and I hurriedly got out my fur-lined coat, which I had not worn for two or three days. The Neva had completely thawed: today it is covered with enormous blocks of ice coming from Lake Ladoga, which sail slowly past like great white birds. And to think that it will be the month of May in four days time!

The Embassy is very disturbed by M. Thomas' proposals. He wants to collect all the French organizations together here, transform the drawing-rooms into offices, put telephones everywhere, and so on. Easy to see that he is not the one who pays. Besides, the Russian *nichevo* will get the better of all this splendid activity: he believes that everything can be got ready in four or five days, that the

[1] Author's note: Princess Léon Radziwill.

43

telephones will be on the tables . . . and that they will work! I shall be rather interested to see that happen.

M. Thomas is to have his headquarters in the ballroom, with his chief of staff in the red drawing-room. As for the big dining-room, they have just brought in a dozen tables: it will serve as a hiding-place, far removed from the bullets, for a whole army of generals, colonels and other gold-braided gentlemen of every rank.

The Consulate is being given over to the Press services. The Consul has got to find another building in the next four days, and remove into it his consulate, his archives, his family, etc. . . . He is, in fact, up against a force of complete administrative inertia which cannot fail to leave him victorious.

People's one thought is to pull down walls, put up partitions, open up doorways, and make holes in tapestries for telephone wires. Poor Embassy!

The Ambassador must be heartbroken to see the vandals installing themselves in his Embassy which he had arranged with so much taste; but he is putting a brave face on it. What worries him much more, and what worries all of us, is to see what the newcomers' politics are going to be. I fear that they will lean heavily to the left and will enter too much into the ideas of their Russian co-religionaries, Kerensky in particular. This is very dangerous for the moderate party in the provisional government, and consequently for us. I tremble for Alsace and Lorraine, which have already cost us so dear!!! What would happen, if the power slips away from the Milyukovs and the Chingarevs into the hands of the Kerenskys and their like, in the event of Germany wanting to make serious proposals on the basis of the *status quo ante bellum*? I very much fear that they would be received with enthusiasm here. As for America, she would inevitably agree, in view of the Wilson plan. There remain the Allies of the West. . . . The English will always get some colonies out of it. . . . But what about us? . . . And anyway, would it not be folly to want to fight on alone, or even with the English, against a Germany supplied by Russia and able to bring up fifty more German divisions against our front line, quite apart from the Austrian contingents, and so on? From this angle, the future looks very black, and the Russians have done us a terribly bad turn by having their silly revolution just at the moment when things were going a little less badly.

From the internal point of view, I can see no improvement as yet.

Anarchy tends more and more to become a chronic condition. Everyone is issuing demands. A few days ago, the college students elected a committee to demand the replacement of the *kissel*[1] they are given for breakfast by soup on weekdays and chocolate on Thursdays and Sundays; to get up an hour later; and the right to stay up until ten o'clock at night. They went to the Duma, where they were received by a minister who congratulated them on their spirit of organization and told them, among other nonsense, that they must *control* their professors.

Consequently, in many colleges there have been elections of the professors by the students. As a matter of fact, it is no crazier than making the soldiers elect their officers. Mme du Halgouet knows a family whose little boy took part in this farce. In his school, the pupils had decided to blackball a professor who displeased them; but one of them pointed out the fact that he only had a year to run before retiring and, with a kind-hearted gesture, the class decided to keep him on for the rest of this year. All this has its comic side, but it seems to me typical of the state of mind which reigns at present.

The person who is the most heart-broken over all this is poor Leonid, who came to me with a long tale of woe. In the midst of all these events, we forgot to celebrate his jubilee. . . . He took advantage of this to remind me of the time when he first joined the Legation, twenty-five years ago. . . . How everything has changed since then! His face lights up at the name of Montebello, only to darken again as M. Albert Thomas walks past in his soft hat and his floppy tie.

He is also distressed for his son who is an officer in one of the Guards regiments and who, he says, sees "his career in ruins". And indeed it can be no joke being an officer at the moment, considering that in his regiment they are obliged to have their meals in the barracks with their men.

This morning I lunched at the Halgouets, with Saint-Sauveur (from the Embassy) and M. Lebourgeois and his assistant. There was much talk of Sweden, and of our stupid policy in that country where previously French influence was so solidly established; we have allowed Sweden to fall completely into the hands of Germany. We still persist in the great argument: "In Sweden everything is for the Boche . . .", thereby pushing them still further in the direction

[1] A kind of jelly.

in which they are leaning. We are unable to understand the elementary truth that "You don't catch flies with vinegar". In Sweden, in Bulgaria, in Greece, in Turkey—it's the same story, everywhere. . . . Alas!

I borrowed *General Durakin* from Annik, which is now allowed since all censorship has been abolished, and I spent some happy moments reliving these old memories. . . . There are so many things in that book which are still true today.

I dined with Countess Nostitz, with the General . . . and Lalaing. The poor General is very gloomy. He fears an attack on Petrograd by the Germans from the sea. His fears are justified by the fact that several German divisions have been withdrawn from the Russian front and have not been identified on our own, and by the Emperor William's recent speech at Oderberg, "Soldiers of my guard, our flag already flies over five capitals. Let us go and raise it at Petrograd, where I promise you we will see the end of the war!" According to him, the German fleet would force an entry into the Gulf of Finland, if necessary by fighting the Russian fleet in the very unlikely event of its still being fit to fight; and that it would protect a landing at about a hundred *versts*[1] from the capital. It is obviously a hazardous operation but one which, in my opinion, would have the biggest chances of success at the present time.

The Countess was fairly cheerful. There was no mention of the article in the *Russkaya Volya*. One has to admit that it was really far too silly: it said that the Nostitzes were at Yalta, and that they formed the nucleus of a conspiracy made to prepare the return of the Grand Duke Nicholas Nikolaievich. . . . How likely it sounds: the Nostitzes working for Nicholas Nikolaievich!

I saw Saint-Sauveur du Creusot. He is naturally distressed by the departure of the Ambassador, whom he dines with every night . . . but he is already starting to make a move towards Albert Thomas.

Friday 27th April 1917

At the Embassy, open disagreement broke out between Paléologue and Albert Thomas.

M. Paléologue and the Italian Ambassador both think that we should support the moderates, that is to say, the old Kadets like

[1] One *verst* = 3,500 English feet.

46

Milyukov. Albert Thomas, on the contrary, only has faith in Kerensky and the English Ambassador, Sir George Buchanan, shares this view.

In any case, the Ambassador acted on his own responsibility and yesterday sent a telegram to the French government, exposing the situation and the danger which would threaten the issue of the war if Kerensky and the Soviets triumph. Albert Thomas, to whom he loyally showed his telegram, telegraphed the exact opposite today, insisting that the situation is improving and that one must have faith in the revolution.

He claims to have forbidden the Ambassador to telegraph in future.

Tuesday 1st May 1917

Today is a total *prazdnik.* . . .

All the restaurants, shops and hotels are closed. No *izvozchiks* and no trams. In the hotels, the people living there have been warned that there will be no men-servants and no maids. Neither will there be anything to eat, and yesterday everyone had to buy provisions for the day. M. Doulcet, who has just come from the Hôtel de l'Europe, tells me that there is not one waiter there . . . not even a hall porter. At the Astoria, they have gone a little bit further still. As there is to be a meeting in the Isaac Square, all the bedroom doors are to stay open from nine o'clock onwards, so that they can be sure that no enemies of the people are hiding there, who could fire on the crowd.

Demonstrators have been marching past the Embassy without a stop the whole morning, with music, choirs, and red flags. Processions of women who all wear a red scarf on their heads. . . . School-children carrying red flags and singing: girls' schools, mixed schools, and even down to the nursery schools.

I am just waiting for the procession of babies, demanding their eight o'clock breast feed.

We all had lunch at the Embassy, which was very agreeable, and where there was, quite naturally, some pessimism. After lunch I went out to 'feel the pulse' of the crowd. The first thing I meet on the little Fontanka bridge is a group of demonstrators. They have quantities of red flags and an immense banner carried by several men, on which are represented a French, a Russian and a German worker shaking hands over a cannon and some broken shells. This banner is all surrounded by a group of civilians in perfect marching order, with fixed bayonets, accompanied by a machine-gun on wheels pulled by a soldier.

The processions follow each other at short intervals as far as the Champ de Mars, carrying flags and red banners with inscriptions and pictures on them. The demonstrators are usually grouped according to their factories. Other processions are divided into corporations, still others into town areas. There is relative order. Red is the dominant colour as, besides the big flags and banners, many of the demonstrators carry little flags and streamers. The sunshine is superb, and all these standards palpitate and float, swell out, and bow low in the violent gusts of wind. The sky is crystal clear and a very limpid pale blue, which makes all this warmly lit red stand out in violent contrast. The ice on the Neva is silver white and is beginning to float slowly past, and the water is a deep violet blue, which still further shows up the immaculate whiteness of the ice-floes. Never before have I had such an impression of colour.

The Champ de Mars presents a most lively picture. It is black with people and above the crowd the thousands of red flags wave in the wind like poppies. The trolley-poles of the trams carry immense red banners with inscriptions. In the middle, round the graves are black flags bordered in red. A few white flags—the white flag is the colour of the International. On the marble palace a great banner with the inscription: "Long live the International!"

Little platforms have been put up everywhere and orators are speaking to the crowd. Others are perched on *lomovoys*,[1] which have been unharnessed and brought here for the purpose. Lastly, in this swarming mass, there are motor lorries full of men and soldiers who manage with difficulty to hold aloft the immense red banners which the wind lifts up and puffs out: they look like ships in full sail, navigating on a black sea swell. They stop from time to time and from these ambulating platforms a bare-headed orator, his hair blowing in the wind, harangues the crowd. Here and there, regimental bands play the *Marseillaise* as it might be played in a circus, and their brass instruments shine and reflect the sun.

The tone of the speeches is fairly violent. They vituperate against the capitalists and the bourgeois. Nobody mentions the war, and one feels that none of these people take any interest in it and have decided to make peace.

[1] Lomovoy—a dray.

After staying there for over an hour, I walked across the bridge in order to pass in front of Kchessinskaya's house. There, the tone is more violent still. Orators succeed each other in the little gazebo which is just on the corner of Kamenno Ostrov,[1] and which would seem to have been built purposely as a platform! There, I listened to a workman in a cap, a student, and then a man dressed in a kind of *kaftan*, whose pointed beard and long red hair were strangely lit up by the sun's rays. Several soldiers spoke too. They all want the end of the war, and they clamour for the 'International'. "Of what use are frontiers to people who have no bread?" "There is only one thing which counts—money. We must take it where we can find it . . . even from the priests(!), and establish universal peace!" The crowd applauds, and seems even more advanced in its ideas than the speakers themselves. Then comes a very young soldier who has returned from the trenches: he describes his sufferings there and concludes with the necessity of ending this war which weighs on the people, thereby letting the Germans in. One voice, however, is raised in protest. . . . So then the soldier, with a really superb gesture, tears off his cloak and shouts: "If there's anyone who wants the war, let him go there: let them take this uniform and leave for the front. But I, I who have lived in that Hell, I am never going back there again!" And the contradictor is booed by the crowd, who give the soldier-orator a real ovation.

I have just got back to the Embassy, rather worn out because I have spent the afternoon on my feet, and the Petrograd pavements are always tiring. Coming back along the quay, I noticed that they have removed the sword from the statue of Suvorov in front of the British Embassy, and that they have replaced it with a red flag.

At any rate it is a little less crowded than before and it seems that the demonstrators are beginning to get tired. Up till now there has been no trouble, and everything went off with singing and speech-making. The passiveness of these people is unbelievable and, although I am used to it, it astonishes me every time.

Thursday 3rd May 1917

Today the situation has suddenly become rather critical. The provisional government has for long been divided over the question of

---

[1] Kamenno Island.

war aims. Kerensky wanted a conference at which the Allies would revise their war aims on the basis of the socialist programme of 'no annexations or contributions'. Milyukov, with the Kadets, wanted on the contrary to honour the obligations undertaken by Russia towards her Allies, in particular those towards us concerning Alsace and Lorraine. The two parties have agreed to send a *note* to the Allied governments. This note, drawn up according to Milyukov's ideas, appeared this morning and has provoked indignation in the Committee of Workers' and Soldiers' Deputies. The soldiers are very worked up against Milyukov, and it seems certain that he will be forced to leave the Ministry. He would be followed in his resignation by the moderates, and the government would fall into the hands of Kerensky and of his party. There is a whole group which goes further still and is insisting on the resignation of the entire government, Kerensky included. If this demand were given in to, there would be complete anarchy. Be that as it may, there is great excitement in the town. Meetings are being held in all the squares. Three regiments have declared themselves against the government, and it is feared that they will clash with those troops who support it. I have just seen two motor lorries go past filled with armed workers, which reminded me of the first day of the revolution. I hope, however, that the situation will sort itself out, because this time it seems to me that the partisans of order are numerous and are not going to let themselves be swamped by the elements of the left. But how can one ever know, in this country? Yesterday we were congratulating ourselves on the *victory* of Milyukov, who substituted a simple note for the conference which Kerensky wanted . . . and today the entire government is tottering.

Friday 4th May 1917

Throughout yesterday there were fairly violent demonstrations. The centre of the agitation was in the Astoria Square, in front of the seat of government (the Mariinsky Palace on the other side of the Moïka, where the Council of Empire used to be). They made a lot of noise, but on the whole no harm was done. The members of the government spoke to the crowd and appeased it by promising to come to some agreement with the Committee.

Today has been a worse day. The demonstrations continued,

particularly on the Nevsky Prospekt, some in support of the government, others against it and against the war. Towards five o'clock two processions clashed near the Hôtel de l'Europe and exchanged a few shots. In the evening, at about nine o'clock, there was another burst of shooting near the English shop.

As there was a great deal of work in the Embassy I hardly went out, and I took no part in the affray. I cannot therefore write from personal experience. But to my mind there has nevertheless been some progress, as there seem to be two mainstreams, and people are fighting. It would therefore seem that at least a part of the populace is trying to break out of the state of apathy and anarchy into which, until now, all were agreed to remain. Most of yesterday's victims were soldiers: consequently, the troops are very angry with the workers, whom they accuse of having stolen arms from the streets! These same soldiers, who today are complaining that the workers are using their arms and stirring up trouble, were shooting in every direction a few weeks ago, and massacring the representatives of order!

It's like Albert Thomas, who reminded us the other day that he had been out in the streets against Briand in the railway strike and who, after having been a minister in Briand's cabinet, comes here to uphold the principles of authority!

Sunday 6th May 1917

The state of anarchy is confirmed and extends further and further every day. Petrograd is no longer the only centre: it's the same everywhere, in Moscow, in Kiev, and confusion and disorder reign. The two influences of the government and of the Committee cancel each other out, and the result of this double authority is chaos and anarchy. Everyone does as he pleases, and from now on it is useless to count on any concerted effort from Russia. A lot of people, Albert Thomas amongst them, still believe in the possibility of a Russian *offensive*, which would revive national feelings. General Alexeiev has solemnly promised us this offensive, but for my part I do not share these illusions. It is possible that the High Command might give the order to attack but, in my opinion, it is incapable of carrying out the order and especially of *organizing* the attack, which is the only real condition of success.

Pacifist ideas are gaining ground daily, and the only formula in the order of the day is 'no annexations and no contributions'. This has *always* been my formula, and I consider that if the butchery were to end without any advantage to any of the belligerents, it would be the best possible lesson to the populations concerned: they would be too disgusted to allow their governments to plunge them into a similar venture for a long time.

But in actual fact France must, at the very least, be able to get out of the war with possession of Alsace and Lorraine, or at least a part of these provinces. I have no false sentimentality about it, and the thought of 'revenge' is entirely foreign to me. But I consider this conquest to be necessary, to pacify feeling in France. Everyone's mind is hypnotized by this question and if we did not obtain satisfaction, at least in part, we would be exposed to the worst disturbances by those people who have suffered from the war, who would be unable to flatter their self-esteem by feeling that, although they had suffered, they had now got what they wanted. The solution to the problem would be more easily solved by giving up some colony or other to Germany, which would give the Germans the similar satisfaction of feeling that they had got something, and would remove all idea of vengeance from them.

But I do believe that if we want to retrieve these two provinces from the war (and they will, alas, have cost us far too dear) and avoid terrible internal upheavals, it is important not to waste another minute.

For what would we do if Germany came to propose peace to us tomorrow, adopting the socialist formula 'without annexations or conquests', and if she took the initiative of getting the populations of Alsace-Lorraine to ask for a plebiscite for these two provinces? It would be impossible for us to accept such an offer, because we know that the inhabitants would vote against us, especially if under pressure from the German authorities. And yet one can be quite certain that, if we refused, the entire Russian democracy would turn against us with talk of 'the sharks of French imperialism', as has already been done here by several newspapers.

But even without envisaging such a pessimistic hypothesis as some such an offer from Germany, which would turn public opinion against us (and not only that of Russia, but of all the neutral countries and even of our new American allies), there are plenty of eventualities to be feared. I am not even thinking of the eventuality of Russia making a separate peace. This hypothesis, although perfectly possible, does not seem a likely one to me for the following reasons: firstly, the Slav imagination, which is nebulous and Utopian, sees things on a larger scale and dreams of a general peace for everyone; secondly, to make peace is to act, and the Russian is incapable of any form of action. But without going so far ahead, and without foreseeing open treachery by Russia in concluding a peace with our enemies and thereby giving them the chance to reinforce, there is at present a situation which is in point of fact just as dangerous. As a result of the confusion, the Germans are able to withdraw a considerable number of troops from the Russian front, and they need only leave weakened units there with some machine-guns, which will be enough to repel any attempt at an offensive, if by some miracle anyone could get the herd to attack.

The failure of the French offensive, in which we suffered losses out of all proportion to the results obtained (I do not dare give the figures), has proved that the influx of enemy troops on our front line is redoubtable. What would happen if Russian inertia became complete and made it possible to get Austrian and Turkish and other contingents into France? The transfer of about fifteen German divisions was enough to annihilate the heroic and admirably prepared effort of the French army, and to transform a very extensive strategic conception, from which we could justifiably hope for first-class results, into a mere tactical operation, brilliant but sterile.

My view is also that the present situation is even more serious than a separate peace by Russia because, in that event, at least we could resort to letting the Germans be paid by the faithless ally, on condition that we received what we want, by way of compensation. Now, in point of fact, the Russian army does not worry the Germans any more than it would if peace were already declared. I must add that a surprise attack on Petrograd is always possible, and a success of this kind for our enemies would make the situation of the Allies regarding their state of *unity* all the worse at the moment of liquidation. Thus we are tied to Russia, and have to suffer the counter-effects of her defeats: and we cannot expect any useful effort from her. It is a pact between fools.

That is how I see the present situation: it has never seemed so alarming to me. The latest news from Rumania is equally very bad, and the contagion has spread to Jassy, which is on the eve of a revolution.

Under these conditions, we ought at least to have a strong man here, who is not afraid to speak out to save that which can still be saved. They are recalling Paléologue at the very moment when his 'strong manner' could produce results. Whatever may be the qualities of intelligence and hard work of Albert Thomas, it is deplorable that they should have sent a man here whose very presence is a concession to socialist ideas. No matter how vehemently he opposes the fantasies of the Russian pacifists, and with however much energy and moderation, the mere fact that it is Comrade Albert Thomas who is speaking divests the words of the representative of France of all their authority.

What is needed here, unless they want to send a general with a dog-whip (which would be much the best solution in a country where all backs are still waiting for the knout), is a very shrewd and very crafty career diplomat, who would know how to compromise the Russian leaders so cleverly that they would have to play our game and lean on us for support. I believe that any politician, and particularly a politician of the left, would be disastrous as an ambassador. Besides, I would be very surprised if they could find one who would risk taking on such a dangerous adventure.

But I repeat, what I would prefer would be a strong riding-whip to threaten all these cowards and make them do something; the military reaction which is sure to be born of all this disorder and anarchy would then have something to lean on if necessary.

But all this promises still to provide us with some very nasty moments. Shubin, whom I saw today, is gloomier and gloomier. The Grand Duke Nicholas Michael himself, with whom Chambrun had a long conversation, has lost his forced optimism of the first few days and does not deny that the situation is getting worse and worse the longer it is prolonged. I fear that in France, where people always see things as they would like them to be, and not as they really are, they are suffering from terrible illusions. Russia will never agree to a fourth winter campaign, and it seems to me impossible for us to obtain a *military* solution to the problem on our own front during this summer's campaign.

Monday 7th May 1917

After lunch I went to see Countess Kleinmichel. The poor woman arouses one's pity. She has been guarded for forty days by a gang of soldiers who stole things from her house, made holes in the pictures, ruined the tapestries, and so on. There were sixty of them who behaved as complete masters in her house and penetrated even to her bedroom. They let no one into the house and they did not even allow her to see her doctor. They stole part of her silver, and the arms which were in the smoking-room, and so on. And now, the big drawing-room has been turned into a meeting-place for the area section of the Workers' and Soldiers' Committee, with wooden trestle tables set up, beside which the little pink chairs are arranged. . . . The floor is filthy . . . no carpet on the stairs, the tapestries have gone, and I felt sick at heart to find the house, which was once so well kept, in this state.

The Countess received me in her bedroom. She is very brave, and views the events calmly. . . . She told me that she has on her the wherewithal to kill herself, rather than be murdered if fresh troubles arise. "After all," she said, "I have lived for seventy years; it's not everyone who reaches this age: one must know how to die." And she has decided to kill herself, rather than submit to the same fate as her Kleinmichel nephew who was an officer at Louga: he was killed by his men after having been blinded, having seen two of his friends murdered, and having his hands cut off. His mother had the courage to go and ask the soldiers for his body, which was no more than a blood-stained bundle which they had rolled in the mud.

The poor Countess has been through some terrifying moments: she was shut up in the Duma for three days at the beginning of the revolution, with a chair to sleep on, in the middle of *gardavoys* who were being brought in as prisoners, several of whom died of their wounds beside her. She was then taken to her house, where she was at the mercy of the soldiers, who came to her bedroom to smoke and describe the massacre of the officers to her: she is still held under some denunciation or some act of vengeance . . . she is as pitiful as a hunted animal. Everyone has got their knife into her, but there is nothing with which she can be reproached . . . Kerensky himself, in his capacity as Minister of Justice, confirmed this to Shubin.

Naturally we talked a bit about everything during the two hours I spent with her. She is particularly shocked by the behaviour of the Grand Dukes. She heard from one of the sailors who was guarding her, and who had taken part in the deputation which went to announce to the Grand Duke Cyril that his rank had been confirmed by election, that the Grand Duke answered: "I am ashamed to belong to the Romanov family: it is not for me to command decent people like you." If this is true, it is hard to imagine anything more cowardly.

She sharply criticized the recent marriages of Leuchtenberg and of Prince Gabriel. . . . The latter, when announcing his marriage to his dancer, is supposed to have said: "She has just won eight hundred thousand roubles gambling: I shall have enough to live on. . . ." A prince of the Imperial house being kept by a tart from the ballet!

Sandro is hardly any better behaved. His wife got her former husband, Ignatiev, to give her a million roubles, and it is with this money that they are setting up house. . . . It all stinks. . . .

Sunday 13th May 1917

The Russians, even those who had tried to serve the new régime have lost confidence. . . . They dare not stay at home.

The Polovtsovs are leaving the Moïka (the Artzinovich house) and are moving into the house on the quay which is opposite the one which they occupied last year, on the other corner. They have offered us their house in the islands, for us all to move into for the summer, but it is unfortunately too far away and even with the car it would be impossible. There is now some question of transferring the French hospital of Lesnoy there so that the house should not be unoccupied, which is highly dangerous at present . . . witness the misadventure which befell Sandro of Leuchtenberg which someone has just told me about.

While he was living love's young dream in Finland, a gang of anarchists arrived at his palace and installed themselves there by force, proclaiming that "he could not need his house, as he was not in it". There are about forty of them there, armed to the teeth, putting the anarchist phalanstery into practice. A piece of red calico is fixed to the door, with the inscription 'Anarchist Club' on it, and red and black placards demand the immediate partition of the land and the International. Up to now, nobody has dared to evict this gang, and the Workers' and Soldiers' Committee has stated that it can do nothing as "all opinion is free in Russia, and one cannot blame citizens for having anarchistic views".

Charming country, where installing oneself in someone else's house is "having anarchistic views", and consequently is not only allowed but recommended.

Yesterday I saw Mme Ermolov, who brought Marie-Claire Mordvinov's jewellery to me, as arranged. She is more pessimistic than ever and can only think about selling up everything and going to live in France. She has sold her wine-cellar to the new club and is getting ready to sell that of her son: she told me that there is more than three hundred thousand roubles worth there! I can understand that she should want to rescue this from the gullets of those brutes, who wouldn't even be capable of appreciating all those treasures.

Wednesday 16th May 1917

I have just come back from the Finland Station, where we drove the Ambassador. M. Sazonov,[1] who was to have left with him to take possession of his Embassy in London, received a note from the provisional government at the last moment, when he had already arrived at the station, ordering him not to leave as Milyukov had resigned during the night.

It was a sad departure. It marks the end of so many things. Few people there: the staffs of the Embassy and the Military Mission, Saint-Sauveur, Darcy, Beaupied, and Mme du Halgouet were also there. No government representatives or foreign diplomats because, officially, the Ambassador is only going on leave. General Nostitz is the only Russian who took the trouble to come: he is a well-bred man.

It was a gloomy little group standing there on the wooden platform, surrounding M. Paléologue who was smiling, and M. Sazonov who was white-faced and tight-lipped: the clouds were low, and a fine rain trickled in dirty rivulets off the metal roofs of the long dark green carriages which formed the background.

The sudden decision of the government not to send M. Sazonov to London proves that the crisis, reopened by M. Guchkov's resignation the day before yesterday, has been still further aggravated, and everyone is worried. 'Mlle Marie' alone, who was very calm and watched over His Excellency's luggage with tender care, seemed happy to be leaving: she had already forgotten the heart-rending farewell to her cat Titi, who has to stay behind in the Embassy.

In a nearby compartment, as happy as a bird let out of its cage,

---

[1] Prime Minister from 1910 to 21st July 1915.

Renée Baltha is installed next to Léon Kochubey, who had already started to tell her one of those stories which are his speciality, and which make our Minister[1] so unhappy.

Further off are Cachin and Moutet, the socialist deputies, who also seem happy to be leaving. One of them (Cachin) when shaking hands with us said: "I'm sorry for you having to stay here . . . with all these madmen."

Thursday 17th May 1917

Russia has slipped further down the dangerous slope. Kerensky becomes Minister for War in the place of Guchkov. Milyukov is expected to be replaced by Tereschenko. Nobody knows yet whether the other Kadets will remain. The situation is serious: and the fact that Sazonov did not leave for London clearly shows the change in Russian policy as it concerns the conduct of the war. The worst is to be feared from Russia, who staged the revolution in order to have peace, and who wants peace at any price.

M. Albert Thomas seems to be hesitating as to what policy to follow, because he can see the danger and realizes that he has perhaps contributed towards this latest development by flirting with the Workers' Committee during the last three weeks, and by encouraging its intrigues against the moderate element in the government. But, with his equable temperament, he has not been discouraged. His policy has undoubtedly produced good results, and he has even succeeded in getting the Soviet to publish a manifesto in favour of continuing the war. . . . But I fear that his methods are not right for this country. One should not treat these people like friends, but one should talk to them like a master. But I am about the only person who feels like this; everyone else wants to cure Russia by the homoeopathic method. . . . I maintain that only a surgical operation can save her: it is very dangerous, but it is the only hope of salvation.

Several people coming from Moscow and Kiev tell me that these two towns are as contaminated as Petrograd. And yet, up to now there have been no serious disturbances in the big centres. It is, rather, a slow disintegration. It is not the same in the country districts. The soldiers charged with keeping order in the surround-

[1] M. Doulcet.

ings of Orel have joined forces with the peasants. They have pillaged the stocks of alcohol and have set fire to all the estates. The newspapers say that the horizon is a red circle every night in this district.

The peasants have taken over the Zamoysky country house and have converted one wing into a school, another into the Mayor's office, one pavilion into a hospital, and so on.

Saturday 19th May 1917

A government has been formed ... young Tereschenko is Minister for Foreign Affairs ... and to think that, three months before the fall of the old régime, he was refused the post of attaché in a small legation. The only public position he has ever occupied is that of attaché to the Imperial theatres; and it was to him that one telephoned, through the *chasseur*, when one wanted a box for the ballet.

In charge of Agriculture there is a citizen who is in favour of the confiscation of all private estates for the benefit of the state. At the War Ministry there is Kerensky, who has declared in his proclamation that he is going to re-establish iron discipline in the army ... whereas, a little further on, he admits that he himself has never submitted to any discipline. . . . It appears that he has good intentions and will make every effort to quell the rising flood. . . . And yet, has he not already been overwhelmed?

Consequently, I cannot share the optimism which is beginning to revive in French circles, following the declaration of the new government. . . . Fine words are not enough to give me confidence, and it is clear that the government is absolutely incapable of carrying out its decisions, since it has neither army nor police. Whether these fine orders are obeyed or not depends solely on the goodwill of the military, as they have no other backing.

Albert Thomas leaves tonight for Moscow; and from there he is to go to the front, to prepare a Russian offensive. . . . There are still some people who have illusions.

Monday 21st May 1917

Albert Thomas sends glowing telegrams from Moscow and manages to communicate his enthusiasm to most of the French people in

59

this place . . . in the chancery they are talking about the impending Russian offensive. Alas! I cannot manage to share these hopes and I can see no sign of improvement. Kerensky flatters himself that he will reorganize the army and restore its military spirit: I doubt whether he will succeed before being overwhelmed, like those who preceded him in power. Anarchy is too attractive to the Russian character . . . and Kerensky can do nothing against it. In fact, his supporters are deplorable: his right-hand man is a *praporchik*[1] called Kuzmin who, at the time of the 1905 rising, led the rioters at Krasnoyarsk and proclaimed the republic there, after having the officers massacred. . . . He was condemned to death; but the Emperor was weak enough to pardon him. One is allowed to distrust the new War Minister's work of regeneration when he has advisers like these. . . .

The economic situation becomes more and more agonizing every day. The greater part of the land will not be cultivated this year, because the few agricultural labourers who have agreed to work are insisting on the eight-hour day, which they interpret Russian-fashion. . . . It means almost certain famine. There are also strikes, particularly in the coal-fields, and Shubin told me that the Minister for Commerce, Konovalov, who is a friend of his, did not disguise his anxiety; he envisages the day when the railways will come to a standstill.

One must therefore have no illusions. It is certain that Russia does not want any more of the war; and one can confirm that at any rate *here* there will be no new winter campaigns. The Allies, therefore, must achieve their own victory before the winter. But can one hope for as much, with all the socialist intrigues and the lassitude which seems general in every country? The future looks very black, under these conditions.

Thursday 24th May 1917

There is complete anarchy in the transport system.

A few days ago, at the Nicholas station, I was present at the departure of the Moscow train. Naturally everywhere was crammed full of people: in the compartments, in the corridors, on the running-boards, on the roofs, and with five or six soldiers piled

[1] An ensign.

into each lavatory. The station-master, judging that it was dangerous for the train to leave under such conditions, tried to make the *tovariches* get off (needless to say, not one of them had paid for a ticket). When this failed, he asked the Workers' and Soldiers' Committee for help. They sent a detachment, commanded by an officer who called on the soldiers to obey. They refused, and they too decided to nominate a committee ... elections took place immediately, and a 'train committee' was constituted in the carriages and on the roofs. This committee naturally decided that they should stay there; as the soldiers said, "Our committee is just as good as the other one because, after all, they are both elected by us."

The Central Committee had to be asked for fresh instructions, and it gave the order to use force. The officer sent his men into the train, to evacuate it. But the recalcitrant soldiers addressed the newcomers thus: "We're going to Moscow. . . . You've never been there? . . . Now's your chance. . . . Come on! Let's all go together. . . ." and they had no difficulty in persuading them. A few minutes later the officer was left standing all by himself on the platform and the soldiers had forced the station-master to let the train leave. It pulled out, several hours late, taking with it not only all the soldiers who had boarded it illegally, but also those who had been sent to evict them . . . all this, in the name of the train committee, which apparently continued to make decisions at will throughout the journey and never missed a chance to tyrannize the passengers who had paid for their seats.

Friday 25th May 1917

There are hardly any demonstrations to be seen. The Russians have ended by getting tired of that too . . . and yet it was their great passion, and nobody can tell how many processions there have been here during these last two months. As a matter of fact, they were a most picturesque sight: the choirs of men and women, the bands playing a slow-motion caricature of the *Marseillaise*, and the prodigious quantity of red flags, standards, banners and streamers. . . . Seen from above, these processions were a fantastic sight: the scarlet line of all these emblems waving above the peoples' heads was superimposed, as with stage scenery, and gave the impression of a single splash of colour, all red above the black mass of the demonstrators. . . . Together with the white of the snow, it made up the colours of Germany. . . . Could it be a symbol?

One of the last processions was that of the 'free women', that is to say the prostitutes, who went to the Taurid Palace led by a band, with beautiful red flags flying, triumphantly making their claims, whose nature I was unfortunately unable to discover.

Now, it is speeches and orders of the day which are the fashion. They are just as useless, and far less picturesque.

Saturday 26th May 1917

The formula of 'no annexations and no contributions' has become an article of faith which nobody here disputes any longer, and in order to make the Russian people understand the claims of France concerning Alsace and Lorraine we have to say. that we want the 'de-annexation' of these provinces.

The formula of the Russian revolutionaries gives me boundless pleasure, and represents enormous progress for humanity. The barbarian who conquered his neighbour, seized the neighbour's field: civilization, by forbidding him to reap the fruits of his victory, has banished war between individuals. Are we on the eve of carrying this progress into effect in the society of nations? It would be the end of armed conflict, which would no longer have the conquest of other peoples' territory as a bait. Perhaps it would mean the establishment of international tribunals, which would judge disputes between countries in the way in which our tribunals judge quarrels between individuals. To those who object that the decisions of these tribunals will be ineffective for lack of a policeman to make people respect them, one can only say that the same objection could have been made in primitive societies where, after all, justice did end in being established.

Besides, if the Allies are victorious some day and if they take advantage of their victory to institute justice and fairness by renouncing all personal profit, and by not insisting on any annexations or contributions from the vanquished, then an international police force will become a reality. In future, any state which wants to violate justice will find its action opposed by the full force of all the other countries, which would unite to make justice respected, as they are doing now against Germany.

The will-power of revolutionary Russia, the intervention of the United States, the efficient propaganda of the socialists of all countries, seem to be bringing us closer to the fulfilment of this dream. . . . I fear, alas, that English selfishness will make this progress of humanity impossible: for England will never allow herself to make sacrifices which do not bring something in. The country which oppresses so many millions of human beings in every climate will never consent to people being able to order their own lives freely, nor to admit that to *conquer* is a crime, like to *steal*.

Sunday 27th May 1917

Kerensky is at the front with Albert Thomas. . . . He makes superb speeches and issues heroic orders of the day in which he only speaks of discipline and imminent offensives. All this is of literary value only, in the state of anarchy in which Russia finds herself.

The time limit which has been fixed for deserters to rejoin their units, under pain of the severest penalties, expires tomorrow—and nobody is worried about it. . . . The soldiers continue to travel about on the trains. Shubin asked an officer-deserter-stoker whether he was not going to rejoin his regiment, and he replied "that he was not so crazy as to give up a good job to go and risk getting himself killed, and that he didn't give a damn for Kerensky and his orders of the day".

The assistant to the Minister for War has had, too, to admit, in an official speech, that out of a detachment of a thousand soldiers sent to the front line only fifty arrived: he mentioned other incidents of the same kind.

It is a fact that the men who have broken all records by overthrowing a three-hundred-year-old régime in half an hour are incapable of imposing their will on the crowd, which they have taught to disobey with impunity.

Monday 28th May 1917

There is undeniably a feeling of general disenchantment and renewed talk of a military reaction . . . names are being mentioned, people assure one that such-and-such a minister would favour a *coup d'état*, and that Cossacks are being sent.

For my part, I would feel very sorry to see the reaction take this form, for nothing is more odious than military rule. We would have to renounce the ideal which the Russian revolution has given to the world, which is a general and lasting peace founded on the right of peoples to rule themselves, without being compromised by the incitements of governments under the pretext of revenge, since all annexation of territory against the wishes of its inhabitants would be prohibited.

However, I hope that, whatever may happen here, the Stockholm meetings will bring us closer to this ideal, and that relations between civilized peoples will stop being like they were in the days of the barbarians. If we succeed in effacing the word *conquest* from the vocabulary of civilized humanity, we will at last have founded international relations on a basis of justice and fairness whereas, up till now, they have rested on covetousness and brute force alone.

Wednesday 30th May 1917

We have just heard of the appointment of the new Ambassador. It is M. Noulens.

The situation is not improving: all the shops in the *Gostiny Dvor* have been shut for two days because of a dispute between the stall-holders and the employees.

In the factories, the demands of the workers are such that many industrialists are thinking of closing their factories down, which will cause still further trouble.

Today, a procession of armed workmen (there were not very many of them, it's true) carrying black flags, marched along the Nevsky Prospekt, shouting "Long live anarchy!"

Thursday 31st May 1917

In spite of the heroic orders of the day, the situation at the front is horrible and Kerensky himself, in one of his speeches, mentioned the regiments which have made peace with the enemy regiments confronting them.

It is even worse in the navy. At Kronstadt the Committee of Workers' and Soldiers' Deputies has been reconstituted, with a majority consisting of Lenin's supporters. It has proclaimed that the town now forms an independent republic and does not recognize the authority of the Petrograd government. At the same time it called upon the government to hand over Kchessinskaya's house to Lenin, and threatened to send cruisers up the Neva to force the government to obey.

Saturday 2nd June 1917

Konovalov, the Minister of Commerce, has sent in his resignation in order to 'utter a warning cry', as he puts it . . . the economic situation is desperate; the workers issue increasingly threatening demands; production is dwindling; the chaos in the transport system threatens to leave the town without food supplies and to leave industry without fuel or raw material. All the factories are faced with having to close down. What will happen when all these workmen are suddenly turned on to the streets, armed with the rifles and machine-guns which are still in their possession?

M. Albert Thomas is due back from the front tomorrow and will soon be leaving for France. In consequence of Ribot's recent speech, in which he says that "a French peace must not be the peace of the socialists, but the peace of victory", the situation is going to be very difficult here, and for him more than for anyone else.

I had lunch today at Donon's restaurant with Poznansky, the legal adviser to our Embassy, who is now a member of the Municipal Council. In the past he was very much to the left and had dealings with the Soldiers' and Workers' Committee. Now, he is worried and pessimistic, and visibly alarmed lest they go for his purse.

Tereschenko was lunching at the next table and I was able to observe him . . . he certainly looks forceful and intelligent but he definitely does not inspire confidence. Poznansky, who knows him well, told me his life story. After studying at the Leipzig seminary, he passed his law degree in Moscow brilliantly, and astonished the jury with his knowledge of Roman law, to the extent that they offered him a full professorship if he would remain at the faculty. But his one ambition was to obtain a position at court, and in order to achieve this he got himself attached to the administration of the

Imperial theatres, where he did not remain for long because of his bad-tempered character. So then he tried to get into the diplomatic service, where they would have nothing to do with him.

At the outbreak of war he got busy with the Red Cross, hoping thereby to earn the court appointment which was his heart's desire. Having once more met with a refusal, he remained in Kiev, where he owns vast factories. When the Committee for War Industries was formed, he was elected president of the Kiev committee and sent as delegate to the Central Committee in Petrograd. With the support of the president of this Committee, Guchkov (who was indebted to him financially), he played an important part and made himself popular by upholding the claims of the workers to be represented. At the congress which took place a few weeks before the revolution, he took the chair in place of the president who was ill, and became one of the leading personalities, with Konovalov and Guchkov, and was all ready to form part of the new government; he was given the post of Minister of Finance which he exchanged for that of Foreign Minister on the departure of Milyukov.

He is certainly, besides Kerensky, one of the most valuable men in the present government . . . but what a strange fate, to become the great man of the revolution and Foreign Minister of Russia at the age of thirty . . . because you failed to become a Gentleman of the Bedchamber.

It is said, besides, that he is thinking of a more permanent position, and many people see him as the future Russian Ambassador in Paris.

Sunday 3rd June 1917

A *tête-à-tête* dinner with Countess Kleinmichel, who was good enough to drink with me the last bottle of French champagne that they have left her. We had supper in her bedroom as there was a meeting in the ballroom of her palace and we could hear the noise of the *tovariches'* voices.

The poor Countess is indeed worn out, and has sold her palace outright complete with all its contents: pictures, collections, silver and china, as well as her *dacha*[1] in the islands . . . she is planning to settle into the Bear Hotel, as she does not want to leave Petrograd

[1] A country house.

until the end of the war, in order to prove the falseness of all the calumnies of which she has been the subject . . . but as soon as peace is made, she will go and live in France or Italy.

In fact, the enquiry which was held concluded that she was completely innocent . . . and yet the examining magistrate insisted on having proof that Boni de Castellane, whose name was mentioned in one of the letters which they seized, "was not a German"! What criminal lunatics!

The Countess is very courageous; she really is a woman of spirit, stout-hearted, and a great lady.

Monday 4th June 1917

People in our countries do not understand what a difficult task the Allied ambassadors in Petrograd have had. The problem they were up against was, in fact, an insoluble one. In order to carry out the policy of their governments and save their own countries from catastrophe, they had to push Russia into an out-and-out war, at whatever cost. So, inevitably, the continuation of a war which *the Russian people were against, ever since the winter of 1914*, was bound to lead to revolution . . . and inevitably this, in its turn, was bound to lead to peace.

Far-seeing Russians, amongst them the Balts who are more realistic than the Slavs, have for long understood this tragic situation and since their country was in any case doomed to be defeated they wanted at least to spare it the horrors of revolution. They justifiably felt that a great people does not perish because the fortunes of war have gone against it; but they believed that any attempt against the régime would topple the whole Russian edifice. As opposed to these conservatives who were branded with the name of Pro-Germans, the ambassadors therefore had to rely on the partisans of out-and-out war, the nationalists (who are as blind as nationalists of all countries), the industrialists (who are obviously interested in the continuation of the war), and on the men of the left. Amongst the latter, there were undoubtedly some who were sincere patriots, prepared to put their country above their political convictions, and who were therefore all the more easily taken in by the mirage-like formula of 'war to the knife', with its appearance of patriotism; but many others knew that the continuation of the war was the surest way of undermining the régime and allowing the revolutionary cause to triumph.

As for victory, and the consolidation of the régime by armed conquest, nobody believes in it since the winter of 1914 ... not even the ambassadors, who tried in vain to convince themselves while proposing this as a goal to the Russian effort. The only thing which surprises me is that Russia should have 'stuck it' for so long. The Allies owe this result largely to the efforts of their ambassadors, whom it is fashionable to criticize today.

Wednesday 6th June 1917

Kerensky has occasional bursts of energy and is trying to take the army in hand again: he has reorganized the courts-martial and ordered them to severely punish all attempts at desertion. All requests to resign presented by officers are refused and General Gurko who, because of the growing lack of discipline has asked to be relieved of his command of the central group of armies, has been put at the head of a mere division. Generalissimo Alexeiev has been replaced by General Brussilov, the victor of Galicia.

But what can all these measures accomplish against the forces of anarchy which are causing the army to disintegrate, and against which all words are useless?

The disruption inside the country increases as fast as the army disintegrates. Chingarev, the Minister of Finance, has just painted a picture of the true situation, in a speech he gave in Moscow. He evoked the spectre of famine, which is inevitable if, as is generally believed, the railwaymen go on strike; and he said that in certain districts there is such a state of want that parents have been killing their children rather than see them die of hunger. The state coffers are empty, and taxes are not coming in. If the liberty loan is not subscribed, it will mean bankruptcy.

Friday 8th June 1917

Yesterday there was a great deal of propaganda for the loan . . . soldiers drove through the streets in lorries decorated with flags and branches, assisted by 'supers' dressed in cast-off clothes from all the theatres of the town. In front of the Imperial Palace there were orators holding forth on a platform surrounded by Roman warriors, musketeers, and peasant girls from Little Russia. I think I even saw a Joan of Arc brandishing a *fleur-de-lys*-ed standard, perched on a lorry which was flying red flags. The whole way along the Nevsky Prospekt one was accosted by women in fancy dress begging for subscriptions. In the square in front of the Kazan cathedral there was a stage with a statue representing 'Free Russia' crushing a German soldier.

I doubt whether these masquerades are enough to reassure the capitalists, because it is not just a question of collecting a few roubles in the streets, but of making people decide to subscribe. Consequently, a rumour is already circulating that if capital continues to abstain, the *liberty loan* will be covered by the seizure of all the money in current accounts in the banks, thus making it an enforced loan. . . . The liberty loan. Oh! the irony of those words.

I went tonight to dine with Shubin in the islands, in Félicien's restaurant. It was a delicious evening; the sky was all orange and green, and the water was wrinkled like a crêpe veil, with luminous silver reflections. There were soldiers in boats singing part-songs in chorus and as they passed, the brightly lit water was disturbed by the movement of the oars, and broke up into big, dark shadows.

Saturday 9th June 1917

A championship wrestling match at the Cinizelli circus. For nearly an hour an enormous negro and a Finlander fought each other . . . these two bodies, one of them of marble and the other of bronze, formed a magnificent group glistening in the harsh brightness of the lamps, their muscles stretching in the effort.

Sunday 10th June 1917

The cost of living has gone up again. Wood costs sixty-five roubles the *sagene*.[1] Certain products are almost completely lacking: it is very difficult to find any meat.

[1] A Russian measure equivalent to about seven feet.

Monday 11th June 1917

The palaces of Peterhof are closed and all the doors are sealed with big red seals. They don't seem to have been broken.

We went for a drive in a car through the immense park, where the roots of the great trees are bathed by the blue waters of the Gulf of Finland. The park is filled with statues, colonnades, pavilions, hermitages, kiosks, boskets, fountains, pools and water follies, each one prettier than the last. I stopped for a long time to look at a pavilion in the style of the Empress Elizabeth, painted bright orange and white, which stands out against the blue of the sea at the end of a great avenue; the branches of the trees seen against the sun allowed some pale green light to filter through. Unfortunately, this splendid scene is defiled by the crowds of soldiers who wander about, all unbuttoned and filthy, sprawling on the lawns and grass walks and reading out their proclamations under the colonnades. We saw a whole gang of them bathing in front of the Montrésor Palace; they were dressing on the terrace, whose marble balustrades were hung with their thrown off clothes and their doubtful underwear . . . the reign of the people is hardly an aesthetic one and when I saw them I thought of how, in the past, in many of the towns of Russia there were placards outside the park gates, forbidding the entry of 'soldiers and dogs'.

We came back by a road which skirted the coast, driving through little woods and wet green fields where black and white cows were grazing, their colour standing out sharply against the green background and the intense blue of the sea. On the horizon the dome of Kronstadt rose above the waves, its outline drawn against an accumulation of billowing white clouds edged with golden light.

Thursday 14th June 1917

This morning we went to the station to say goodbye to M. Albert Thomas, who is leaving for France, where his presence has become necessary in order to 'direct the socialist party'!

His stay here has certainly contributed towards slowing up Russia in her fall down the fatal slope, at any rate for the moment. The effort he has made during these last two months is superb. Never in bed before one o'clock, always up at six, making up to eight speeches a day, taking part in all the important meetings, going to see the members of the government and of the Soviet: receiving industrialists and French notables, dictating diplomatic telegrams, briefing journalists, concerning himself at the same time with internal Russian politics, the socialist movement, the Stockholm conferences and general policy, at the same time as directing his Ministry of Munitions from afar. Always smiling, never tired, he is the most prodigiously active man anyone has ever seen. And with all this, he is a man of a subtle turn of mind and very cultured, with artistic tastes, new and daring ideas, an extraordinary gift for organization, and an absolutely first-class talent for oratory. This disciple of Jaurès has kept the imprint of his master, not only in his thought but in his eloquence, his gestures, and almost in his outward appearance. The only thing I have against him is that his outlook is too rosy . . . in Russia and elsewhere, and that he perhaps has illusions. But I would not be surprised to learn that he pretends to be more optimistic than he really is, in order to carry his group along with him.

There was a crowd of people at the station, and M. Albert Thomas found a kind word and a smile for each one of them.

Kerensky, who sat up with him until three in the morning, came to see him off. . . . His legs were encased in leggings and he was dressed in a kind of dung-coloured uniform, with one of those half yachtsman's half chauffeur's caps on his head . . . which have, alas, been adopted by other heads of state. This get-up, apeing uniform, was enough to put me off and gave me a wrong impression of the man who was thus rigged out. For a socialist minister, I much prefer Albert Thomas' bowler hat and floppy tie.

Monday 18th June 1917

A group of anarchists have installed themselves in the Villa Durnovo, that ravishing country house a few *versts* above Petrograd whose colonnades are mirrored in the Neva. The government has been trying in vain for two weeks to evict them, by serving them with summonses and orders of the day . . . the anarchists remain there, as they know there are no police . . . this is an example of what people call 'Kerensky's forcefulness'.

Tuesday 19th June 1917

A dinner at the Embassy given by M. Doulcet in honour of the departure of Basili, who is going to take over the Russian Embassy in Paris.

For the moment the quiet of the streets is apparently undisturbed, although the 'militiamen' ordered to do police work are on strike; but the state of anarchy in which Russia has been for the last four months is no better, and the results are being felt everywhere. The value of the *rouble* continues to drop, in spite of the fact that all foreign investment has been forbidden, which is in fact concealed bankruptcy since Russians are forbidden to pay the sums which they owe abroad. The foreign exchange department has had to bring the official rate down from 59 to 52, but one can easily change money at 80.

The industrial situation is hardly more cheerful. Many factories have used up their reserves and have informed the government that they will be obliged to close at the end of the month. The workers' demands are more and more exorbitant. Raw material and fuel are becoming scarce and prices are rising. The closure which most of the factories are up against threatens to bring fresh trouble with it. There is again talk of a railway strike, which would make the situation still more serious.

Thursday 21st June 1917

People are very worried by the publication, on M. Albert Thomas' advice, of a decoded telegram addressed by the Swiss government to its minister, M. Odier. This document proves that Germany sought to initiate talks with Russia, through the intermediary of the Swiss government and the socialist Grimm. But if this first attempt failed, another one will succeed. It would be madness not to see that Russia *wants* peace. The army will never agree to embark on a fresh winter campaign. The soldiers only stay at the front now because the weather is fine, and because they are well fed and are living in the open air without much to do and without having to take too many risks; in most sectors the Germans take good care not to fire on them and disturb their *siestas* in the sun, but as soon as the first autumn rains start to fall . . . they will leave their summer rustication to continue this *farniente* in their *isbas*[1] . . . unless they prefer to settle into the castles and the houses of the bourgeois.

Only the Cossacks still go on fighting . . . it is in their nature, and it amuses them. Moreover, they fight just as happily against the 'comrades' as against the enemy. Major Segonne met a *sotnia* taking a group of anarchists to the police station; the anarchists had seized the printing works of the newspaper *Russkaya Volya* and had been dislodged by the *sotnia*. He told me that the sight was a pleasure to witness. . . . Needless to say that the anarchists, who had been soundly thrashed with a *nagaika*,[2] were released the same evening with the apologies of the government. As a result, in certain circles people are counting on the Cossacks and expect wonders from the 'Congress of Cossacks' which was to have opened yesterday. I do not share this opinion and cannot believe that the Cossacks could provide an *element of order*. They make admirable agents of repression, but they must be directed, otherwise they are just brutes who pitch into everyone indiscriminately, just for the fun of pitching in. . . . How low must we have sunk, to expect salvation from a Congress of Cossacks!

Friday 22nd June 1917

Lubersac, who has just returned from the front, is more pessimistic than ever; anarchy is gaining ground and the artillery, which up till now had resisted the infection better than anyone, is beginning to be contaminated. The filth of the troops is beyond all belief and as a result there are epidemics, scurvy and typhus having claimed many victims. He mentioned the names of several officers who have been murdered by their men. One of them was buried with great pomp by the very men who had killed him. They had invited the Germans, and it is said that a German band marched at the head of the funeral procession.

There are many cases of Russians fraternizing with Germans. Sometimes it ends badly: in one village the Russian troops had invited the Germans to a big banquet, but the German officers who

[1] A cottage, or peasant's house.
[2] A whip, or scourge.

came refused to sit down at the same table as their men and the Russian soldiers. The *tovariches* were offended, and it ended in a battle. . . . I do not know whether it is one which is mentioned in despatches.

Saturday 23rd June 1917

People were greatly dreading today, as the extremists had announced that there would be demonstrations against the government. It was being said that forty thousand workmen and soldiers were to take up arms, and that they had made a plan to arrest the members of the government. Luckily, this time the Workers' and Soldiers' Committee decided, after a stormy night session, to support the government and it sent delegates to the factories and barracks to dissuade the malcontents from putting their plan into operation, and to advise them to postpone it to another day.

The government, fortified by the support of the Soviet, prohibited the demonstration and gave orders for the troops to disperse. . . .

Although the government has not got the strength to enforce its orders, the day has passed without incident . . . perhaps because it was very hot and the *tovariches* preferred to stay at home. At Tsarskoye Selo, on the other hand, there apparently were some skirmishes, and shots were fired last night. People there are rather worried and the Grand Duke Paul, with whom I was supposed to be dining, with Countess Kleinmichel and Shubin, sent a telephone message telling us not to come. As we were therefore free that evening, we all three went to dine at Félicien's restaurant, where Countess Kleinmichel drove us in an open car. Everything was very quiet.

A day or two ago Countess Kleinmichel saw an officer who was on the commission sent to the palace, to see the Emperor and to make sure that he is being guarded. The Emperor is resigned to his fate, and anticipates all the restrictions put on him, asking the sentries who accompany him on his walks: "May I go along this path? Am I allowed to sit?" . . . He met the commission of enquiry with all his accustomed good nature, shaking everyone by the hand and assuring them that he had no complaints. At that moment the Empress came in: she was very haughty. She kept her hands behind

74

her back and when they asked her if she had any complaints, she is said to have answered: "I have only one wish, that you do not permit yourselves to interrogate me, as there is nothing in common between you and me."

Today I lunched at the Danish Legation. M. de Scavenius feels as I do that there can be no question of an offensive on the Russian front. He is very pessimistic about the internal and economic situations. Nevertheless, he somewhat consoled me by telling me that lassitude is beginning to be felt in Germany too. He has come back from Copenhagen, where he had been recalled by his government, and according to the impressions he received during the course of his journey, he does not believe that Germany is able to start a new winter campaign, although he says that "one should expect a great deal from Germany's pride and from her powers of resistance".

Sunday 24th June 1917

Yesterday, at a big revolutionary meeting in the Modern Circus, some practical joker shouted: "Here come the Cossacks." . . . In a second both speakers and audience vanished into thin air . . . and the circus was empty.

Thursday 28th June 1917

The government's situation is becoming more and more shaky. We are expecting fresh trouble, and big demonstrations are announced for Sunday. . . . On my way to the Embassy I met several lorries filled with soldiers and workmen armed with rifles.

Nevertheless, I do not believe that danger comes on a date fixed in advance . . . the row will happen some day when one is not expecting it.

Friday 29th June 1917

Kerensky is at the front with Brussilov, in order to take command of the famous offensive. . . . This appears to be a joke, if I can judge by the condition of the army as I see it inside the walls of the capital.

Several units are well known to favour Lenin, in particular the Paul regiment, the Finland regiment, the *chasseurs* and two machine-gun regiments. The rest are hardly any better and the men one sees get more and more dishevelled and badly turned out. . . . They no longer obey any of the regular authorities, and an officer told me that in order to be listened to (for there is no question of giving orders), he had to dress himself up as a student.

Naturally, all these people do anything which enters their heads. The guards at the Fortress are refusing to let out some prisoners who have been acquitted (amongst them the Vyrubova),[1] in spite of the government's order to set them free. At the Kchessinskaya house, which has at last been evacuated by Lenin, the detachment of the Paul regiment which is guarding it has made common cause with the anarchists: they have installed themselves there under the protection of those very soldiers who had been ordered to forbid them access. The Villa Durnovo remains under the control of the anarchists, who have set up a 'directory committee' there, in spite of several orders from the government to restore it to its owners.

General Gurko, who renounced all responsibility for the direction of his army group and was put at the head of a mere division, has refused to accept the command: he will only agree to go to the front as a private soldier, as his conscience does not allow him to take any responsibility, not even that of commanding a section, because he has not got the means to make himself obeyed.

The situation in the navy is bad, too. The agitations in the Baltic fleet have, however, somewhat quietened down; but they are worse than ever in the Black Sea fleet, where the crews have forced their officers to surrender their arms, as "they might use them to encourage the counter-revolution".

Admiral Kolchak, the commander-in-chief, has left his post, as he does not want the continued responsibility of commanding such fanatics. From the top of the bridge of his battleship, he threw his sword of Saint George into the sea—he was given it in the war against Japan, and his sailors were trying to take it from him.

Sunday 1st July 1917

All circulation is forbidden on account of the big demonstration

[1] Anna Vyrubova, who introduced Rasputin to the Empress.

organized by the Soviets, ostensibly in favour of a peace conforming to the ideals of the revolution, but in reality against the war.

Everything is quiet up to now, although the extreme left-wing newspapers in the last few days have been full of attacks against the Allies, whom they accuse of prolonging the war by refusing to accept the Russian revolution's peace plan. There was even talk in these pages of "burning the entrails of the Allied Imperialists on the graves in the Champ de Mars". . . . Decidedly, we are very popular here! What a lot of ground has been covered since the frenzied ovations of the beginning of the war!

I went to the Champ de Mars, where the processions from various quarters of the town were converging. They are led by military bands, whose brass instruments are all tarnished and dented. The women are dressed in light-coloured linen and carry red banners. Because of the heat, the groups are followed by barrels of drinking-water drawn by horses. By order of the government, the inhabitants also have to place receptacles of water at the doors of their houses, to refresh the demonstrators. . . .

I did not meet any armed men, but the expressions on the faces are not good, and seem to have got worse since the time of the last demonstrations on the 1st May. Perhaps it is simply that when they are more covered up in winter clothes, I appreciate them better like that. As for the soldiers, they get dirtier and more unbuttoned.

The inscriptions on the banners are more and more violent, but one has got so used to them that one no longer pays any attention to the inevitable insults against the bourgeois and the property owners.

On the other hand, I was struck by the number of them which were directed against the government and against the Duma: one of them which crops up the most frequently is "Down with the *ten* capitalist ministers". Naturally, the greater part of the inscriptions are against the war: "Enough of the war", "Bread and peace", etc.

I saw the Preobrajensky regiment go past, and the Lithuanian regiment with its officers, and with banners saying: "Greetings to the International".

All this is significant, and it would be dangerous to allow oneself to have any illusions. And yet, many people persist in believing in a fresh offensive in Galicia.

It is possible that Kerensky might succeed in stirring up a few divisions with his eloquence; he is at present at this front line, which has been the least contaminated up to now, and he could have some local success, which is all the easier because the enemy will not offer any resistance. But I cannot believe in any serious or lasting military operation, with the state of mind prevailing at present.

This is the opinion of Scavenius, whom I went to see. It is also the opinion of Major de Maleyssie, in whose house I dined last night, with Chambrun. The Major has no illusions and agrees with me that anarchy and lack of organization will bring Russia up against famine, which will force the government into the peace which everyone here wants.

Perhaps it would be wise for us to act before that moment occurs, and make an advantageous peace with Germany . . . so much the worse for the Russians, whose complete inaction since the revolution amounts to a *de facto* armistice.

Monday 2nd July 1917

I went to spend the day at Terisky with Countess Nostitz. In the evening Lalaing arrived from Petrograd, bringing the news that the Russians have launched an offensive and are supposed to have taken ten thousand prisoners!

Wednesday 4th July 1917

The news from the front is still good. The offensive appears to be a real victory. One does not know whether to attribute this result to a kind of resurrection of the Russian army (anything is possible in this country) or to the fact that our enemies' situation is worse than we had dared hope. And yet, in Russian circles, where people always tend to be pessimistic, they say that the losses, particularly of officers, are appalling and out of all proportion to the results obtained.

Thursday 5th July 1917

Although I cannot believe that the successes in Galicia will have any lasting effect on the general situation, I must however admit that they have restored a little prestige to the government, which has even had the courage to prohibit the demonstrations planned by Lenin's supporters in protest against the offensive. It has even arrested a few of the anarchists from the Villa Durnovo without, however, daring to order its evacuation.

The victory also seems to have somewhat raised the morale of the army. The Cossacks gave a fine display, accompanied by one or two cavalry regiments, and for the first time since the revolution I got the impression of seeing mounted troops. They rode through the town led by military bands, with bunches of flowers on their carbines and lances, some of them standing on their saddles carrying huge photographs of Kerensky, just as in the past they carried pictures of the Emperor.

Basically, the mentality of the people has not changed at all, and in spite of all the democratic formulas, one feels that what these simple-minded souls need is a leader. It does not matter whether he is Kerensky or the Tsar, provided that he is the incarnation of their ideals, that they can attribute every virtue to him, and that they can venerate his image as they do the ikons.

Friday 6th July 1917

This evening I watched a demonstration of territorials, several thousand in number, who marched along the Nevsky Prospekt demanding "Bread and Peace". . . . What a contrast to the cavalry celebrating victory.

It is hard to imagine anything more dishevelled and dirty than this troop of ragged men with long hair and shaggy beards, their pale, vacant eyes staring out of weatherbeaten hairy faces, walking like animals and dragging their feet. Some of them were in uniform with *dvornik*'s caps; others, dressed like *moujiks*, wore military headgear, caps or even fur hats in spite of the stifling heat; some were in tunics, others in threadbare greatcoats or in ill-assorted bits of old uniform, with open collars and no shirts, battered blue enamel teapots hanging from their belts and filthy spoons stuck inside the uppers of their boots. They carried red notice-boards with inscriptions in watery ink, and as they marched they gnawed hunks of black bread or chewed sunflower seeds. This tatterdemalion army made a lamentable impression of poverty, savagery, and fatalism.

It is a crime to take men away from their homes and their work, and then leave them in a state of total want: the first thing to do is to demobilize all these poor wretches, who are quite justified in their demands for bread, and who are of no use in the war.

Tuesday 10th July 1917

Reports from Germany state that the Russian successes have led to deep despondency, in a people who are suffering dreadfully. The recent budget talks in the Reichstag seem to me significant: the Catholic Centre rallied against the government, with the cry of "no annexations". If the Germans were clever they would put forward a peace on this basis to the Allies, with proposals to simply evacuate the territories they have occupied. No amount of bluff would then be able to persuade public opinion to carry on the war for much longer under these circumstances. Furthermore, the hero's part would be taken over by the Germans who would now be defending their fatherland, and would derive fresh courage from their sense of doing right. For them, it is the only hope of salvation, especially if American intervention becomes serious and if, against all appearances, the armies of revolutionary Russia which one had thought of as out of the running, continue to go from one success to another. . . . But it will also be the end of all the hopes which the war politicians had raised in us, and in our country which is over-excited and hypnotized at the same time, there is the risk that this disillusionment will bring a serious reaction with it, especially after so many sacrifices have been made.

Wednesday 11th July 1917

Russia is definitely the land of surprise. At the moment when every-body believed the army to be completely breaking up, every day brings news of fresh victories and today it is announced that Kalish has been taken, with considerable loot.

Here, it is really impossible to try and foresee any logical con-sequences to the events or to judge the affairs of this country with plain common sense. Events never develop in the normal way, and there are always dramas.

There is something immoral about the victory of this disorganized, louse-ridden army, led by a petty little socialist lawyer. . . . All our ideas about discipline, "which is the principal strength of armies", are contradicted by this herd, in which each man does as he pleases, where officers are murdered, where each company has a *soviet* of delegates, and where even the plans of campaign are argued about. In spite of all this, or "perhaps because of all this", as Chambrun said in a sudden flash of wit, the army is victorious. Jaurès would have been triumphant.

But this can hardly last and we shall have a terrible awakening when the *tovariches* have to face Germans, with their machine-guns and their heavy cannon, instead of the Austrians who have decidedly "had enough of it". And yet these successes, however fleeting they may be, have had a beneficial effect and have slightly strengthened the provisional government, which seemed about to give up.

Thursday 12th July 1917

I have just come back from Tsarskoye Selo, where the Grand Duke Paul gave a dinner-party on the occasion of his birthday.

The Grand Duke, in a dinner-jacket with the ribbon of Saint George in his buttonhole, had Countess Kleinmichel on his right and Mme Polovtsov on his left. Princess Paley had on her right the Grand Duke Boris, who has at last been set free, and on her left Chambrun. The other guests were the Grand Duchess Maria Pavlovna II, who wore a very pretty white crinoline dress with wonderful pearls, Vladimir Paley, Mita Beckendorff, Stopford, Armand de Saint-Sauveur, General Efimovich, and so on.

The wines were remarkable, and Chambrun praised a Musigny so highly that the Grand Duke ordered the glasses of his French guests to be filled once more. The service naturally was very good . . . but several of the servants had moustaches and two women were helping: a sign of the times. . . .

After dinner the little princesses, Irene and Nathalie Paley, who are really charming, acted three little plays in the big Empire ballroom: the plays were in French verse composed by their brother Vladimir, and were: a *marivaudage* with ravishing Pierrot and Pierrette costumes, a little Persian story with very 'Bakst' dresses (also designed by Vladimir), and a short topical drama called 'Monarchy'.

Princess Nathalie Paley played the part of a boy King with great charm. She looked absolutely delightful, with her beautiful hair, in a red velvet suit with a black silk sash and the grand cordon of a decoration on a ribbon round her neck. Her elder sister, who grows more and more like pretty Countess Kreutz, was a young Nihilist dressed all in black.

To end up with, Vladimir Paley and the Grand Duchess Maria Pavlovna acted a comedy in Russian.

The whole thing was delightful, and that evening spent so far away from the revolution did me good . . . how pleasant life could still be if only men were sensible . . . we sadly enlarged on this theme as we drove home from the station with Countess Kleinmichel in her open barouche, on the most diaphanous of white nights.

Sunday 15th July 1917

M. Noulens, our new Ambassador, arrived this evening with his family.

Monday 16th July 1917

The crisis which has been hatching for several days, following the resignation of the Kadet ministers, blew up this evening.

At four o'clock we were informed by telephone that armed demonstrators were massing in front of the Mariinsky Palace, the seat of the government, and in front of the Duma.

Shortly afterwards we saw motor lorries driving past full of workmen and dishevelled soldiers with their rifles and machine-guns. At the same time armed men went into houses to requisition motorcars, just like they did in the early days of the revolution.

I was able to prevent them from taking our car, and I arrived at the garage with a small picket of uniformed French soldiers just in time to argue about it with a patrol of *tovariches*: I drove it under safe escort to the Embassy, where it stands in the courtyard next to the military mission's cars, which we were able to rescue. The Halgouets' new car is in the hands of the revolutionaries: revolvers in hand, they forced the mechanic to put the magneto back into working order, which he had dismounted in order to immobilize the car. Jean de Saint-Sauveur, who was returning from Kamenno

Ostrov, saw the Belgian Minister's car being stopped in the street: they made him and Mme Buisseret get out and the car drove off, occupied by ten or twelve *tovariches*, with a machine-gun resting on the hood and a red flag flying alongside the Belgian one. . . .

Last night at about one o'clock, accompanied by a soldier, I went to the Liteiny Street telegraph office to make sure that the new Ambassador's first telegrams were sent off.

The whole street was filled with a troop of soldiers: some were arguing, others were sitting on the edge of the pavement, some were lying in the roadway. I could not find out what they were doing there, but the whole scene, lit up by the wan glimmer of these white nights, made a very bad impression on me.

Tuesday 17th July 1917

A day of waiting, which reminds one of the first days of the revolution. The morning, however, was relatively quiet, although all the shop windows are closed. The shooting began in our part of the town at about one o'clock and was fairly heavy on the corner of the Mokhovaya and the Pantelemonskaya. But I had the impression that they were mostly shooting in the air. And yet the passers-by were running wildly to hide in doorways: two cabs had been abandoned in the street, their drivers having run as fast as their legs would carry them and in spite of their long *armiaks*,[1] to take shelter under an archway.

I went out at about two o'clock with Jean de Saint-Sauveur to see what the situation was like. Liteiny Street is very agitated and has the appearance it had in the bad days: lorries full of armed men and machine-guns drive through the middle of the crowds of *tovariches*, most of whom have rifles. Workmen, and soldiers. A lot of sailors. Nearly all of them have turned their cap ribbons with the names of their ships on them inside out, so that they cannot be identified.

We went as far as the corner of Sadovaya Street and the Nevsky Prospekt, where there had been a considerable affray. In fact, the *tovariches* must have been shooting each other: as the government made no attempt to suppress the outbreak, there cannot have been a fight, properly speaking. And yet some people had been wounded and were being carried into motor ambulances. The roadway was

[1] Peasant overcoats.

littered with caps and sticks, lying among the debris of plaster knocked from the walls by the bullets. In a corner near the offices of the '*Novye Vremya*' broken chairs and furniture were piled up among parcels, out of which spilled face-powder and ribbons from a looted shop.

Tovariches are breaking into houses and one can see them through the window-panes, walking about in the rooms under the pretext of conducting searches. They are always haunted by the thought of machine-gunners posted on the roofs, and while some of them search the rooms, others keep watch below, noses in the air and guns at the ready.

Armoured cars mounted with machine-guns go past, with red flags carrying inscriptions: "Down with the government", "Peace at any price". . . .

I walked back to the Embassy by the quays, where I saw the steamers which brought the sailors from Kronstadt. Further on I met a disbanded regiment, with unbuttoned men with their rifles slung across their backs, in their hands, or under their arms as though they were out shooting: they dragged their feet and were all mixed up with the women and the bands.

Groups of civilians, all armed, walk endlessly past the Embassy shouting . . . one of these gangs stopped and started to threaten, insisting on all the windows being shut, as they were afraid of being shot at . . . overloaded lorries full of *tovariches* with the usual machine-guns race past, making all the windows rattle.

The government, which was helpless at first, even sent in its resignation during the course of the afternoon and asked the Russian congress of the Workers' and Soldiers' Committee to take its place. But the Committee having refused and even given it a vote of confidence, the government somewhat recovered, and at about five o'clock it took the decision to restore order.

It started by sending out some Cossacks, so that they should be seen, and from my window I saw several *sotnias* going past in fairly good order: they were patrolling the quay without coming into conflict with the demonstrators, who continued to circulate with their lorries.

Towards seven o'clock the Central Committee of Workers and Soldiers which, unlike the local Petrograd Committee, has a majority in favour of maintaining order, issued a proclamation to the comrade soldiers asking them to postpone their demands and help the government to keep order in the town, while their brothers are doing

84

their duty at the front. But the motorcars carrying these proclamations were stopped by the demonstrators and the proclamations destroyed. When I returned to the Embassy, under a very black and stormy sky, the Neva was covered with thousands of sheets of white paper which slowly followed the current, lit up by a slanting beam of wan light which made them stand out sharply against the dark colour of the water.

I had hardly got in when a loud burst of firing made me run to the window: the crowd was fleeing madly, riderless horses were galloping among running soldiers who were throwing away their arms . . . some Cossacks came charging out of Sergevskaya Street, turned round in the street and came to take refuge in my courtyard. The shooting was very sustained, and I even heard several cannon shots mixed up with the roar of thunder. A torrential downpour of rain started at this exact moment, washing the streets in a flash and transforming them into rivers. As soon as the deluge had somewhat lessened, I went back to the Embassy, where I found everyone in a state of great agitation. In the waiting-room, an officer and several unhorsed Cossacks had taken refuge.

I left again with Gentil to find out what had happened, and we met M. Diamandy,[1] who was trying to get back to his Legation, escorted by two sailors of the guard.

Liteiny Street was a heartrending sight: dead horses, their skins taut and shining from the shower that had just fallen, lay in the wet roadway between the pools of water, some of which were tinged with red. We counted twelve dead horses between the corners of Spalernaya Street and Sergevskaya Street, but there were others in the direction of the Nevsky Prospekt. A lot of inquisitive people had already gathered to rob the horses of their harness, but we did not see any more armed men. Neither did we see any dead or wounded: we are told that there are a great number of them, which seems probable considering the number of horses killed. There is a huge bonfire opposite the Arsenal which is reflected in the pools of water, where bundles of the Committee's proclamations are being burnt.

This is what happened. A *sotnia* riding along the French Quay coming from the Troitsky Bridge was attacked by demonstrators posted on the Liteiny Bridge, who opened fire on it. Some Cossacks fell, and the frightened horses wheeled round. The main part of the troop surged into Liteiny Street at the gallop, going towards

[1] The Rumanian Minister.

the Nevsky Prospekt, while riderless horses and groups which were more or less out of control rushed through the two adjoining streets, Spalernaya and Sergevskaya. I had seen them debouching from there from my window. In short, nobody knows for certain whether they were fleeing from the bullets or whether they were charging. In any case the result was the same, and the area was cleared. The demonstrators fled too. They had even abandoned their armoured cars, which they only came back to fetch later when the panic was over; then they disappeared in the opposite direction to that taken by the Cossacks. They are said to be 'entrenched' near the Finland Station. The cannon shots were fired by two pieces of artillery from the battery set up outside the *Jardin d'Eté*, under the command of Rehbinder: several shells were fired in the direction of the Liteiny Bridge to support the operation of the Cossacks, or to protect them in their flight.

Having spent the evening ciphering, towards one o'clock in the morning I took the telegrams to the Ministry for Foreign Affairs to make certain that they were sent off, as all the post offices are closed. Everything was quiet again, a fine drizzle was falling and the streets were deserted.

In Millionaya Street I was stopped by a Cossack patrol which let me pass as soon as I had made myself known. Government troops are massed in the Winter Palace square: Cossacks, armoured cars, and artillery. Cossack sentinels gallop round and prevent people from approaching.

At the Ministry I saw Tatichev, who confirmed that the day had been critical. But according to him the government has recovered and has decided to re-establish order by using force if necessary. It appears that they considered the idea of constituting a Public Safety Committee, consisting of Tseretelli, Nekrassov and General Polovtsov, but this plan was discarded by those who were not in it.

Unfortunately the government has not much armed force at its disposal, as the great majority of the troops do not want to take sides either for or against it. It appears too that the Bolsheviks are in the same situation . . . the soldiers are quite prepared to walk about with rifles, but they do not want to be regimented and have to fight as units. In their independent state, they can always resort to running away and joining the side which wins. In spite of everything, according to Tatichev the government can still count on the Preobrajensky regiment (half of which has unfortunately been dispersed to mount guard on the banks, the ministries, etc.), on Rehbinder's two cannon, on two or three cavalry regiments, two Cossack regiments and sixteen armoured cars. On the rioters' side are the regiment of Grenadiers, the sailors of Kronstadt, the Paul regiment, seven or eight armoured cars and, it is said, four cannon. Nevertheless, Tatichev is fairly confident, because they expect the arrival of troops who support the government.

As I was coming back from the Ministry I saw a large mob of soldiers along the branch of the Moïka Canal which joins the Neva after passing under the Hermitage Bridge: I walked up to them. They were soldiers of all arms, who had got together to rescue a little cat which had fallen into the canal and was mewing despairingly and floundering about, with its white body showing up in the black water of the canal. All these people, who were shooting each other a few hours ago, had come together to save the poor beast and to give a leg up to one of their number who had not hesitated to jump in the water to effect the rescue . . . what worthy people they are, basically!

Wednesday 18th July 1917

This morning General Polovtsov issued an order forbidding the inhabitants to go out, and ordering them to keep their doors locked. The streets are deserted, and the town is a dead place. It is raining. . . .

The Liteiny and Troitsky bridges are up, thus cutting off all communication between the two banks of the Neva. The Liteiny Bridge is guarded by the Preobrajensky and the Troitsky Bridge is in the hands of the Paul regiment, which is on the side of the demonstrators.

My impression is that things are rather better. The government appears to have pulled itself together and to have the wherewithal to carry on the fight. But the two parties are clearly frightened of each other and are reluctant to have a confrontation.

Thursday 19th July 1917

The government announced yesterday evening that it is going to have Lenin and the ringleaders arrested and accused of treason.

It claims to have proof of their having received money from Germany. It seems to me that this accusation must be false, at any rate as regards Lenin, who is a sincere and dedicated man. But this accusation will enable the men who make it to pose as patriots and incorruptibles, and thereby regain some popularity.

Be that as it may, the government having mustered sufficient troops, took the offensive this morning and had the Peter-Paul Fortress surrounded, also the Kchessinskaya house, which was the headquarters of the rioters. The latter gave themselves up without firing a shot, when they saw that action had been decided on. During this operation security was well organized and access to the quays was strictly forbidden to the public. In fact, it was feared that the rioters might bombard the town with the Fortress cannon and the artillery of the three destroyers from Kronstadt which had come to their assistance. But for once the extremists were even more frightened than the government and its troops, which is saying a good deal.

Friday 20th July 1917

The Germans have reopened the offensive in Galicia, and seem to have scored some important successes in the Tarnopol region.

In town, order does not seem to have been completely re-established, and again today there was serious trouble in the area near the Nicholas station, where rioters fired on the troops when they appeared. During the night there was a big fight, and from my house I could hear the battle, which took place at about midnight near the Admiralty. The rifle-fire went on for over half an hour, and in the silence of the night one could very distinctly hear the sound of two machine-guns of different range firing almost the whole time. It appears that the fighting was very severe, but that the government troops were victorious.

Saturday 21st July 1917

Prince Lvov has relinquished his responsibilities as President of the Council and the government has once more been reorganized.

Kerensky and Tseretelli, who are the strong men in it, seem determined to restore order. They have sent for a lot of troops, in particular the Cossacks, who are very worked up and out to revenge their comrades . . . and especially the horses, which are their personal property.

In fact, the comrades are not remarkable for their courage. The other day the midday cannon went off at the moment when an armed troop of about a hundred sailors was marching along the quay . . . every one of them went flat on their stomachs!

Sunday 22nd July 1917

As everything was quiet yesterday, I took advantage of the fine weather to go off with Colebrook and spend the night in his little sailing boat on the Gulf of Finland. Sunrise over Kronstadt in a riot of gold and purple was a marvellous sight. Unfortunately a wind rose at the same time as the sun and soon blew up into a storm, forcing us to take shelter at the mouth of the maritime canal. Towards evening we were able to reach Strielna, and from there I came back by train. It was full of families who had spent their Sunday in the country, in happy ignorance of the events.

Friday 27th July 1917

Russian troops are retreating and running away everywhere. Nobody knows where they will stop. "On the Volga," General Polovtsov said to Chambrun. I am well aware that he is apt to look on the dark side of things, because he was sacked after the recent events. They say that he is to be replaced as Governor General of Petrograd by Lieutenant Kuzmin, a friend of Kerensky. But the Commander-in-Chief, General Kornilov, is hardly more optimistic. In fact he declared in a published letter that it was useless to think of launching an offensive before the end of September (?!), and that the whole army must be brought back. So the Germans know where they stand: Russia is virtually in a state of peace, at least until the month of September, since the commanding general has proclaimed that he will not mount any military operations before that date . . . and that he is incapable of doing so. This promises happy days for the

French front, where our enemies will now be able to send still more fresh troops.

Saturday 28th July 1917

The funeral of the Cossacks killed in the rioting took place today in Saint Isaac's. The ministers took part in the ceremony and carried the coffins as far as the door of the church. Troops marched past, with the Cossacks in perfect order but with the other troops far from brilliant. The procession went along the Nevsky Prospekt as far as the *Lavra*[1] of Saint Alexander, where the burial took place. The parents walked behind each hearse, accompanied by the friends of the victims, and it was touching to see these worthy peasants, who had come from the Urals or the Caucasus to follow their sons' coffins, being comforted by other Cossacks, who were full of solicitude for the mothers of their brothers-in-arms. Then followed the dead Cossacks' horses, in their harness; one of them had been seriously injured and was limping pitifully behind its master's coffin. On another horse the dead man's son, a little Cossack of about ten years old, had been put up into the saddle.

At present, the Cossacks are the only element of order. It is said that they have received large rewards for keeping order, from various banks. Whatever the truth may be, one can count on them for the moment. But although this may be sufficient for Petrograd, I doubt if they will be able to stop the landslide in the country districts and at the front.

Monday 30th July 1917

I wrote to M. Paléologue to tell him how much worse the situation has become since he left. I really cannot join in the wave of optimism of so many French people here, for whom everything once more becomes rosy when they see a regiment march past in a slightly less disordered state, or when Kerensky has made some resounding proclamation. I say, and I repeat, that Russia is out of the running for a long time . . . it is up to us to act accordingly, and to see if we are to go on with the game and how we ought to play it, depend-

---

[1] Monastery.

ing on what cards we have in our hand, which I ignore. But the important thing is not to harbour any illusions, and not to count on a trump card which we haven't got. . . .

It is true that, by way of compensation, Siam has declared war on our enemies: so everything is all right! and long live our Siamese brothers!

Tuesday 31st July 1917

I met Kerensky again today, in his khaki uniform (he still does not dare dress like a Cossack), installed like the Emperor in the Imperial Rolls-Royce, with an aide-de-camp covered in shoulder-knots on his left, and a soldier sitting next to the chauffeur. . . . I don't call these people revolutionaries, but just "you clear out and make room for me" people, and I much prefer Lenin to these "just-look-at-me" men—at least he is an honest and sincere man.

Besides, the great man of the Russian revolution[1] is in reality nothing but an inspired fanatic, a case, and a madman: he acts through intuition and personal ambition, without reasoning and without weighing up his actions, in spite of his undoubted intelligence, his forcefulness and, above all, the eloquence with which he knows how to lead the mob—all of which shows how dangerous he is. . . . Fortunately, the career of a personality such as this can only be precarious.

Nevertheless, for the moment he is the only man on whom we can base our hope of seeing Russia continue to fight the war, so therefore we must make use of him . . . but I fear that he has some terrible disappointments in store for us, in spite of his blustering and in spite of the Draconian measures he has proclaimed. And yet, in Russia you never can tell . . . perhaps the people will lie down like good dogs as soon as they see the stick.

Wednesday 1st August 1917

The material side of life becomes more and more difficult, the price of everything is prohibitive and it is a real problem to find the most indispensable commodities. It is very hard to find meat, and the

[1] i.e., Kerensky.

price is very high. Even horse meat costs one rouble eighty for a Russian pound of four hundred and ten grammes. Milk is equally scarce, and the farm at Lesnoy where I had an order has warned me that they cannot continue to supply me.

Luckily the Embassy, under the intelligent direction of Halgouet and Colonel Caillaux, has organized a food supply service which provides us with the most necessary products.

Saturday 4th August 1917

Last night there was a big meeting which consisted of the resigning ministers, the influential members of the Soviet, and the Committee members of the old Empire Duma. What a mix-up, and what confusion. . . . The newspapers talk of a 'historic night' . . . but nothing emerged from it all except speeches. While it was going on, armed thugs broke into the Palace of the Senate, tied up the men who were guarding it, and carried off a silver statue of Catherine the Great and other valuable objects! . . .

At the front things are going from bad to worse. The army is retreating in utter confusion. General Erdeli, in command of an army and the victor of Kalish a month ago, has been murdered by troops whom he was trying to stop from running away.

Following Tarnopol and Chernovitz, it is announced that Kamenz Podolsk has been taken by the enemy. This leaves the Rumanian army, which had been so well reorganized by the French mission, in a terribly dangerous position. Can one expect the Rumanians to make fresh sacrifices, and will they consent to abandon Moldavia, as will doubtless be necessary? Will they not rather listen to the peace offers which our enemies will not hesitate to make?

Be that as it may, here are the Ukraine and the Kiev district—the real granaries of Russia—on the verge of falling into the hands of our enemies, like Belgium and the North of France, Poland and the petrol producing districts of Galicia and Rumania. If Moldavia is included, can one really hope to reduce them by starvation and famine?

The Germans are intriguing very skilfully in the Ukraine, and it is greatly to be feared that by encouraging the passion for independence they will find the same complicity which they were able to count on in Poland and in the Baltic states, and which they are planning for later on in Finland. If they succeed, the road to Odessa will be open to them, thereby giving rise to great hopes in the East.

It is with these gloomy prospects in view that the fourth year of the war is now beginning. . . .

Sunday 5th August 1917

Dulong has come back from a journey on the Volga and is sickened by what he saw. The confusion in the provinces is beyond all imagination. All the French people he saw in Rybinsk, Nijny and Kazan are in despair.

Monday 6th August 1917

The German Chancellor's speech revealing the secret agreements concerning the left bank of the Rhine has had a considerable effect here, and has given the newspapers a good excuse to attack "the French imperialists who plan to make conquests with the blood of the Russian people".

I am convinced that the Germans obtained information on all this through the treachery of the Russian Ministry for Foreign Affairs. They got their information from someone who saw the file without having had it in his hands for long, because the Chancellor made a few mistakes, which M. Ribot pointed out in his speech. But there are certain details which prove that the person who gave the information had at least skimmed through the file.

Tuesday 7th August 1917

At last, after more than two weeks, Kerensky has been able to form a ministry, after a fashion. But everyone here reckons that this arrangement is not going to last. The Kadets who are part of it joined it in their capacity as individuals, and without the knowledge of their party; the socialists are annoyed at having to share the power, which they want to keep for themselves.

As for Kerensky himself, his popularity is diminishing. Chambrun went with old Prince Peter Karageorgevich to the music-hall in the Nevsky Prospekt, and told me that people cheerfully applauded the portraits sketched by a lightning artist. . . . Rasputin, Goremykin, and even Stürmer had their little success; but an icy silence and even a few whistles greeted the appearance of Kerensky on the screen . . . it's nothing much, but it is a symptom in this country where they only love those who succeed. I still remember the day in the cinema when the picture of the Emperor at the front appeared, and a voice shouted: *"Glupichkin na voinye*. . . . The simpleton at war." A few weeks later, it was the revolution.

Wednesday 8th August 1917

Everyone is interested in the battalions of women soldiers who exercise in the courtyard of the Paul Palace on the Fontanka . . . people talk of the 'heroism of the Russian women' and they get all excited about it . . . as for myself, I feel that it is rather unpleasant histrionics. As far as fighting goes these women can only be thinking of the rough-and-tumble!

Tuesday 14th August 1917

What strikes one about the present events is the lack of men . . . the Kadets, who stirred up so much trouble in the opposition under the old régime, have shown themselves to be lamentably incompetent when in power. It makes one wonder whether the Emperor wasn't quite right in not calling on their help. If he had given them power, far from saving him they would have precipitated his downfall, because they have shown themselves to be doctrinaires, muddlers and blunderers. . . .

During the first days of the revolution one of these brilliant theoreticians came to see Shubin, completely panic-stricken. Shubin expressed astonishment at his being in such a state at the moment when the event which he had spent his whole life preparing for was actually taking place. . . . "Yes," his visitor replied, "the revolution is all very well, but it is not happening the way I wrote about it in my book. . . ." The whole history of the Kadet party is contained in that answer.

In spite of the efforts of the new ministers who are said to be full of good intentions, disorder and waste increases everywhere: there has never been so much stealing or so much bribery. The thirty-five motorcars from the Imperial garage, which were sufficient for the needs of the Emperor and his court, are no longer enough for all these democrats and the numerous parasites who are helping them to devour what is left of the finances of unhappy Russia, and the newspapers have announced that they are going to requisition another thirty. In the islands one meets the new masters of Russia, and people of their kind take their ease in the court motorcars which used to be so well kept, and which are now dirty, with flaking paint and dented mudguards. The old carriages too, formerly so elegant with their impeccable teams of horses driven by scarlet-coated coachmen, are now in a dreadful state: the horses are broken down and no longer in well-matched pairs, and the *tovariches* and their worthy companions pile into the carriages, with lousy green caps on their heads. And while Kerensky lives in the Winter Palace and sleeps in the Emperor Alexander's bed, the Tsar is travelling to Siberia. . . . The Tsar in Siberia! It seems like a dream . . . it's true that it is perhaps the road which will lead him back to the throne. Is it not from there that most of the men of today came into power? Meanwhile, the Imperial railway line which linked Tsarskoye Selo with Petrograd is being demolished, and the rails and the sleepers are being taken away to be used elsewhere.

Wednesday 15th August 1917

People are rather disturbed by the account of an interview with Count Pourtalès[1] which has appeared in the German newspapers. In it, the former German Ambassador describes the days which preceded the declaration of war; accuses Paléologue of having urged on the war; and talks about a dinner-party in the country house of one of the great ladies of St. Petersburg, at which a secretary from the French Embassy is supposed to have announced the news of the Russian mobilization twelve hours before publication. General Sukhomlinov, the Minister for War, who was at the dinner, seemed to know nothing about it. It appears that the reference is to a lunch-party at Countess Kleinmichel's *dacha* in the islands, which took place on Tuesday 28th July and not on the 30th, as Count

[1] Count Friederich von Pourtalès who, in spite of his French name, was German Ambassador to Russia, 1907 to 1914.

Pourtalès says. Chambrun, who sat between Countess Kleinmichel and Mme Sukhomlinov, spoke only of the declaration of war between Austria and Serbia, a piece of news which he had just learnt from M. Rivet and which General Sukhomlinov did not yet know about, although he received confirmation of it during the course of dinner. It is not therefore possible to take this incident as a proof, as is claimed by Count Pourtalès, that Russian mobiliza- tion was a coup planned in advance with the agreement of the French Embassy without the knowledge of the Minister of War himself.

Friday 17th August 1917

There is much discussion of the Pope's encyclical, addressed to the 'Heads of Nations' who have so misunderstood their duty up to the present and have put their ambitions above the true interests of their countries: in it, he urges the demented world to listen to the voice of wisdom and moderation.

This letter comes at the moment when all hopes are turned towards the two 'Internationals' which, as Romain Rolland said in 1914, had up to now failed in their mission: these are the Catholic Church and Socialism, which appear to be at last emerging from their torpor and trying to make their voices heard. It will be interesting to see whether these two doctrines, supposedly enemies but in reality so close to each other, will join together to encourage the greatest catastrophe in all history or whether they will remember that, after all's said and done, both of them are founded on the great principle of human fraternity.

The Russians are furious because the name of Russia is not even mentioned, and because the Pope's proposals establish Russia's defeat and the fall of the Slav world. They blame the Pope for preparing the Austrian peace . . . but that peace, whatever anyone may say, is also the peace of France, who has no interest in dividing up Austria-Hungary for the benefit of the Slav nations and one day seeing what is left of the monarchy joining up with Germany, to make her stronger than ever.

If the Pope's voice were listened to, the peace of Europe would be assured for a long time because his proposals are, on the whole, a realization of the legitimate aspirations of peoples. What I admire above all in his encyclical, with its high moral tone and its really splendid final sentences, is his appeal to the spirit of moderation and mutual concession, which would not impose on any party any of those unforgivable humiliations which would be the cause of further 'revenges'. . . . As long as this spirit of moderation does not reign among the States, there will be no lasting peace.

Monday 20th August 1917

We only know a few details about the Imperial family's journey. The departure from Tsarskoye took place in the early morning. Kerensky made the effort, and was at the station: apparently he even got the troops who were there to keep order, to present arms.

The town of Tobolsk, where the Tsar and his family are to be interned, is a long way from the railway. Rasputin was born near there. The Grand Duchesses are supposed to have told Kerensky that the Empress's dearest wish is to build a big church there, so that people can pray to God for the martyr. . . . I have no doubt that the future cathedral will be dedicated to Grischa and will be the centre of a cult which will very soon become popular. . . . Saint Grischa Rasputin, the patron saint of the *tovariches* . . . it's just what they need. In fact, one has to admit that there is something impressive about the fulfilment of the prophecies of this man who never ceased to foretell that, if he met with a violent death, the Empire would collapse during the month after his disappearance. It is understandable that the events which followed Rasputin's murder should have struck the imagination of the Slavs.

Tuesday 21st August 1917

The town is now perfectly quiet and there are no more meetings or demonstrations in the street, but Bolshevik theories continue to attract converts, and the latest elections in the factories will help to swell their majority on the Workers' and Soldiers' Committee.

Wednesday 22nd August 1917

Transport is becoming more and more difficult, and the rolling stock is in a state of terrifying dilapidation. On the Finland line I saw some surburban trains composed entirely of cattle-wagons crammed with crowds of people, compared to which the crowds which invade the Paris *métro* on a race-day are nothing.

Selys told me that as he wanted to spend his Sunday holiday in the country at Peterhof, he took the train. It was full to bursting point: people had climbed on to the roofs, and were sitting astride the buffers or hanging on to the steps on the wrong side of the train. He himself could only find room on a step, and when a train passed in the opposite direction, he saw the steps of another carriage give way under the weight and the human bunch of grapes disappear beneath the wheels . . . fourteen people were cut to pieces and killed.

As a result of accidents, the number of carriages grows less every day and the fewer there are, the more they overload the remaining ones, which makes them wear out all the faster. The same applies to the engines. The railwaymen no longer obey orders and go on strike at the slightest pretext, thereby holding up the traffic for hours to suit themselves. Accidents are increasing. If this goes on, and if the Americans do not perform a miracle (which, for my part, I think they are quite incapable of doing), there will be famine in the big towns and at the front.

Saturday 25th August 1917

There is again a certain amount of excitement in the town. Cossack patrols and machine-gun carriers are massed in the Winter Palace square, ready to intervene. During the last few days one has felt that things were going badly again. . . . One feels it, like one does when one knows that a storm is coming, even though one cannot yet hear the thunder.

Sunday 26th August 1917

The Pope's letter continues to cause interest in political circles, and it really seems as though the Allies are about to make another mistake.

Even if it is admitted that the Holy See's concrete proposals are not in our favour (which in fact I do not myself believe), we ought to take advantage of everything in the letter which could go into our programme: the rights of peoples, justice, disarmament, arbitration, the society of nations (these almost complete the socialist formula), and especially the preliminary evacuation of occupied territories. We ought to stress all this so that we can proclaim that "the Pope is with us". Instead of which we deliberately fling him back into the enemy camp, and we think we are being very clever by printing in our newspapers that "the Pope is a Boche". In doing so, we really are playing into the hands of our adversaries, who well know how to profit by it, and I would have thought that it would be much more cunning to catch the Holy Father in his own trap—that is, if he really wanted to set one for us—and to enlist him by force by making use of the arms which he has given us.

But alas! Vandervelde is right: "The masses live, weighed down by a frightful superimposal of scourges: that of kings over nations, of war over kings, of famine over war, and of stupidity over everything else. . . ."

Monday 27th August 1917

The big democratic conference of Moscow is opening in a stormy atmosphere. Generalissimo Kornilov is in opposition to Kerensky and has threatened to resign and Savinkov, the assistant to the Minister for War, on whom the optimists placed great hopes, has left the government because no one would listen to him. In Finland, and in the Ukraine, the situation is getting more and more worrying . . . not to mention the front: the Germans are only a few kilometres from Riga.

Wednesday 29th August 1917

The news from Moscow confirms that the conference has been a success for Kerensky and his government. The Kadets rallied: they did not dare to withdraw their support from him.

They were counting on General Kornilov to overthrow the government, but his performance was lamentable. He did, in fact, make a sensational entrance into the Assembly Room, followed by an escort of Cossacks from the Savage Division,[1] with their enormous fur hats; he was greeted by a storm of applause from all the right-wing deputies, who stood up to acclaim him. But his speech was of such mediocrity that his supporters were discouraged.

So for the moment the *coup d'état* which the General and the Kadets seem to have planned thus appears to be impossible, at least in Moscow. A lot of people think that General Kornilov could still tempt the army with it, with the support of the Cossacks and the Knights of Saint George, who have just joined together to form a brotherhood.

Kerensky, on the other hand, was very eloquent. His speech was not of course what people expected, that is to say a well-documented statement by a head of state setting out a programme of reform and proposals for remedying a difficult situation, but a brilliant and fiery improvisation . . . in which, however, there is nothing more than fine words. But it's what the Russians want: they can get even more drunk than the French themselves on eloquence and empty phrases, without looking to see what lies behind. So Kerensky was able to grip the whole assembly.

Alas! mere words are not enough to feed the people or put a stop to anarchy!

Thursday 30th August 1917

Chambrun came back from Moscow three days ago, and this morning we took him to the Finland station, as he is leaving us for good. This departure, coming after that of M. Paléologue, marks the end of the brilliant Embassy in the Empire of the Tsars, and I felt a real pang at parting from this companion, who is so shrewd and so well-read, whose gaiety is so truly French, and who will leave such a great gap in our midst.

On the way to the station I saw a long train full of German and Austrian prisoners who looked well turned-out, in contrast to the Russian soldiers guarding them. I was struck by the extreme youth

[1] The Savage Division consisted of Circassians, who were famous for their courage and cruelty. They were allowed to wear their own clothes but all wore the same head-dress. The Division was regarded as an élite regiment rather like the British Commandos in the Second World War.

of most of them . . . which doubtless explains why they managed to get captured by Russian *tovariches*, who only know how to run away now, and which is hardly the way to take prisoners.

Friday 31st August 1917

At the Moscow Assembly all the parties made solemn declarations on the necessity of going on with the war until the enemy is driven out of Russian territory, proclaiming that Russia will never make a separate peace. . . .

I feel suspicious, because one of the ways in which the Slav mind works is by making false allegations in order to get at the truth, and if there was so much talk about war it means that they are thinking of peace. . . .

Let us therefore beware of mistaking all these fine declarations by those two swindlers called Kerensky and Tereschenko for the words of gentlemen.

Sunday 2nd September 1917

The palaces and the private houses of members of the Imperial family and of the aristocracy are falling into the hands of the bankers and the Jews. The Grand Duke Dmitry's palace, the Oldenburg palace, and the Grand Duchess Olga's palace have already been sold. It is sad to see a whole world coming to an end in this way.

Tuesday 4th September 1917

Today's news is hateful. Yesterday the Germans occupied Riga, several regiments having run away without a fight. The General Staff is planning to evacuate Dvinsk and bring the front line back to the line of Pskov and the lakes, in order to avoid all danger of being turned back on the north. I hope that they will not be reduced to this extremity because it would bring the enemy to within two hundred kilometres of the capital, which would then be at the mercy of their aeroplanes. No air-raid defence has been planned, and I am thinking of the effect which bombs would have if they fell on a town seething with excitement, where the inhabitants are only waiting for the chance to pillage and kill each other.

But the Russians are such *nichevo*-ists that the announcement of this new defeat has left them practically indifferent: they are in fact so used to catastrophes that nothing disturbs them any more. Well! we must just hope that the bad weather will stop the Germans, because one really cannot rely on the *tovariches*.

Wednesday 5th September 1917

The men produced by the revolution, who have clamoured so loudly for the right to be free, are if anything more intransigent and more merciless towards their adversaries than the men of the old régime.

Old Stürmer has died from the ill-treatment he was forced to undergo in the Fortress: General Voyekov, too, is practically blind, and in spite of the advice of the doctors they have refused to move him from the damp cell where they are slowly murdering him, like they did Stürmer. Count Fredericks is still in the French Hospital and is getting much weaker.

Meanwhile they are busy unearthing 'monarchic plots'. The worst they have found so far is a so-called conspiracy of which the 'head' is supposed to be Mme Ivanienko! As is her habit, she was jabbering away on the telephone, which led to her arrest and to that of a certain number of her friends, who don't know what it's all about. But Kerensky has saved democracy from a great peril!

Nevertheless, his popularity is waning and he is the object of violent attacks. People tell scandalous stories about him, and the latest pretext for these is his divorce, and his re-marriage to one of his sisters-in-law, who is a very young student at the Conservatoire. . . . Amongst the people, it is said that he has got divorced to marry the Tsar's daughter, and that he is going to become Regent. . . . It's the kind of story they love here, and the Slav imagination is busy embroidering on these fantastic themes . . . we shall see it all later on at the opera with some Chaliapin, or at the ballet with some Karsavina. I can just imagine the scene, with sets by Bakst, and numerous interludes: the murder of Rasputin and the treachery of Sukhomlinov will complement the episode of the false Dmitry, the scene of the begging monks, or the intrigues of Marina in *Boris Godunov*. After all, perhaps it is one way of making the most of the tragic events which we are living through, and if a master-piece emerges from these 'times of trouble', there will always be that.

The rate of the *rouble* is ninety-seven *roubles* to one hundred francs.

Thursday 6th September 1917

The weather is horrible today: everything is grey, the pavements are sticky and the Petrograd wind is blowing in gusts at the street corners, where it whirls in every direction, while torn clouds gallop overhead in a crazy saraband. And yet the sky is beginning to light up, and the setting sun, which is quite near the Fortress now, has pierced the ragged clouds with a bright gold shaft. It illuminates the quays with a golden light and sharply picks out the masts of a schooner anchored in front of the Embassy: they stand out like shining metal against the dark grey background of the clouds and the surging water of the Neva. . . .

All this produces an impression of autumn . . . almost of winter, and one feels it all the more acutely because the summer has really been superb.

This approach of winter has something agonizing about it under the present circumstances, and I wonder what disillusionments and what catastrophes it will bring us. Since the capture of Riga the situation seems desperate from the military point of view. The Germans have made a further advance of about twenty kilometres and it is thought that it will be impossible to stop them before they reach the line of the Pskov lakes. And even there one can hardly rely on anything except the winter to prevent them from reaching Petrograd, as the herds of *tovariches* will offer no resistance. But what will happen in the spring?—that spring from which the Allies expect victory. . . .

From now on, people are thinking of evacuating Petrograd. The departure of the government would be justified under some pretext or other, such as establishing itself in Moscow, the historic capital and the centre of the land of Russia; they would take advantage of this to include Petrograd in the military zone, which would allow them to declare a state of siege and to try and re-establish order. . . . But I doubt whether these plans are to the liking of the *tovariches* and the Bolshevik workers, and I fear that the announcement would only provoke fresh trouble.

The thought of this departure has thrown everyone into a panic, and there is a continual stream of our compatriots coming to the Embassy to ask if they ought to leave at once. The most absurd rumours are circulating and are accepted with the most naïve credulity.

There is talk of plots being woven against the revolution and the government has had the Grand Duke Michael, and the Grand Duke Paul and Princess Paley arrested in their palaces; also Vladimir Paley, whose letters to the Grand Duke Dmitry, which have been seized, are said to be the cause of all this agitation. At the same time, riots are being predicted and everyone, with an air of importance, produces absolutely reliable information as to the date on which they will break out.

The government sets an example of discord . . . the different ministers contradict each other and are attacked by their respective newspapers. Resignations are announced every day, and the crumbling edifice is patched up with great difficulty.

Friday 7th September 1917

General Efimovich came on behalf of the Grand Duke Paul to give me the details of his arrest, and to beg me to reassure Countess Kreutz who is at present in Stockholm, and with whom he can only communicate with difficulty.

The arrest took place on Monday. It was the actual day on which there was a small dinner-party at the palace, and all the guests were arrested within forty-eight hours. They were released after this time had elapsed but they cannot communicate with the Grand Duke and his family, who are being kept under close watch in the palace and the garden, but are apparently not being ill-treated. They are hoping for a decree of banishment, as though for the coming of the Messiah, which would allow them to go to France; and they talk about Boulogne as if it were the earthly paradise.

Everyone would like to emigrate, but it is difficult because of the impossibility of taking money out, or of being sent sums of money from Russia. These sums are limited to five hundred *roubles* a month—less than five hundred francs, as the rate is one hundred and seven *roubles* to one hundred francs. One could buy treasures here for a cheque of a few thousand francs on Paris.

The government itself seems to have decided to abandon Petrograd for Moscow; not so much because of the possible arrival of the Germans, but because of the difficulty of supplies. This departure would also enable them to include Petrograd in the military zone and to try and establish a little order there.

The bad weather makes me think that the Germans will not be able to cover the remaining four hundred kilometres as far as here, although they cannot be meeting with any resistance. Nevertheless, it appears that they are reinforcing the Riga army with effectives from other fronts, including even some Guards units; which seems to indicate that they will attempt something all the same. It would obviously be to their advantage because, apart from the effect which their entry into the Russian capital would have on morale, they would seize the Petrograd factories which alone produce almost as much munitions as the whole of the rest of the country. They would cut off all communication between Russia and Europe for the duration of the winter, because the port of Archangel is blocked by ice and there is no railway which joins the Murmansk line without passing through Petrograd. There remains Vladivostok!

Saturday 8th September 1917

The internal situation is still far from brilliant. One has the feeling that there is increasing disagreement between Kerensky and Kornilov, and that the extremist parties are taking advantage of it to gain ground.

In the latest municipal elections, which now take place every two months, the Bolsheviks had sixty-seven seats, having only had thirty-seven in the month of June.

The populace, which had at first accepted the fall of Riga philosophically, is now seized with panic and is trying to get out of Petrograd at all costs. In Kanyuchennaya Street I saw a hundred-yard-long queue of people waiting for tickets outside the Wagons-lits office. There was such a scramble at the Nicholas station yesterday that several people were suffocated by the crowd and killed.

Sunday 9th September 1917

Robert de Flers asked me to lunch alone with him at the Hôtel de l'Europe and I spent a delightful hour there, although there was not a crumb of bread to be had and we had to sweeten our coffee(!) with cherry jam. . . . But with such a good talker it is enough to enjoy the conversation. The Duc de Luynes came with him from Rumania and left this morning for Paris.

At about five o'clock I went to the Moscow station with Major Gallaud. The booking-hall, the platforms and the lines were full of people camping in the midst of their luggage, waiting to leave by any available train. It was only with difficulty that one could push a way through the mountains of luggage which cluttered up the entrance. Soldiers, *tovariches*, and women with their children were either squatting on the platforms or sitting on their bundles, surrounded by bags, bursting packing-cases tied up with ropes, wooden trunks painted in bright colours, nondescript suitcases, Samovars, rolled-up mattresses, household utensils and gramophone horns.

Others were stretched out on the ground, sleeping resignedly while waiting their turn, like animals asleep in the slaughterhouse.

A train which was being assembled was stormed by the crowd right in front of me. People even climbed into the carriages by the windows, and piled into the compartments and corridors with their parcels. It is incredible what a lot of people can fit into one carriage. There must have been several layers of them!

We questioned one or two of these people, who told us that they had been there for two days, and that before that they had queued for tickets for the same length of time.

It is real panic, and the number of wretched people camping like this in the station can be estimated at eight thousand. Most of them are worknig-class people driven by irrational fear, who want to return to their villages, where they think they will be safe. But there are also well-to-do people, such as officers and their families, and so on. I was told of a case of someone offering a thousand *roubles* for a place in a luggage-van . . . in no matter what direction!

Monday 10th September 1917

Last night I was called to the Embassy by telephone, with the news that General Kornilov had announced the fall of the provisional government and was marching on Petrograd. One has known about the discord between the commanding General and Kerensky for some time, but I never thought that it would lead to such serious conflict so quickly.

Herewith begins the age of the *coup d'état* and the *pronunciamento*, and free Russia need no longer envy the *macaques* of South America for anything.

I got to the Embassy at the same time as M. Noulens, who had just returned from the Ministry for Foreign Affairs, to which he had been summoned by Tereschenko, whom he found trembling with fear at the thought of losing office, which he values so highly. He told him the facts of the situation: Kornilov had informed Kerensky through the intermediary of M. Lvov,[1] that in view of the danger which threatened the country, he had decided to take over as dictator, and that he was offering him the office of Minister of Justice in this new government. Naturally, the vain and sensual petty lawyer, who believes himself to be the master of Russia because he sleeps in the Emperor's bed, could not resign himself to taking his hand out of the till: he answered by having M. Lvov arrested and declaring Kornilov "a traitor to the fatherland". The Generalissimo retaliated with a proclamation in which he describes Kerensky and the ministers as "tools of the German General Staff". The government representatives to the armies aped our own Revolution by calling themselves 'commissars', and he has had them all put in jug.

Meanwhile, while all this was going on, the government gave full power to Kerensky, who constituted a Committee of Public Safety consisting of eight members, deprived Kornilov of his rank, declared Alekeiev generalissimo, and announced a state of siege in the capital.

But during this time Kornilov has had Alekeiev arrested, and is marching on the capital with an army corps and the Savage Division. The 'men of order' are pinning all their hopes on him, quite forgetting that less than six months ago it was this same general who, when he was Governor of Petrograd, did not hesitate to give the order for the arrest of the Empress, by way of appeasing the extremists.

Nothing new has happened this morning: the population still goes about its business, piles into the trams, and queues outside the

---

[1] M. Lvov, former President of the Holy Synod, not to be confused with Prince Lvov, leader of the first revolutionary government.

shops, without a moment's concern for what is happening and showing the most complete indifference. They've had enough, and nobody is in the least interested in these ruffianly goings-on.

At midday a rumour started that there had been an encounter between government troops and those of the generalissimo, commanded by General Krymov, somewhere near Luga, and as there are some fiery southern imaginations in the Embassy, somebody even heard the gunfire. . . . The news came that the troops of the capital had gone over to Kornilov and had arrested all the members of the government. I wonder what they will think up next. We really know nothing, and are just waiting. I imagine that it will all fizzle out, and that all the gossips will soon be saying the same thing. As Robert de Flers says, to be called 'traitors to the fatherland' and 'tools of the German General Staff' are almost conciliatory terms for these fine fellows, and one can take it that this is the beginning of negotiations.

Besides, the ground for agreement will be easy to find: sharing the booty will be quite sufficient, as has been proposed by the foreign ambassadors and ministers who have met in solemn council at the English Embassy, and who have offered to act as mediators between the two parties. Sir George went to present the proposal to Tereschenko, who welcomed him as though he were the Messiah, and the Belgian general de Ryckel, who is the *doyen* of the military attachés at Headquarters, has been charged with communicating it to Kornilov, who I am quite sure will send him packing. . . . I believe in fact that if Kornilov holds firm he will succeed, and I look forward to seeing him make a clean sweep of all that rabble and, I hope, hanging them. . . . So I think that the step which the Diplomatic Corps have conceived is most unwise: one should never interfere in family quarrels.

Tuesday 11th September 1917

The populace seems to support General Kornilov, whom they are counting on to restore order. All is quiet in the factories. I lunched at Donon's restaurant with Armand de Saint-Sauveur and Baranovsky, who told me that the factory employees are working better than they have done for a long time. They are visibly alarmed.

The General's entry into the capital is expected to take place tonight. And yet the government is very loudly proclaiming its determination to reduce 'the traitor' and not to negotiate with him: it has finally rejected the mediation of the diplomatic representatives which Tereschenko seemed so happy about yesterday evening.

Wednesday 12th September 1917

The situation seems to be veering round again. In view of General Kornilov's tardiness, the workers have pulled themselves together and have started holding secret meetings again. The government, for its part, having taken control of the press, has managed to create the impression that it is the strongest side and that Kornilov is at its mercy. It is the best way to discourage his supporters, as the longer things drag on the more readily will they believe in his defeat. He is losing adherents with each hour that passes—people are so cowardly here.

One must admit that Kerensky has played his cards well. He has proclaimed himself Generalissimo, as all the Generals (Alexeiev, Klembovsky, etc.) have escaped, and he has concentrated all power in himself, wielding it like a real autocrat. In this way he did not hesitate to suppress the '*Novye Vremya*', which was not going the way he wanted it to.

Meanwhile Kornilov parleys and dawdles instead of marching into the town. After having taken Gachina and Luga, his vanguard got to within a few kilometres of Petrograd, where it went into some trenches two *versts* away from those which had been dug by Kerensky's troops for the defence of the town. It is a new front line, greatly appreciated by the *tovariches*, who run no risk of getting hurt at that distance. Besides, the delegates of the opposing troops made haste to fraternize, as is customary . . . as though they were dealing with Germans. . . .

The result of this situation is that the heads of both parties are powerless: it is the soldiers who are the real masters. They will be the winners, and whatever the result of the crisis, the Soviets will become increasingly stronger at the expense of the future government, whatever it may be.

The danger is all the greater because Kerensky has been weak enough to distribute arms to the workers for them to go and fight Kornilov's troops . . . how will anyone ever be able to take them away again! So there they are, once again masters of the town, and it is greatly to be feared that this venture will have disastrous results.

Thursday 13th September 1917

Kornilov's troops are still in their trenches on the outskirts of Petrograd. But the Generalissimo himself is still at Mohilev, in a state of incomprehensible inaction.

People are beginning to say that this venture is the result of an intrigue hatched by Kerensky to get rid of the Generalissimo, whose popularity annoyed him. Apparently Kornilov is the victim of a trap, into which he has fallen headlong. According to this version Kerensky asked the Generalissimo, through M. Lvov, to send troops to Petrograd to maintain order, as it was threatened by the Bolsheviks. Then, knowing the General's fiery nature, he must have found some pretext or other to exasperate him. Kornilov, falling into the trap, flew into a temper and issued his proclamation: he wanted to use the troops, who were already marching towards Petrograd, to overthrow the government. But Kerensky was counting on a sudden reversal of feeling by the troops: when they saw that there was no trouble in Petrograd, they would turn against the Generalissimo for having misled them and for trying to use them as an instrument against the revolution. That is what in fact happened: the forward columns sent delegates into the town, who ascertained that everything was quiet and then persuaded their comrades not to advance.

This theory of Kerensky's intrigue is confirmed by the more than suspicious behaviour of Tereschenko, who manœuvred between the two parties. Last Saturday, on the eve of the crisis, he left for Stavka at the same time as General Caillault. During the journey he was handed a telegram from Kerensky announcing that he had received Kornilov's ultimatum, and asking Tereschenko to return. Before complying with this request, he telegraphed to Kornilov to assure him of his friendship and to apologize for not being able to go to Stavka. And a few hours later he joined with Kerensky in declaring Kornilov to be a "traitor to the fatherland".

But in spite of all his Machiavellism Kerensky must at one moment have feared for the success of his enterprise when he saw the Generalissimo's troops entering Gachina and Luga without firing a shot, all the generals rallying to the movement, and all his supporters disappearing, to the point where nobody was willing to take on the post of generalissimo. Kerensky only got away with it through determination and through his ability, which one has to grant him. It is true that on this occasion too he was pretty unscrupulous. In fact, he lied in the most shameless fashion by declaring that the Allied representatives had given him their *co-operation* and their *support* against Kornilov. It is to be feared that the real Russia will for long bear a grudge against the Allies for their venture, which was dangerous enough in itself because it represented intervention in internal affairs, something which Russian pride will not suffer, and it was made still more dangerous by the untruthful way in which Kerensky's government presented it.

Friday 14th September 1917

Kornilov's attempt has not yet been liquidated, but it seems doomed to failure. A rumour is already going round that he has surrendered and has been arrested.

This business is indeed becoming more and more mysterious. Thus, Savinkov, to whom Kerensky two days ago had given the post of Governor of Petrograd for the purpose of defending the capital against Kornilov's army, has just resigned, as it has been established that he was in collusion with the Generalissimo. Kerensky then offered his job to General Krymov, the same man who was in command of Kornilov's troops: Krymov accepted the appointment, and went to the Winter Palace, where he blew his brains out . . . all this is incomprehensible to the Western mind, and these intrigues are worthy of the 'times of trouble', when there were as many as three False Dmitrys at the same time.

It is said that this morning Kerensky had a telephone conversation with Kornilov, during the course of which the two enemies deplored the disaster (like in *La Belle Hélène*), tried to outdo each other in patriotism, and remarked to each other that because of their quarrels the front was now open, "which breaks our hearts". Kerensky asked Kornilov if he could rely on him in the fight against the enemy without. Kornilov gave him his word, and Kerensky drew up a proclamation announcing that Kornilov would keep his post as Generalissimo until a successor had been appointed, and ordering him to obey in all matters concerning operations against the enemy. . . . As Robert de Flers says, they guarantee his authority until the day they hang him. Is it a farce, or a Shakespearian tragedy?

Saturday 15th September 1917

The conflict between Kornilov and Kerensky is going to take a back seat, because a far more dangerous struggle is in preparation between the government, supported by all those who want relative order, and the Soviets, who have realized the extent of their strength as a result of this venture, and who are preaching to the *tovariches* to revolt against all authority.

The government is struggling amid endlessly renewed difficulties and it is impossible to succeed in forming a cabinet. With every hour a new arrangement is announced, and with every hour there are new resignations, sent in and then withdrawn, and fresh bargainings. A certain man, whose allegiance had been obtained, backs out because a certain other man has been promoted too. It's a real 'Russian salad'.

Naturally the parties of disorder profit by the situation and hope to impose a Bolshevik government. A coalition cabinet seems impossible . . . it is the decisive moment for the Russian revolution. Will it be a victory for the comparatively moderate parties, or for the party of the extremists?

I am also distressed by the constitution of the new French cabinet, from which the socialists are excluded, and which seems to have been a real *coup d'état*. . . . I fear that it may be the end of the holy Union!

Sunday 16th September 1917

The new government, a real Directory of five members consisting of Kerensky, the inevitable Tereschenko, Nikitin, a general and an admiral, seems to have decided to leave Petrograd and take shelter with the Bolsheviks, and steer a bit to the right.

There is no cabinet, properly speaking, because no appointments have been made, and the five members of the government all look after the general direction of affairs of State together.

The Soviets are furious and the former minister Chernov has presented an ultimatum in their name demanding, amongst other things, the partition of the land and the immediate conclusion of peace with Germany. The Soviets have given the government ten days in which to answer, and after the Russian 13th September they will enforce their ideas by any means they think fit. In particular, they have announced a congress of the general council of all the Soviets. All this is very dangerous, because it is clear that the Bolsheviks are no longer an undisciplined party which goes spontaneously into the streets to proclaim its rights, but a powerful organization directed by leaders who lay down the policy. Even the quiet of the last few days proves the strength of the party discipline and makes one all the more apprehensive of the violence which is predicted on the expiry of their ultimatum.

Monday 17th September 1917

Last night the Republic was proclaimed. Nobody is interested. As for myself, I thought that it had been done a long time ago.

One of the five men who form the Directory is Admiral Verderevsky. He is the admiral who, in the latest disturbances, was asked by the government to stop the sailors coming from Kronstadt and who, instead of doing his best to obey, communicated the order which he had just received to the Workers' and Soldiers' Committee, putting boats at its disposal to go to Petrograd and arrest the government.

The decree announcing his appointment as a minister is couched in roughly the following terms: "The admiral . . . is appointed a member of the government. . . . Proceedings against him in connection with the Kronstadt affair have been suspended." It really is a farce. No sooner out of prison than you are in power. One of these days Kornilov will become Kerensky's War Minister and will be the strongest supporter of the régime.

Tuesday 18th September 1917

I went this morning to the Finland station to see off M. Buisseret, the Belgian Minister, who has also been recalled.

Today the government proclaimed the Republic, in order to satisfy public opinion . . . and seized the opportunity to double the price of bread. A theoretical price, in fact, because there is none to be had. This last measure, because it affects their interests, has hit the people far more than the platonic demonstration by which it was hoped to distract their attention. When one has nothing to eat, one doesn't give a rap for the Republic.

In the South, the supporters of order seem to be the masters of the situation. General Kaledin, *hetman* of the Cossacks, has entrenched himself with a fairly strong army at Novo Cherkassk. He has declared that all Southern Russia is with him, and he is threatening the government with the starvation of the capital and the Northern provinces.

Kerensky's position, between Kaledin's Cossacks and Chernov's Bolsheviks, is clearly critical. Besides, his popularity has greatly lessened and it appears that Tereschenko, always so good at sailing with the wind, is seeking to supplant him. He is said to be in favour of a swing towards the right, and to be pushing Kerensky into an agreement with the Kadets.

Wednesday 19th September 1917

Bad news from Finland. The massacres of officers continue. At Viborg half a dozen of them were thrown off the bridge into the river and finished off with gun-shots. At Helsingfors the sailors murdered several naval officers with blows from a hammer. Murders like these are said to be happening almost everywhere, but they have been kept from the public.

Thursday 20th September 1917

Dinner at Donon's restaurant with Armand de Saint-Sauveur. He is not much more optimistic than I am, and believes that the situation is getting worse. The factory workers are clearly waiting for the word of command to go out into the streets, and people are greatly dreading the 25th and 26th September, the dates on which the Soviet ultimatum to the government expires. The Embassy is guarded by a detachment of French gunners sent from Moscow in case of trouble. The new Municipality has a Bolshevik slant, as might be expected after the latest elections, which gave the Bolsheviks sixty-seven seats on the Municipal Council.

The executive committee of the Workers' and Soldiers' Council has sent in its resignation in a body, and it will be replaced by a committee which is further to the left, which is saying a good deal.

Chernov, the former minister, is in open conflict with the government and he will doubtless become President of the Soviet, which will make him master of the situation. He is a fanatic, who has not been sobered down by his rise to power, and there is everything to be feared from him.

Friday 21st September 1917

Robert de Flers left this morning. There had been some question of his coming back here, to take charge of propaganda; but he is very discouraged, and he confessed to me that a few days spent in Petrograd had been enough to make him lose his optimism, which he had managed to keep in spite of the disasters in Rumania.

Monday 24th September 1917

At dinner last night with Prince Gorchakov everybody was very pessimistic. M. Narichkin, who came in during the evening, said that peace must be made at all costs by giving the Germans everything they want. The whole of Russia *basically* thinks the same as he does: but there are still people who dare not say so.

Tuesday 25th September 1917

Mita Beckendorff, whom I went to see, told me that the Grand Duchess Maria Pavlovna II and Prince Putiatin were able to celebrate their wedding in the Pavlovsk palace. The Grand Duke Paul was not allowed to attend. On the morning of the wedding, the local Soviet apparently forbade the Queen of Greece to dress her staff in livery . . . in the name of liberty.

Tonight I dined in Contant's restaurant with Armand de

Saint-Sauveur. We saw Prince and Princess Radziwill there, as well as Mme de Derfelden, back from the Caucasus, who was dining with her escort of horse-guards, as close as possible to Gulesko. He was making a hellish noise, rolling the whites of his eyes and twisting himself into contorted attitudes while playing *Allah Verdi* or the *March of the Hussars* in every octave and with every known variation. While dining in this elegant circle I thought of Etienne de Beaumont's apt observation when, during the early days of the revolution, he pointed out to me that the most important events seem like mere incidents to the people who live through them, and that one continues to live one's life, attaching importance to minor worries and preoccupied with small details. It reminds one of the expedition to the country which Anatole France describes so well in *Les Dieux ont soif*, when the characters go out painting landscapes, picking flowers and making love while people are slaughtering each other in Paris.

Wednesday 26th September 1917

Everyone is more and more concerned with the departure for Moscow, although nothing has yet been decided. And yet things are being moved . . . ministerial archives, valuable furniture, the collections of the Grand Duke Nicholas Michael and the Prince of Oldenburg, and the pictures and statues from the Hermitage. It is a strange sight to see barges anchored along the quays, hastily roofed over with planks, and guarded by soldiers in lazy and abandoned positions, while long lines of *lomovoys*, high on their wheels with the bright red accent of the wooden hoops on their harness, bring up packing-cases which other soldiers unload and carry into the barges.

I spent a good while idly contemplating this *genre* picture, its background the splendid scenery of the Neva, all blurred in the cold autumn light which bathed everything in blue mist: the gold spire of the Fortress, the red ochre of the palaces, and the rostral columns of the Stock Exchange. The slippery pavements and wet wood smelt of mushrooms and when one passed close to the groups of soldiers, one breathed a whiff of the leathery smell which is so characteristic of Russia.

The democratic conference opened yesterday. It is thought that Kerensky will not be able to weather the storm and will be forced to go: the parties of the left are wary of him because he has given himself the airs of a dictator since the Kornilov affair, and the parties of order have long ago lost faith in him and accuse him of talking too much and doing too little. He nevertheless scored a certain success yesterday when he pronounced his own panegyric, but this success would appear to be ephemeral. There is talk of the socialist Tseretelli as a possible successor; up to a point, he has the qualities of a statesman. If he does not succeed in winning power, it will be a Bolshevik government . . . and then there is everything to fear.

But after all, it is perhaps best that the crisis should come to a head as soon as possible and that the abscess should burst, as it is inevitable anyway . . . and so much the worse for Russia: if we set about it in the right way, we could still score an advantage for France by making a peace which would repay her for her sacrifices.

Sunday 30th September 1917

Today, with great interest, I again saw the collections in the Ethnographical Museum, which they opened specially for the Ambassador: the aerial coffins and the iron amulets of the Shamans of Siberia;[1] bones carved by the Samoyedes[2] and the Tunguses;[3] clothes and utensils from Great and Little Russia, from Red Russia and White Russia; Finnish sledges, carpets and embroideries from Turkestan and the Caucasus; Persian ceramics, Buddhist idols from Pri-Amur[4] and Manchuria, and arms and harness from Bokhara and Samarkand.

By the time one leaves the Museum, one has understood what Russia means: the achievement of the Tsars is comparable to that of the Roman Empire, which imposed its administration and its power on peoples with just such differing civilizations and origins. But Russia without an empire is not even a geographical term and does not correspond to anything real. If things go on as at present, this word Russia will soon have lost all meaning. There are Shamans

[1] The Shamans are the priests of Shamanism, the ancient religion of the Ural-Altaic peoples; their office is hereditary and their chief assistants are ancestral spirits.

[2] The Samoyedes are a tribe of the Ural-Altaic group scattered over a vast area from the Arctic Ocean to the White Sea.

[3] The Tunguses are a branch of the Mongol-Tatar family and cover a wide area in the Amur basin and Central and Eastern Siberia.

[4] Pri-Amur is the Province of Amur, formed by the basin of the river Amur.

in clothes made of fish-skin with hundreds of iron charms hanging all over them, or half-savage Circassians, or those slant-eyed Manchurians, whose mentality is so different to our own: how can one expect people like these to vote? In any case it is Utopian to want the *moujik* of the Russian plains to play a part in the conduct of state affairs: he still harrows his field with a tree-trunk with the branches left on, and grinds his corn with a hand-turned wooden grindstone.

The men who claim that they can turn these people, who are so far removed from what we call 'civilization', into citizens of a great, unified, centralized republic should spend a few hours looking into the glass show-cases of the Ethnographical Museum, and they would realize that in overthrowing the Empire they have destroyed the only thing which kept Russia united.

Quantities of ill-assorted objects were piled up in the big pink marble hall, which it appears were from the Anichkov palace and had been moved there for safety. It is incredible that these people can have lived surrounded by such bric-à-brac, when they could have had the most beautiful things in the world: there were Japanese screens from the bazaars, portraits done from photographs like the ones one sees in concierges' lodges, stuffed monkeys under glass domes, and the most hideous furniture! The horror of the objects transported there is almost unbelievable, and they were part of the surroundings of the Dowager Empress of all the Russias! In the heap I saw a magnificent Chinese *cloisonné* enamel, mounted as a *jardinière* with metalwork from the ironmonger's, and further on a ravishing eighteenth-century terracotta statuette with a wonderful patina, mounted on a pedestal made of parrot green plush!

Count Tolstoy, Director of the Imperial Museums, who accompanied us, told me that the pictures and the most valuable objects in the Hermitage left for Moscow yesterday in a train of twenty-seven carriages, guarded by the pupils of the *Ecole Militaire*. There remain to be moved the antiquities, the Houdon statues, the glass from the Kerch treasure, the collections of china. . . . Count Tolstoy is doing what he can to keep them in Petrograd. It is certainly far less risky to leave all these beautiful, fragile things in the Hermitage.

Tuesday 2nd October 1917

There have been no political demonstrations in the last few days and the Bolshevik attempts, which there has been so much talk about and which were supposed to coincide with the work of the democratic conference, have not materialized. But disorder and anarchy increase, and the scene in the streets is a reflection of what is happening everywhere. There are no police, the trams cart people about hanging on like human bunches of grapes, and the *izvozchiks* drive as best they can on broken-up roads between mountains of wooden paving-blocks awaiting the pleasure of the road-menders in the middle of the streets.

In spite of the absence of police, there have been relatively few crimes and burglaries. It must be because stealing and pillaging call for *action*, which hardly enters into the Russian temperament whereas to let everything go you only need to let yourself go.

It is to be feared, however, that certain foreign elements may take advantage of the situation and that the *tovariches* will follow this example. Gentil tells me that in the building where he lives an apartment was completely ransacked at eleven o'clock in the morning. We're in for some happy days.

Thursday 4th October 1917

There have been a great many speeches at the conference, but up to now nothing has resulted from it. It seems, however, that it will be possible to form a coalition government, which would include some Kadets and some industrialists alongside the socialists. The conference agreed to the principle of a coalition, but with a very weak majority. It now only remains to apply the principle, and this does not appear to be an easy thing.

It seems, too, that on Tseretelli's initiative the conference agreed to convoke a sort of provisional Parliament until the Constituent Assembly meets, which would support the government and provide a means of keeping it in touch with public opinion. It is hoped that in this pre-Parliament the bourgeois and even the peasant elements would balance the worker and soldier elements, and that this assembly would counterbalance the influence of the Soviets, from which the bourgeois and the peasants are excluded.

But it is to be feared that the extremists, whom Kerensky so unwisely armed at the time of the Kornilov affair, will oppose all attempts at organization with force. Tonight they walked out of the conference hall, refusing to associate themselves with the resolutions of the conference.

Saturday 6th October 1917

In the provinces, the hostility of the peasants towards the workers is increasing and the *moujiks* are refusing to sell their products to feed the workers, whom they accuse of having caused the economic crisis through their idleness.

The workers are doing less and less work because it does not provide them with a living, and because on their part they do not want to do anything for the peasants who refuse to supply them. It is a vicious circle which makes the economic situation more serious every day. The result is armed conflict, pogroms, and disorders of every kind. A detachment of Alsace-Lorraine prisoners returning to France by Archangel was caught in one of these affrays near Vologda and several of them were wounded.

Sunday 7th October 1917

On the way home from a matinée at the Cinizelli Circus with little Anik du Halgouet, who delighted us with her remarks, I walked through the *Jardin d'Eté*, which was looking delicious in its autumn finery. The sun made great splashes of light on the bright yellow trees and the golden leaves littering the avenues, and on the marble statues. This symphony in gold was wonderful and I enjoyed my few minutes' walk, while I breathed in the smell of mushrooms and of the countryside which rose from the damp leaves; and I amused myself by dragging my feet through them, in order to hear the soft, dull, rustling noise which they made.

Monday 8th October 1917

Kerensky has at last been able to form a government which conforms to the skilful balancing of parties laid down by the democratic conference after so much palaver. The moderates hold an important place in this government.

The railwaymen went on strike yesterday and are claiming a rise in pay. It is estimated that five milliard roubles would be needed to provide the credit with which to satisfy their demands. There can be no question of it in the present state of financial distress. The government hopes that they will agree to negotiate and that the strike will be of short duration, because if it were prolonged it would mean famine. We still have some provisions in the Embassy, but in the Alexandre Benois' house, where I spent the evening round the *samovar*, we drank tea without sugar and Mme Benois told me that people are short of everything.

Tuesday 9th October 1917

On orders from their governments the Allied ambassadors today took steps to issue a solemn warning to Kerensky and to convey their anxiety to him. The American Ambassador alone found an excuse to abstain. Kerensky received them in the Winter Palace, in the company of Tereschenko. Sir George Buchanan, the doyen, read them the joint declaration. Although this was expressed in the most moderate terms—too moderate, in my opinion—it violently irritated the despot's vanity, and he walked out exclaiming: "You forget that Russia is a great power!" The Tsar also refused to listen to Sir George in similar circumstances: a few weeks later, he lost the crown!

It is said that the Germans are planning to bombard the capital with their zeppelins and aeroplanes . . . people can talk of nothing but this eventuality, which fills *tovarich* and bourgeois alike with terror. During the last few days there have been dress rehearsals in case of an attack, with the sounding of sirens, the mobilization of firemen, and the putting-out of lights. It is all too childish, and would anyhow be practically useless as there are hardly any cellars. . . . Meanwhile, they have put out the few gas lamps, which anyhow did not light the town, and to ward off a problematical danger they are running the certain risk of accidents in the dark streets, where everyone does as he pleases owing to the absence of police; the *izvozchiks* sleep in their drivers' seats, unharnessed *lomovoys* are left abandoned right across the streets, and the *tovariches'* motor lorries hurtle at full speed along the partly destroyed roads.

Sunday 14th October 1917

The Germans have occupied the islands of Dagö and Osel, and it is feared that this new German base will threaten the Russian right wing and force them to modify their front line by strengthening it on the Gulf of Finland rather than on the Gulf of Riga. This new line from Narva to Pskov by Lake Peipus would bring the Germans still nearer to Petrograd.

The town is quiet, but anarchy is increasing in the provinces. In the Caucasus, some brigands quite simply removed the railway lines to stop a train and rob the passengers. There are said to have been about fifty victims. Charming country!

Monday 15th October 1917

Carriages have more or less disappeared from the towns, and the few *izvozchiks* charge five *roubles* to go from the Embassy to the Hôtel de l'Europe . . . before the war one did the journey for twenty-five *kopeks—chet vertak—*and one turned one's back on them in scorn if they asked for *poltini*, that is to say, a half-*rouble*. The trams are packed, dragging real human 'grape-bunches' along with them.

One has to queue to buy the smallest thing. Useless to think of buying a packet of cigarettes in a tobacco shop; one has to go through the intermediary of the soldiers, who have nothing to do so spend their day queuing and profit by it to hold their little meetings. Then they sell for more than double. This is how one can also get chocolate, which can only be had in rations of tiny boxes, for which there are endless queues, because Russians adore sweet things. The soldiers sell them in the streets, the bars of chocolate at eighteen *roubles* the pound.

It is generally thought that the Germans will not make any attempts on Petrograd before next spring, but that they will make sure of a strong base at Reval and perhaps one in Finland. It is therefore feared that the Russians will have to retreat as far as Pskov, with disastrous results for the town's supply system. This is effected largely through Pskov and the railway line from Pskov to Smolensk, from where the centre of Russia is reached: it is true that this involves an enormous detour, but it avoids using the Nicholas railway, which is already over-loaded.

In any case, air attacks are to be feared . . . but they have thought of every way of guarding against them: the few gas lamps which still remain intact have been painted blue.

Thursday 18th October 1917

The great families are obliged to part with their most precious mementoes, in order to live. I went with Colonel Caillault to see Mme Narichkyn, who has a bust of Marie-Antoinette which she wants the Louvre to buy. The chief lady-in-waiting of the Court, having been unable to follow her Sovereigns to Siberia, has taken refuge in a small apartment in Sergevskaya Street, where she received us very graciously. . . . With her Bourbon profile, she still looks like a daughter of Louis XV and seems remarkably young . . . even though she saw the 1848 revolution in Paris and remembers that month of June quite well. The *biscuit de Sèvres* bust which she showed us is quite exquisite. It was given by Marie-Antoinette herself to Mme Narichkyn's grandfather, who accompanied the Comte du Nord on his journey to France. It is a unique example, all the others having been destroyed during the French Revolution, and it would be highly desirable if the Versailles Museum or the Sèvres factory could buy it, rather than it should one day grace the parlour of a Transatlantic pork merchant.

Saturday 20th October 1917

The opening session of the pre-Parliament took place today, and marks the end of Kerensky. . . . His speech, which it was assumed would have the usual effect, was heard with general indifference and the deputies, who are in fact more or less chosen by the government, gave his tirade an icy welcome. Moreover, the Allied representatives were not much more successful, and barely half the deputies stood up to applaud and turn towards the diplomatic box when Kerensky spoke of the Allies. . . . The majority were silent if not actually hostile and did not budge. . . . Russia, even official Russia, no longer conceals the fact that she has had enough of the war, and that she holds the Allies alone responsible for its continuance.

Under these conditions, the end cannot be long in coming. When one compares the peace programme of the Soviets with the manifesto of the neutral socialists of Stockholm, with the Pope's encyclical, and with the declarations of the French socialist minorities, one observes striking analogies showing in which direction the current is shaping which will bring us peace. In view of such unity of outlook in Petrograd, Stockholm, Rome and Bordeaux, it is high time to listen to the voice of reason, instead of adopting the too easy attitude of answering all these unanimous manifestations of common sense from such different circles by saying that they are all 'German inspired'.

The really sensible thing would be to make all our arrangements for peace in advance, because any day could produce a disaster in Russia, which would make our position less good at the moment of liquidation.

Tuesday 23rd October 1917

The opposition between the Bolsheviks and the government has taken on a fiercer character since the first session of the pre-Parliament which opened today, Saturday's session having only been an opening ceremony. The Bolsheviks left the hall in a body, announcing the breaking off of all ties with the government, and threatening to achieve their purpose by whatever means they consider suitable. It is a real declaration of war.

Wednesday 24th October 1917

The government seems to have given up the move from Petrograd for the moment, as a result of the opposition shown by the advanced parties to any departure for Moscow. To disguise its climb-down, it is pleading the excuse of having to make room in Moscow before being able to move the administrative offices which are now in Petrograd; and it has let it be understood that, in the present state of the railways, this operation could not be carried out before January.

It is also being said that there is no hurry, since the Germans appear to have halted in their present positions.

In reality, the government has given in to the Soviets, where the extremists have taken a very firm stand against the transfer of the capital to Moscow, considering it to be a counter-revolutionary plot which they have decided to oppose with force.

Thursday 25th October 1917

Luncheon at the Bear with Labonne, who has just arrived accompanied by M. Weill, socialist deputy for Alsace in the Reichstag, who crossed over into France on the declaration of war. They are going to try and explain the question of Alsace and Lorraine to the *tovariches* and to show them that the return of these two provinces to France conforms with the new 'no annexations' charter, and that it is indispensable for the future maintenance of peace. I doubt whether the *tovariches* will be interested in these questions of right. . . . They only want one thing: the end of the war.

Those of them who recognize that the question of Alsace is one of primary importance (as Kuhlmann himself recognized, moreover) are trying to find a compromise solution to the problem, which would look after the interests of both parties but could be applied immediately such as, for instance, the independence of these two provinces; or the creation of a buffer state on the Rhine consisting of Luxemburg and Alsace, a sort of Lotharingia which would separate the enemy brothers. . . . The Soviet diplomats cannot see that a solution of this kind would satisfy nobody . . . except perhaps the Alsatians, or at least certain among them. But then, who gives them a thought in this business? When two litigants quarrel over an oyster . . . the interests of the oyster never come into it.

Friday 26th October 1917

Kerensky is becoming more and more unpopular, in spite of certain grotesque demonstrations such as this one: the inhabitants of a district in Central Russia have asked him to take over the supreme religious power, and want to make him into a kind of Pope as well as a dictator, whereas even the Tsar was really neither one nor the other. Nobody takes him seriously, except in the Embassy. A rather amusing sonnet about him has appeared, dedicated to the beds in the Winter Palace, and complaining that they are reserved for hysteria cases . . . for Alexander Feodorovich (Kerensky's first names), and then Alexandra Feodorovna (the Empress). . . . To add to his misfortune, apart from the similarity of first names, Kerensky happens to have as aide-de-camp a certain Vyrobov. . . . What a subject for cheap gibes!

Sunday 28th October 1917

M. de Scavenius told me that General Verkhovsky, who is now Minister for War, was at one time page to the Dowager Empress. She even saved him from dishonour as the result of a gambling scandal. . . . In spite of this, when the revolution started, he went himself at the head of a gang of *tovariches* to the palace of his benefactress, and with real sadism he removed all the objects which she most valued, such as her religious books and her letters from her mother. Then he forced her to sign the 'requisition form' in the name of Marie Romanov. He then presented this document to one of his companions in crime, telling him that "it may be worth money later on", a sordid detail which gives a good picture of this sorry specimen.

According to what the Danish Minister told me, he had to intervene several times with Kerensky and Tereschenko in the most strenuous fashion to protest against the way in which the Dowager Empress is being treated. She is a Princess of Denmark.

He is sickened by the cowardice of these two men.

Monday 29th October 1917

Luncheon at the Embassy with the representatives of the French press in Russia: Naudeau, Marchand, Antonelli and Pelissier. I could see that I am not the only one to see things in a gloomy light. All these men, who frequent the news rooms and are in constant touch with public opinion, are still more discouraged than I am, and do not hide the fact that the situation *here* is desperate. Russians of every class have had enough of the war, and the force of inertia of this whole people is more dangerous to us than the violence even of the Bolsheviks, because against this force of inertia there is nothing to be done.

Tuesday 30th October 1917

M. Georges Weill, the socialist deputy from Metz, who came to Russia to explain the French claims to Alsace-Lorraine, has been coldly received. As he came out of the assembly, he heard a delegate saying to one of his colleagues: "Well! so we have to be hospitable towards foreigners and allow them to talk a lot of nonsense like that!"

Wednesday 31st October 1917

Dinner at Countess Kleinmichel's, with Count Keller and Sigismond Wielopolsky. After dinner in came old Princess Soltykov, the Scaveniuses, Nicolas de Mingrélie, Bezak, young Countess Keller, and Yonine, looking superb dressed as a wild Cossack.

I talked at length about the situation to Princess Soltykov and Scavenius. Like everyone else, they are frightened of the demonstration which the Bolsheviks have announced for Friday. There was also a lot of talk about Sir George Buchanan's imminent departure: according to rumour he too has been recalled and is due to leave quite soon, probably at the same time as Tereschenko who is due to appear at the Paris conference next week. The 'dummies' from the bridge tables came to join us round the *samovar* in turn. The evening passed very agreeably and it was after midnight when I walked home with Bezak, after a little supper. It was a most beautiful night, and the moon lit up the great golden turnip domes of the Church of the Resurrection with silver haloes; it was a real fairy-tale scene.

Thursday 1st November 1917

A big French propaganda film describing France's war effort was shown in the cinema today. There were a lot of people: all the boxes were occupied by Allied diplomats, the stalls by the *tovariches* and the balcony by the Court and the town, friendly neutral diplomats, people of fashion, press representatives, actors and so on. The film, which was not without interest, showed models of guns and aeroplanes, and gave statistics showing the progress we have achieved in the making of tools. All the Russians who saw it seemed very impressed by the prodigious effort made by France . . . but they have no intention of imitating it. Some of them even said, "With such splendid guns and such quantities of munitions, you can go on with the fighting . . . but how can you expect us to make war, when we have nothing?"

One must have no illusions, all Russians want peace and the best of them are almost rejoicing at the disasters on the Italian front, hoping that it will bring the end closer.

This wish to have done with it is understandable in this country, which is in a state of upheaval and complete anarchy and is on the eve of famine, and one really cannot blame them for it. But under these conditions all 'propaganda' efforts are useless . . . here more than anywhere else.

Friday 2nd November 1917

The Bolshevik demonstrations which had been announced for today did not take place, the extremist leaders having decided to postpone them until later.

But conflict will inevitably break out between the Bolsheviks and the government. . . . The situation is all the more serious because the populace is exasperated by the rising cost of living. Tereschenko's speeches to the provisional council have displeased everyone, and tonight there is talk of his resignation and of that of the Minister for War, General Verkhovsky. . . . But at least in as much as it concerns Tereschenko, it must be a false rumour: he is much too keen on holding office to relinquish it without being absolutely forced to.

Saturday 3rd November 1917

After an excellent performance of *La Passerelle*, in which Mlle Didier was charming and Hasti screamingly funny in the part of a manservant, I went to end the evening in the house of young

The French Embassy at St. Petersburg, July 1914. *From left to right:* Comte Charles de Chambrun, First Secretary; Marquis de Laguiche, Military Attaché (*third left*); M. Doulcet, Counsellor to the Embassy; Commandant Gallaud, Naval Attaché; Comte de Robien, Attaché; M. René Dulong, Secretary; and (*seated*) Monsieur Paléologue, the Ambassador

A soirée at the Town Hall, St. Petersburg, July 1914. *From left to right* (*see stars*): Count Tolstoy, Admiral Le Bris, Comtesse de Robien, Comte de Robien

The liner, *France*, carrying the French President, Monsieur Poincaré, arriving at Kronstadt, July 1914, on the occasion of the President's State Visit to Russia

The arrival of the French President at St. Petersburg. Monsieur Poincaré is seen talking with the Emperor, Nicholas II

Countess Keller. There I heard that old Princess Urussov arrived this morning from Lapotkovo, her estate at Tula; she fled from there without being able to take anything except the clothes which she stood up in. The peasants have burned and pillaged everything.

Sunday 4th November 1917

An engineer from *Russky Renault* told me that in the last few days the workmen, who are all armed, have spent the greater part of their time in the courtyard of the factory, drilling with their rifles and their machine-guns. . . . A promise of happy days to come. . . .

In fact, there is a feeling of anxiety in the air, because there was nobody one knew at the ballet, which Colonel Caillault took me to with Lady Georgina and Miss Muriel Buchanan. They were doing *Paquita*, with La Smyrnova, Will and Lyukom. The last two ladies were enchanting in the *pas-de-deux*.

After the performance I went to have supper in Prince Argutin-sky's house, with Alexandre Benois, Somov, Mme Karsavina and Bruce.[1] Benois is very busy working on the scenery and costumes for *Petrouchka*, which is due in the month of January.

Monday 5th November 1917

Mme du Halgouet left for France this morning at the same time as Dulong.

Luncheon at Countess Keller's, with Mme Roggers, where we heard some of the appalling details about the pillaging and burning of the *château* at Lapotkovo. Old Princess Urussov was ill, and the peasants dragged her out of bed and left the unfortunate woman for several hours in the courtyard, shivering with fever and cold, while they ransacked everything and squabbled over the furniture and clothes. Not one of them would agree to lend a cart to drive the poor woman to the station and it was some Austrian soldier prisoners who took pity on her and saved her from being murdered by taking her to the station. Those peasants behaved like savages. They dug up the body of the Princess's son, who had been killed at the beginning of the war, to see if they could find any jewellery or medals

[1] Mr. H. J. Bruce, married to Mme Karsavina.

on it; then they left the corpse half out of the grave, all blackened but still quite recognizable. Not one man could be found in the village to help the Princess and her daughters, who had in fact been very kind to their peasants and had done them a great deal of good. The priest himself, who had been supported by them, refused to help them. . . . And these are those very same peasants whose gentleness and patriarchal customs are praised by Tolstoy, who wrote a few kilometres from there! . . . There is moreover something very disconcerting about these outbreaks: it is a kind of sudden madness. In fact a few days before, these same peasants, while dividing up the land on the estate between themselves, had decided to protect their former masters and declared that they would not allow them to be insulted, even verbally. Then all at once they burst in in a fury, pillaging everywhere and burning everything . . . without even having the excuse of drunkenness, since there was no alcohol there.

Dinner with Armand de Saint-Sauveur at Contant's restaurant. He is very worried about the situation. The town is in a fever and trouble is expected tonight. It is said that General Verkhovsky, who has left the War Ministry, is in agreement with the Bolsheviks and that he has gone to the Soviet headquarters in the Smolny Institute to take charge of the movement against Kerensky.

Tuesday 6th November 1917

In spite of our fears for today, everything has been quiet. Besides, the government had taken precautions, and had raised some troops who are believed to be reliable. I watched the women's regiment going along the Embassy quay, with bands and machine-guns, beautifully in line, with their rifles held straight on their shoulders, with fixed bayonets. One could have mistaken them for a splendid Guards regiment of the old days. I am told that they made several arrests: nevertheless, the peace was not disturbed and I drove round for part of the afternoon without any incidents.

Wednesday 7th November 1917

Yesterday's quiet was deceptive. In fact, during the night the Bolsheviks pulled off the surprise attack which they have been planning for a long time. . . . They are now in possession of the telegraph office, the stations, and the departments of state: in short, they are masters of the capital. The government collapsed like a house of cards without the least resistance, and the apparent order has not been disturbed. Tereschenko has disappeared since this morning; and Kerensky has fled in a car belonging to one of the secretaries of the United States Embassy, as last night the Bolsheviks took good care to immobilize all the cars which he could have made use of. . . . He is said to have gone to the front to bring back some troops.

The Soviet has distributed proclamations saying that it is now in power, that the whole garrison is under its orders, and proclaiming immediate peace and the partition of the land.

To all appearances the town is completely quiet. There are not even any of the usual lorries with their loads of *tovariches* in heroic poses, and in spite of the hallucinations of a few madmen, there has been no fighting. A few patrols are circulating; Armand de Saint-Sauveur was arrested by some soldiers of the Paul regiment and taken before a kind of tribunal, which treated him with the greatest courtesy and gave him a safe-conduct for himself and his motor-car. . . . It is true that, a hundred yards further on, some other soldiers seized his car in spite of the safe-conduct: as it had been issued by the Soviet of a different regiment, to them it was not valid. But they too were very polite and promised to send back his car when they would no longer need it.

Lescaille went to Headquarters to get a guard for the Belgian Legation. He was told that there was no longer a Headquarters, and they very kindly took him by car to the Soviet, who will send the guard tomorrow. He is anxious to know whether he can accept, and whether his acceptance will be considered as a recognition of the new order of things. I told him that in my opinion he must make sure of the guard on his Legation before anything else and that in fact . . . once in power, the Bolsheviks will be just like the people who went before them, and that nothing will be changed.

Yonin, too, went to the Soviet to ask for petrol for the English general to whom he is attached. There were some difficulties at first because they said that the 'Savage Division', whose uniform he was wearing, was for Kerensky and the '*burjui*'. . . . Apparently he answered that he had served the Emperor before, and that now he was serving his country . . . but that he had never been for Kerensky . . . and he got as much petrol as he wanted.

Thursday 8th November 1917

The night was not as quiet as the day. Having found the 'Little Palace' closed, where I was supposed to dine with M. Vuagenat and Pingaud to hear Milton sing, we had supper instead at the *pension* Choisy where we found most of the actors from the Michael Theatre, with whom we passed the evening very agreeably.

I left at about eleven o'clock and as soon as I got into the street I could hear heavy firing and the crackle of machine-guns and, dominating everything, the ominous thunder of cannon-fire, preceded by a great glow which lit up the dark sky like lightning. Some *tovariches* whom I questioned told me that fighting was going on at the Winter Palace. Near the Champ de Mars very well-ordered security troops prevented me from going any nearer. So I went home, where I found Armand de Saint-Sauveur who had spent the evening at the Narodny Dom, where Chaliapin sang. He came back by tram without the slightest difficulty although a hundred yards away cannon were being fired.

According to this morning's information, the battle was fairly heated. The Bolsheviks had decided during the course of the evening to seize the Winter Palace, the government's last stronghold. It was being defended by a few *junkers* and by the women's battalion, who had entrenched themselves inside the Palace and in the square, behind mountains of firewood, where they were defending themselves with machine-guns and grenades. The Palace was surrounded by Bolshevik troops who set up a battery of about twenty machine-gun vehicles in front of the Ministry of Foreign Affairs, and installed two cannon under the red archway of Morskaya Street. In addition, the cruisers which had brought the sailors from Kronstadt were moored broadside on to the Palace, firing their guns. Firing was also coming from the Fortress, which had been in the hands of the Bolsheviks since the morning. Under those conditions, the defenders could not hold out for long. . . . It is impossible to know the casualty figures . . . all information on the subject is contradictory . . . three hundred women soldiers are said to have been killed, but this figure seems to me exaggerated. The others gave themselves up and have been shut up in the Preobrajensky and Pavlovsky barracks, where they are at the mercy of the soldiers, who are making the very most of the opportunity.

After lunch I went as far as the Winter Palace. I stopped at Countess Kleinmichel's house, where I found Mme de Scavenius and we went together to the Square. There were a lot of sightseers who were being canalized very courteously by the security force of sailors and Bolshevik soldiers, who prevented them from going near the Palace or on to the quay. The whole façade is literally riddled with bullets, which have made thousands of white flecks on the red plaster of the building. Some windows are broken, most of them pierced with holes: I counted ten holes in a single window. On the other hand, under the red archway where the battery of guns stood, all the windows are in fragments. The projectiles used were shrapnel and not explosive shells, which explains why the building was not demolished. And yet, just on the corner of the side which faces the quay, part of the cornice has been knocked off by a shell fired from one of the cruisers. A big destroyer with four funnels is anchored near the Palace bridge, opposite the Stock Exchange. The cruisers are moored a little further downstream, alongside the English Quay.

The Soviet has published a second manifesto, abolishing the death penalty, announcing that negotiations for a separate peace are to start at once, and ordering all revolutionary organizations to assist in arresting Kerensky, on whom they have not yet been able to lay hands.

The Bolsheviks have not, in fact, formed a government and are in disagreement with the other parties of the left, which are refusing to co-operate. But for the moment they are masters of the situation and they have locked up all the former ministers in the Peter-and-Paul Fortress, including Tereschenko, which gives me particular pleasure. In fact they are most courteous and have issued *laissez-passers* to the members of the Diplomatic Corps, and safeguards for their apartments. All is quiet in the town. Order is being maintained by pickets of sailors and soldiers, and I went unmolested to dine with Mme Barelly and M. Mimeur at the Hôtel de l'Europe and came back by tram without any difficulty.

Friday 9th November 1917

The Ministry has still not been constituted and it is generally thought that the Bolsheviks will not be able to remain in power under these conditions. I must admit that this is a disappointment to me, as I cannot deny having a certain sympathy for these men who at least have an ideal. Much as I hated the revolution, the only result of which was to instal a seedy-looking barnstormer in the Winter Palace instead of simply leaving the Emperor there, the more do I feel drawn towards the Bolsheviks, who dream of a future of peace and fraternity for all humanity. What seems to me the most hateful is the hybrid rule of bourgeois republics with imperial policies. If autocracy has had its day, if the aristocracy must disappear because it did not know how to fulfil its mission, then let it be in favour of a universal democracy in which all peoples are brothers and in which property will be fairly divided, and let the new state of things mark some progress in the happiness of men. . . . But there is nothing more odious than a glorified riff-raff . . . Kerensky in Alexander's bed. Lenin at least, like Christ of old, brings something new and talks a different language to that of the governments of today. . . . They are perhaps dreamers, but I prefer their dreams to the gross realism of the 'get-out-and-let-me-in' people of the first revolution.

In the provinces, the Bolsheviks seem to be in an even more difficult position than they are in the capital. There is no news from Moscow. Some people maintain that they are masters there like they are here; others claim that Rodzianko and General Kaledin have formed a Kadet government there. It is also reported that the Cossacks have established a government on the Don and that Kornilov, who is supposed to have taken advantage of the disorder to escape from prison, has set one up too. That makes a lot of governments for poor Russia, without counting yesterday's government shut up in the Fortress, and the Tsar at Tobolsk, and of course without counting the governments of Finland, the Ukraine, the Caucasus or any others. . . .

I lunched at Donon's restaurant with Armand de Saint-Sauveur, who had asked me there. He is rather annoyed because the banks are shut and he doesn't know how he will be able to pay the workmen in his factories tomorrow.

During the afternoon the disagreement between the Bolsheviks and the other left-wing parties seems to have become accentuated. It appears that the Municipal Council, which published a protest against the *coup d'état*, will have to take over the direction of the opposition movement. But for the moment public opinion is undecided . . . nobody misses Kerensky but people hesitate to rally to the Bolsheviks because they feel that their success cannot last. The most absorbing question is the problem of supplies: there is only enough food for two days and if, as people are saying, the railwaymen come out against the Bolsheviks and stop the trains from running, it will mean famine.

Nevertheless, the Bolsheviks are taking over the various administrations and have sent Commissars to take possession of the Ministries. The civil servants do not seem inclined to serve them, and are opposing them with the force of inertia. Trotsky went to the Ministry of Foreign Affairs at about three o'clock and called all the staff together and asked them to go on working for the new régime. After a short discussion all the officials, including also the subordinate employees, refused and handed in their resignations, leaving Trotsky somewhat disconcerted. . . . But everything will sort itself out if he sets about it in the right way. And yet it is very strange that the people who rallied so quickly to the first revolution should show such scruples today. . . .

On the other hand, all the soldiers are for the Bolsheviks because every one of them, even the Cossacks, wants peace above all. I cannot therefore believe that Kerensky will be able to raise any troops to fight against them. Nevertheless, people are saying this evening that he has arrived at Tsarskoye Selo at the head of an army. If this is true, it will end like the Kornilov affair did.

Meanwhile, all is quiet. I dined at the Danish Legation, where the Scaveniuses had invited me to share their revolutionary meal with Countess Kleinmichel, to whom they have extended their hospitality. They were naturally rather upset by the cannonade of the night before last which happened practically under their windows, but like me they are very surprised that everything went off in such orderly fashion.

It appears that the streets adjoining the Palace were closed from nine o'clock onwards, and soldiers were stopping people from going through and warning them politely that shooting was soon going to begin.

Tonight too everything is quiet, and I walked home along the quays. It is very dark, and half melted snow is falling. Only a few gas lamps are lit, and the sentries at the head of the Troitsky Bridge are crowding round a bonfire. It makes a huge circle of firelight against which the soldiers in their big astrakhan fur hats are outlined, and their guns with fixed bayonets reflect the glow of the flames. . . . Practically nobody in the streets.

Saturday 10th November 1917

According to the information which I have been able to collect, it appears that the fighting at the Winter Palace was less murderous than was at first believed. Among the dead, Prince Toumanov is the only one mentioned by name. He was Assistant Chief-of-Staff to Kerensky, and he crept under an attic bed to hide when the Palace was taken, and was discovered there by the assailants: his body was afterwards found in the Moïka. It appears that the Kronstadt sailors shot a number of *junkers*, and some women soldiers were killed during the fighting. On the other hand, the ransacking of the Palace is said to have been done by thugs, who got into the building on the heels of the Bolsheviks and destroyed everything. It has been impossible for me to verify this, as one cannot get inside. However, the hospital which occupies the centre of the building has not suffered and the wounded remained there throughout the battle, during which time the windows of the rooms used by the hospital remained brilliantly illuminated, to prevent them from being shot at. But all these dear Russians are so clumsy that those windows got just as badly riddled by bullets as the ones which they were aiming at, as did the windows in the Admiralty, although the building was empty.

The gunners in the Fortress did not do much better, and at a range of about four hundred yards they missed the target with almost every shot, sending their shrapnel either into the water at their feet, or else to the devil. And yet the Palace made a lovely target . . . seeing them at work like this, one realized why they did so little damage to the Germans, who consider a spell at the Russian front to be a rest-cure after Champagne or Artois.

The day has been fairly hectic. . . . We were expecting Kerensky's Cossacks to arrive at any minute, having been told that they were at the gates of the town, but up to now they have not appeared. According to some people, they are at Tsarskoye, according to others at Gachina or Dno. It will end like it did with Kornilov's army.

And yet the Bolsheviks were noticeably on edge. . . . Part of the day was spent shooting, and a few innocent spectators have been the victims of this stupid pastime. . . . Near the Hôtel de l'Europe I saw a young girl who had been killed in this way by a stray bullet. A large crowd gathered round the wretched corpse and an orator started a tremendous speech, waving a handkerchief soaked in the victim's blood. . . . What riff-raff!

Sunday 11th November 1917

During the night the rumour that Kerensky's troops were approaching was confirmed. The *junkers* have once again taken the offensive, thinking that reinforcements were arriving. At about nine o'clock this morning they even succeeded in occupying the central telephone exchange in Morskaya Street. This triggered off some fighting in the streets. The Bolsheviks, helped by all the thugs—and by the hooligans, as they are called here—to whom in their folly they distributed arms, have started a horrible hunt everywhere for students, which is like what happened before to the *gardavoys*. They were openly slaughtering in the streets all those on whom they could lay their hands. Outside the Military Mission, in Gogol Street, a car in which some *junkers*[1] were trying to escape had broken down, and the Red Guards massacred the young men who were inside it. . . . Their mutilated bodies lay on the pavement for part of the afternoon.

More violent fighting took place in the various military schools, which the Bolsheviks ended by occupying. The Vladimir School defended itself with great courage and the Bolsheviks were only able to take it by using cannon. After their victory they behaved disgracefully and murdered a great number of the besieged.

Meanwhile trams and cars are circulating as usual and it does not occur to all these armed thugs, who are themselves in rags, to remove the fur-lined coats of the bourgeois driving past in cars. They are not really bad at heart, and in any other country days like these would have been much more terrible.

I was able to get about undisturbed all day. I lunched with the Ermolovs, and I dined with Mme Lindes and came back along the Liteiny Prospekt, which was very dismal and wrapped in a thick fog. The fog made great haloes round the few street lamps, in which the

---

[1] Used here in the sense of young men of good family who were students in the military schools.

silhouettes of the Red Guards with their guns and their bayonets appeared immense and fantastic.

Monday 12th November 1917

The situation is just the same. We have still heard nothing definite about Kerensky's troops. I feel more and more convinced that it will all end in a compromise. It is announced that the Railwaymen's Union, wishing to avoid bloodshed, has proposed to mediate in the formation of a socialist government in which the Bolsheviks would be represented: at the same time it is threatening to declare a general strike if its proposals are not accepted, which would cut off everyone's food supplies.

I have just come back from dining with the Scaveniuses, who have returned to their Legation; they left it for two days to camp in the Austrian Embassy, which is under the protection of Denmark, because Kerensky's troops were expected to arrive at any minute and Sergevskaya Street seemed less exposed than Millionaya Street, which is so near the Winter Palace and the guns of the battleships.

Everything is quiet in the streets, in spite of the total absence of police. However, a guard service has been organized in the various houses. The tenants keep guard in turn and thanks to these precautions, and more particularly to their natural apathy, the robbers have not ventured far. . . . However, I am told that two or three were arrested in my street last night.

Tuesday 13th November 1917

Kerensky is still not here, and I don't think that he will get here for some time. There have however been some battles during the day round Tsarskoye, which the Soviet troops regained at the end of the afternoon. Kerensky's position seems rather bad: he has only got Cossacks and Cossack artillery still with him. The infantry regiments go over to the Bolsheviks as soon as he gets them up from the front. Consequently it is very difficult to form any exact idea of the position of the two sides, and Claude Anet very aptly describes it by comparing it with one of those cakes where there are alternate layers of jam and pastry. From Petrograd to the front there are alternate slices of Bolshevik troops separated from each other by slices of government troops, which are all reduced to a standstill and all encircled by each other. Meanwhile trains circulate between the different sides, who are parleying at one moment, fraternizing at another, and fighting at the next. Things are a complete mess from Petrograd to the front, where the Germans are very careful not to fire a single shot, but advise the Russians to go and settle their little business at home.

This afternoon I went to the flea market to see if by any chance there was anything there from the pillaging of the Winter Palace. But I saw absolutely nothing of any interest. In fact, most of the shops were shut.

Just as I was leaving the Embassy, Armand de Saint-Sauveur came to fetch me with his car to go and dine at Contant's. The Nevsky Prospekt is quite deserted and there are only a few soldiers and armed workers keeping watch round big log fires at each cross-road. The restaurant too was empty and apart from our table there were only two that were occupied, one by Colonel Langlois, and the other by three Jews who the head waiter told us were policemen. Saint-Sauveur tells me that in the factories the workers are working more or less normally, and are taking it in turns to shoulder arms, or to mount guard in the streets, or to 'go to the front'.

We talked about the events of the last few days. One of his engineers witnessed a horrible scene. Some Red Guards, on the hunt for students from the military colleges, got hold of a boy of fourteen who was wearing the uniform, ran him through with their bayonets and threw him into the Moïka, like dung on the end of a fork, while his mother who was with him fell unconscious in the road. It is appalling, and those people who sent out these unfortunate young men, at a time when they could get no help whatever, bear a very great responsibility, as it was only to be expected that the exasperated Bolsheviks would take terrible reprisals.

Wednesday 14th November 1917

I meant to go this morning to Tsarskoye Selo and the 'front', in order to get some information which is less fantastic than that which is given out here, but the Soviet troops who regained Tsarskoye Selo the day before yesterday have pushed Kerensky's men back as far as Gachina. It is too far away, and as I did not want to risk not being able to get back, in case the trams were not running, I had to give up my plan.

During the morning I went with Lieutenant-Commander Fradel to the Smolny Institute, in order to obtain car-licences and petrol rations for the Embassy cars.

The Institute, formerly a school for the young girls of the nobility, is a large building in the Empire style painted yellow with white pediments and columns. Its austerity is in contrast to the rococo domes and the pale blue buildings of the monastery of the same name, which one passes on the way there, with its small-paned windows and its wrought iron balconies. Armoured cars and field guns are in position outside the gates, and quantities of motorcars are lined up in the courtyard. Two naval cannon stretch out their necks under tarpaulins on either side of the entrance, guarded by some sailors grouped around a fire, ready to defend the Soviet in case of attack by the 'Kornilovians'.

In the entrance there is a continual coming and going of dis-hevelled soldiers, armed *tovariches*, Red Guards and women, and this teeming crowd reminds one of the early days of the March revolution in the Taurid Palace. . . . Control is very strict, and to get into the building one has to have a *laissez-passer* which is issued in a little ante-chamber, where we had to queue for a long time. As soon as our turn came and we had made ourselves known, they gave us our cards without any difficulty and with them we passed, one at a time, before the guard composed of workers and sailors, and through a doorway almost completely blocked by tables and chairs. The vast white corridors were a strange sight, with the never-ceasing movement of soldiers and *tovariches*. The floor is littered with newspapers, proclamations and cigarette ends. Nevertheless, there is some attempt at organization and on each door a placard indicates the purpose of the building: regional Soviets, Soviets of professional associations, Commissariats, supplies, and so on. We wandered about on three floors, where you could hardly see the end of the immense corridors, absorbed by the whole scene and not hurrying overmuch to find the office in which we had to do business. When we had had enough of it, we went downstairs again and went to get information from the 'commandant', who occupies a room near the entrance. The *praporchik* who fulfils the function of com-mandant spoke French and was most amiable, as indeed were all the people we had to deal with. He got someone to take us to the special Commissariat in charge of issuing *laissez-passers* for motorcars and petrol vouchers. I was struck by the scenes of activity in all the offices. Women sit at typewriters, long-haired students, soldiers and non-commissioned officers work in the middle of the din, and I admire their patience, because they get disturbed all the time by *tovariches* here and *tovariches* there . . . soldiers who have been on sentry duty and who want a meal, others who need ammunition for the 'front', and still others demanding cars. There is continual agitation, and yet it all seems to be 'sorting itself out' and one must admit that everyone goes about it with great good will. We were really given a very good welcome in spite of our '*burjuis*' status, and all these worthy people were naïvely straining their ingenuity to say a word of French to us—'*bonjour*' and '*merci*', and so on. There were types there whom it would have been interesting to sketch: soldiers in big woollen caps camping on the staircases; Jewish students with greasy hair; young men with inspired expressions and the faces of apostles and visionaries; and Red Guards with guns slung across them and revolvers at their sides. We talked for some time to a sailor, a colossus who carried his gun by a string, with its bayonet fixed: he had come back from the front, and described the vicissitudes of the fighting. He told us that the workers fight courageously but that they have no leaders. . . . "It's lucky the sailors are there," he added. He confirmed that the Bolsheviks have occupied Tsarskoye, and he thinks that today they will try to take Gachina.

After luncheon I went with Armand de Saint-Sauveur as far as the Winter Palace. Two big destroyers and two other smaller ones were getting under way with the help of numerous tugs. We watched them moving upstream, lit up by a ray of orange-yellow sunshine which outlined them in gold against the grey background of the Fortress, where only the spire shone out in splendour. They dropped anchor near Smolny. Two cruisers are berthed at the English Quay. The evening is peaceful. There is a dull booming noise in the distance, which is probably cannon fire.

Thursday 15th November 1917

A good many desertions are occurring among Kerensky's troops, who have retreated beyond Gachina. The Cossacks themselves, who are discontented, ill-fed and under-paid, are going over to the Bolsheviks, who seem to be masters of the situation here. In Moscow, too, events seem to be turning out to their advantage, but according to the latest news, the fighting has been fierce. Apparently there has been shooting in the streets with heavy calibre guns, and there have been a number of killed and wounded. Material losses are also said to be considerable: the Kremlin, where the supporters of the old government had dug themselves in, is badly damaged and two of the oldest cathedrals have been burned down.

But one must always make allowances for the Slav imagination and I hope that the battles of Moscow will prove to be like the bombardment and capture of Tsarskoye Selo. If one believed what people are saying here, then the Bolsheviks have burned down the town and massacred part of the population. Most fortunately, the bombardment made a great deal of noise and did little damage, and the so-called mass murders boil down to the killing of two of the inhabitants, the director of the power station and a priest.

But, nevertheless, the peace-loving people living in the town have been through a worrying time. I dined at Contant's with Armand de Saint-Sauveur, who was able to telephone to Princess Paley. She told him that the Grand Duke Paul had been arrested and taken to Smolny, and has just been released after having been shut up there for nearly two days. Dinner was excellent and a lot of people were there. Gulesko played the '*Nord Express*' with more gusto than ever, but I must admit that I was rather irritated by this gang of twenty strapping fellows striving to amuse a few idlers, when people are killing each other perhaps only a few *versts* away. . . . But then, that is Russia in a nutshell, with its morbid charm, its contrasts and its incoherence.

Friday 16th November 1917

Kerensky's supporters have laid down their arms. His General Staff have given themselves up, and he himself has fled. So now we are rid of this grotesque character, and with him the régime which issued from the revolution has collapsed too: it only succeeded in alienating everyone and in becoming an object of ridicule, defended by a few Cossacks, a battalion of women and some children.

The Bolshevik government has not yet been constituted, but it is thought that by tomorrow this will be an accomplished fact.

I am waiting impatiently to see the 'workers' and peasants' government' at work. How will these people with an ideal translate their dream into reality? In any case they cannot do worse than the puppets of the 'provisional government'. Let us hope that the International, which to a certain extent had been realized by the aristocracy before and which was destroyed by the nationalist bourgeois, can be reconstituted by democracy and the proletariat. The workman and the peasant have something in common, no matter in what country they are thus classified, just as there was something in common between a peer of France and a prince of the Holy Roman Empire.

It is the bourgeois, vain, selfish and grasping, who created that nationalism which encourages their ignorance of foreigners and fills their coffers. They are the people who are responsible for the policy of imperialism, as much in Germany as anywhere else. It is their newspapers which during peacetime dreamed only of drums and flags, and which are still blowing the trumpet to prevent the voice of the people being heard. . . .

Since the International of the Church has gone bankrupt and that of the intelligentsia is too weak to make itself heard, let us put our trust in the International of democracy, while at the same time we regret the good old days of the aristocratic International, and the elegant solution which consisted of stopping a massacre with the wedding of a princess.

Saturday 17th November 1917

The town is still quiet and it is impossible to get any idea of what is happening from the look of the streets, where the trams and *izvozchiks* are circulating as usual, where everyone is going quietly about their business, and where customers line up in long queues outside the bakeries and food shops. The almost total absence of motorcars is due to the petrol shortage. At night fires burn at the main cross-roads, where soldiers and Red Guards bivouac adding a picturesque touch to the dark streets. The town has been put in charge of a military commandant subordinate to the Soviet, a

Colonel Muraviev, who has shown himself to be forceful. He has published a *prikase* ordering the guards responsible for keeping order to execute on the spot any individual found pillaging, or breaking into those houses where all the tenants, except those at work on national defence, have to mount guard in turn. This order lays down certain formalities for searching houses and specifies that searching the houses of representatives of foreign powers is forbidden, under any pretext whatsoever. . . . All this bears witness to a concern for order, which we have grown unaccustomed to since the revolution. It is true that a decree has appeared at the same time which shows up the new order of things in its true colours. This decree, which regulates the allocation of all the land to the peasants, begins with these words: "Private property having been abolished . . ." This does not suit either the former owners or the peasants!

The officials in the Ministries are still on strike, but the telegraph people have started working again, or at least in part, as we have received a few telegrams. Until yesterday evening, in fact, the German radio services were our only source of information and it is through them that we learned of the fall of the government in France. I hope that Albert Thomas will be part of the next arrangement. He is the only one of our political people to have had any direct contact with Russia and to have understood its importance from the point of view of the war.

Sunday 18th November 1917

One rather forgets about the war, because of what is happening round one. But the Germans don't forget about it. It is believed that they are planning to occupy the Aland Islands and make a landing in Finland. All the reactionaries are building high hopes on their arrival. There is a story that when he entered Riga, the Emperor William arranged for an orthodox service to be held and had prayers said for the Tsar. A rumour is also spreading that he has set at liberty the officers of a division who had been delivered to the Germans by their men with their hands tied, and that he has had a certain number of the soldiers of this division shot, and others scourged. This news, whether true or false, is much discussed in bourgeois circles, where they make no secret of the fact that they are hoping for the coming of the Germans. Without exaggeration, one can say that they would be welcomed by almost the entire population. . . .

The Bolsheviks, moreover, are in a difficult position . . . the populace already blames them for having not yet made peace or distributed bread. They are also accused of using old régime methods, prejudicial to liberty, by suspending the newspapers which are hostile to them and prohibiting meetings. . . . It is being said that "their hands are drenched in blood". It's true that they don't wear kid gloves!

Besides, they are having trouble among themselves, and this very day several Peoples' Commissars have resigned. The new régime depends entirely on two men, Lenin and Trotsky. But the extremists, especially among the sailors, are already accusing them of not acting . . . since the war is still going on and the age of plenty has not returned. Some day perhaps these two apostles of Bolshevism will seem very Menchevist in relation to men of more advanced ideas. The Municipal Council of Petrograd was elected a few weeks ago with the Bolsheviks triumphant, to the dismay of the bourgeois: now it embodies the hopes of all the elements of reaction and is the centre of resistance against the new government. It was the same with the Kadets in relation to the old régime, and with Kerensky in relation to the Kadets.

From the external point of view, the situation is even more difficult. In fact, no foreign country has yet recognized the government of Peoples' Commissars up to the present. . . . And yet it is just as good a government as the preceding one, and there has not been much change in Russia. There is neither administration, nor cabinet, nor police, and things are exactly as they were in the days when all this intricate machinery worked, more or less badly. The Bolsheviks have proclaimed a general peace . . . and the war still goes on: they have partitioned the land . . . but the peasants had already seized it without permission. And so why should there be such scruples, and why refuse to recognize this government under the pretext that it is the 'outcome of riots'? As if all governments, starting with Kerensky's and going as far back as Merovaeus', hadn't also at some given moment been the 'outcome of riots'. It is America who is being the most intransigent, and who is the most obstinately refusing to have any relations with 'the revolutionaries of Smolny', even for obtaining petrol or for the safe journey of a courier. These sewing-machine and canned pork merchants really do go a bit far, and they are rather too ready to forget in what way free America was founded.

But it is up to France to take the initiative in recognizing the Petrograd government, because we cannot cut ourselves off from Russia. . . . Alas, we appear to be a long way from doing so, and people continue to have illusions. The agency telegrams describe the American effort in glowing terms, as if anyone could really believe that a few thousand amateur soldiers could compensate for the onslaught on our front of a hundred and fifty divisions. These consist of German, Austrian and Turkish troops which are at present still at this end of the front line, and that is without counting nearly two million prisoners whom the Russians could send back. Looking at the tiny portion of the front which is held by the English after three years of war, and with four million men under arms, is quite enough to be able to appreciate American co-operation at its true value, and to realize what can be expected of them after only a few months of war and at such a distance from their base.

Compared with these facts, of what account are the so-called Bolshevik atrocities which fill the French newspapers . . . and where blank spaces in the columns lead people to believe in still worse horrors. . . . This campaign is all the more inadmissible because these same newspapers never breathed a word of all the horrors and all the vileness committed by the February revolutionaries at the time of the collapse of the Empire. In truth it all boils down to a few hundred victims in Petrograd and in Moscow, a dozen broken windows, and a few corners knocked off the painted plaster by machine-gun bullets. These are the 'atrocities' which provoke the righteous indignation of well-meaning people . . . those same people who, nevertheless, coolly remark that "the last offensive did not cost very much".

Monday 19th November 1917

The government of Peoples' Commissars has still not been constituted, and well-informed people say every night that it cannot last "another day". . . . And yet in spite of these assurances the Bolsheviks are still masters, and I cannot imagine who there could be to even compete with them for power. The people, moreover, are bored with the whole question, and each one goes about his business. There are not even any more sentries or Red Guards at the cross-roads. It no longer amuses them to mount guard round a camp fire, and they have all gone back to their homes.

The politicians argue, in the midst of the indifference of the masses. The social democrats are forming a coalition with the revolutionary socialists and the Mensheviks excommunicate the Bolsheviks, who offer to compromise with I don't know who. . . . Parties are founded, cartels are established, people make mergers, Committees are formed, and so are committee Councils, and council Committees: they all claim to be saving the country and the world. All these debating societies are designated by initials: these pacifists have the same manias as the General Staffs, and as a result it is impossible to make head or tail of it. Each day one hears of some new split and some sensational new patching-up; there are announcements that a new army is marching on Petrograd, that the Cossacks are arriving in Moscow, that railway-lines have been cut, that the Germans are landing on every coast . . . and each day passes in peace and quiet. All these reports are untrue and even if they were true they do not interest anyone, and people in the street and even in the drawing-rooms can only talk of the best way to get hold of a sack of flour or a few eggs.

The Ministries are still empty, for lack of employees. At the Foreign Ministry Trotsky is pursuing Neratov, who is said to have gone off with "all the secret treaties". He is apparently rather disappointed not to have yet had an answer from Germany to his peace proposals, and he is beginning to foresee the problems of foreign relations. Rumour has it that he is thinking of handing over his post to Baron Rosen, the former Russian ambassador to Tokyo and Washington. . . . And that is how the socialists abolish diplomacy! . . . by appointing a diplomat as Minister for Foreign Affairs! There is no bourgeois government which would have the sagacity to do as much.

However that may be, the choice appears to be a fortunate one. Baron Rosen is indeed a remarkably intelligent and shrewd man, who judges events objectively. He has not been infected by the epidemic of madness which rages all over the world, and has dared to say what he thinks in a letter published in the *Novya Jizn*, Gorky's paper. It is this letter which has caused him to be banned by 'well-meaning' people and which has drawn the attention of the Bolsheviks to him: they will find in him a true friend of peace, but one who knows all the difficulties standing in the way of its conclusion, and who should know how to negotiate it cleverly without getting carried away by the generous illusions of a Lenin or a Trotsky.

Tuesday 20th November 1917

Lubersac has just come back from the Dvinsk front and has given me some picturesque details on the state of the army in that sector. The Germans march about between the trenches, led by their bands and followed by the music-loving *tovariches*, and enemy soldiers come to buy tobacco on the other side of the Russian lines without any bother.

And yet General Niessel has come back from a tour of inspection at the front and is full of optimism because he heard shouts of "hurrah" as he walked past, and because he saw a few men marching more or less in line. Little does he know that the whole thing was faked for his benefit, according to a truly Russian tradition of politeness which has survived everything. . . . He was taken to a sham Soviet with well-chosen supernumeraries, and the troops whom he saw marching past are rather reminiscent of the ones at the Châtelet. It was always the same supers, both officers and Cossacks, who made up the guard of honour which came with bands playing to meet him at his train in the morning, whom he reviewed at mid-day dressed as artillery, and whom he saw again in the evening dressed as cavalry. . . . The General was taken in, as also was Catherine the Great some time before. . . . Ever since Potemkin, the art of putting on a show with theatrical scenery has been a Russian speciality.

The most serious thing is the complete absence of food supplies. The distribution of bread will cease on Saturday in that section of the army where Lubersac is stationed. In order to survive, the army staffs have to send out detachments behind their lines, which go to the extremities of Russia armed with machine-guns, in order to seize the trainloads of corn or flour which have broken down on some railway line, and bring them to the front . . . this fact alone is enough to show the state of general disorganization.

This evening we received the first official communication from the new government, notifying us of its succession, and proposing the conclusion of an armistice between all the belligerents while awaiting the opening of peace negotiations.

The document is typewritten on cheap quality paper and contained in an envelope addressed in Russian to "the Embassy of France", and it could well have been mistaken for a circular and been left to lie about on a table. Of course it is very democratic. It is written in pretty bad French, but with an obvious concern for courtesy. It ends with an appeal to the 'noble French people' to put an end to this 'incomparable butchery' (*sic*), and is signed by Trotsky.

Whatever happens, this scrap of paper marks a new era, and I have even preserved the envelope itself: some day it will be interestting to find it in the Embassy archives.

The Ambassador immediately telegraphed Paris to ask for instructions, as the mere fact of acknowledging receipt would be to enter into relations with the government and recognize it as an established fact.

In my opinion, moreover, it is very regrettable that this recognition did not happen earlier, and I never can understand the tactics of isolating oneself from the adversary rather than getting into contact with him, finding out what he is driving at, and getting the advantage of him. To break with Russia, which certain people are pressing for, would once again be playing into Germany's hands; by our departure we would leave the field clear for her to establish the most rewarding of colonies. Even if Russia makes a separate peace, we should release her from her promise and not break with her. This could be questionable from the moral and sentimental point of view, but from the realistic point of view, which is the only one which ought to count, there can be no possible doubt. Without seeking further, we need only consider the milliards of French money in Russia, which have not been balanced by similar Russian investment in France. Under these conditions it would be France who would suffer from the results of the reprisals policy into which people are trying to drag us.

Thursday 22nd November 1917

There has been some talk about a monarchist plot which has been discovered during the last few days, and about the arrests which have resulted from it. The plot, which I had already heard about before it was discovered, was in fact no secret and had been organized by some bankers, landlords, officers and Cossacks . . . but they all chattered, some of them were guilty of treachery, and it ended in all the leaders being arrested in the Russia Hotel on the Moïka. Among them is Purishkevich, one of the murderers of Rasputin, who tried in vain to escape by disguising himself as an hotel waiter and offering to help the Soviet envoys in their search for this same Purishkevich and his accomplices. But his stratagem was discovered: he was the first to be arrested, and the list of all the other conspirators was found on him.

The Bolsheviks seem to have been more worried by the resistance put up by M. Shipov, the director of the State Bank, and his employees, which is still going on. The Commissars have ordered them to hand over a certain number of million roubles, and they are opposing this demand with all the force of inertia. The Municipal Duma is supporting the Bank and has delegated several of its members to guard the building and oblige the Soviets to use force and break open the safes, which action could then be exploited to their disadvantage. The government is pressed for money, and in the morning of the day before yesterday it tried to send out a military expedition against the Bank: I saw it passing along the Liteiny Prospekt, with bands playing, Red Guards, soldiers and sailors. The procession arrived at the Bank, followed by lorries for collecting the money. . . . But at the last moment the Commissars retreated and did not dare to use force. But this cannot last long, and if the Bolshevik government remains in power, it will soon end by getting the better of the resistance it is meeting. In any case, it is clever of it not to fall into the trap which has been set, and not to give in to the temptation to impose its will by brute force.

Meanwhile, the government is carrying on with its programme of socialization and has issued a decree purely and simply abolishing the bourgeois newspapers. Its explanation of this attempt against liberty is that paper and printing should be for the use of all, that is to say, of the masses. It would therefore be unfair to let the capitalist bourgeois keep their newspapers, as they are a minority and through their money they occupy a position in the press which is out of all proportion to their numbers. This measure would only be a temporary one which would cease on the day when all distinctions of class and fortune will have disappeared, then all citizens would have equal shares in the newspapers. . . .

A decree has also appeared reserving the monopoly of all advertisements, notices, etc., to the State, and another one ordering the requisitioning of all furs and warm clothing for the army. Each apartment will have to contribute a certain number of furs, and the 'house committees' are ordered to strictly supervise the enforcement of these regulations.

Friday 23rd November 1917

Trotsky has wasted no time, and as soon as he had proposed the conclusion of an armistice with Germany to the Allies, the council of Commissars ordered General Dukhonin to open negotiations with the enemy, and gave the order to all front-line units to cease hostilities. This order received an enthusiastic welcome from all the regiments. As for the Generalissimo, he tried to get out of it by saying that his business was to make war and not to discuss peace, but he had to send in his resignation. He has been replaced by the *praporchik* Krylenko, one of the best-known Bolshevik leaders, who immediately took steps to carry out the order of the Council of Commissars as quickly as possible.

At the same time, the Soviet government this morning started the publication of the 'secret agreements' . . . it seems odd to see all these documents published in the newspapers, when we used to lock them up in the strong-room with such care and with so many keys. . . . What is even odder is the speech in which Trotsky announced this publication, which reveals a candid ignorance of what is known today as 'secret diplomacy'. He seems to be quite shamefaced at not being able to produce beautiful hand-written documents on parchment, sealed with impressive seals, and he seems surprised that it all consists of mere "correspondence and files". . . . He is still back in the days of the ceremonial procedure of Vienna!

But he adds that, such as they are, the documents are even more "cynical than he could have imagined". He ends with some most disagreeable remarks about the Allies, notably the Americans who, he says, came into the war to do business rather than to defend right and justice. . . . For a Bolshevik, it's not so badly observed. . . . But there are certain things which you have no right to say, once you are Minister for Foreign Affairs.

The town remains quiet; and yet the Bolsheviks seem to fear attempts against their authority, because they have reinforced the Smolny guard and have had a big gun-boat, the *Kibinetz*, sent from Kronstadt to defend them against attack. It saw it coming up the Neva late yesterday afternoon, and I stood for nearly half an hour watching the picturesque scene. . . .

It was getting late, and in the background one could just make out the shape of the Fortress, the outlines of its architecture picked out in gleaming snow. The grey mass of the ship stood out in the mist with its turrets and its slender masts, and little tugs sent up rockets of smoke into the sky as they helped it to move slowly up the river, which was covered with ice-floes whose wan whiteness contrasted with the dark colour of sky and water. The Troitsky Bridge had been opened, and a crowd was waiting to cross over it again. . . . In the tangle of low sledges and red tramcars waiting in long lines, interested and anxious spectators were moving about in the dusk, and gathering in groups round the guards' log-fires at the entrance to the bridge, where they stood out against the glowing flames like actors in a shadow-play.

Outside the Embassy of England stood the carriages of the Allied representatives, who were in conference with their *doyen* as a result of Trotsky's letter to the Diplomatic Corps announcing the establishment of the new régime. The *chasseurs* in their green livery and their shoulder-belts, waited on the pavement talking to the imposing coachmen, wearing caps with cockades and all muffled up in braided *armiaks*. The chauffeurs drowsed at the wheels of limousines which, according to the custom adopted by the Diplomatic Corps since the revolution, sported the flags of their owners' countries.

In spite of help from the tugs, and because of the currents and the ice-floes, the *Kibinetz* had great difficulty in getting through the narrow space provided by the opening of the bridge, which was not intended for ships of such heavy tonnage. So they decided not to try and reach the Liteiny Bridge the same evening, and dropped anchor in front of the Embassy. From the big bay window of the Chancery, through the darkness of the night one could see the outline of the ship, which seemed enormous, with its port-holes lit up and its coloured signal lights. . . . Of course somebody had to say that it was there to threaten the Embassy with its guns, but early this morning it went on its way in the direction of Smolny.

Saturday 24th November 1917

I went to see the Grand Duke Paul and Princess Paley in Countess Kreutz's apartment, where they have taken refuge while waiting to be allowed back to Tsarskoye Selo. I found the Grand Duke wonderfully courageous, relating the details of his arrest and of his detention at Smolny with great good humour. But they went through some terrible hours as after the fall of Kerensky they were at the mercy of the red hordes. The Princess showed remarkable presence of mind. She at once got in touch with the Tsarskoye Selo Soviet and arranged for one of its leaders, a sailor called Dybenko, to come to the palace. He arrived at the moment when gangs of victorious Bolsheviks had invaded it and were about to pillage the cellars containing several thousand bottles of wine. With truly admirable vigour he took control and forced these men to come out of the cellars; then he put the Grand Duke into a car and drove him to Smolny.

It seems that the Bolsheviks were rather embarrassed by their prisoner. They wanted to move him to the Fortress, then to Kronstadt, which could have had tragic results. The Grand Duke was very insistent, and protested so strongly that the *tovariches* allowed themselves to be persuaded. He heard them saying: "He's a nuisance, that man, he doesn't want to go anywhere." Finally, after a great deal of palaver they decided to leave him at Smolny, where they shut him up in a room guarded by a squad of sailors. The Grand Duke, moreover, has no complaints about his guards: some of them even addressed him as "Comrade Highness"! They found an armchair for him and settled him into it; one of them then begged him to read the newspaper to them and explain it, and they asked his permission to smoke while listening. The Grand Duke naturally agreed, and it must have been strange to see this Romanov in general's uniform and wearing the order of Saint George, with his majestic look and superb presence, reading *Pravda* to a group of four dishevelled sailors. He sat on a rickety armchair in one of the great white halls of the former school for the girls of the nobility, the sailors listening to him with that look of concentration which one sees in the simple folk of this country, squatting on straw-bottomed chairs and smoking their cigarettes, with their rifles with fixed bayonets propped between their booted legs. . . .

Meanwhile the Princess lost no time, and with the help of a devoted doctor she managed to convince the Committee that the Grand Duke Paul's state of health did not allow of his being treated as a prisoner. The Bolsheviks were afraid that he might die on their hands, and they ended by setting him free on condition that he promised in writing not to leave the capital without authorization.

Sunday 25th November 1917

An evening at the ballet with the Alexandre Benois and the Destrées. They were doing *Swan Lake* with Smyrnova: Fokina and Feodor-ovna danced the Spanish *pas-de-deux* in a remarkable way, and Spezizova was enchanting.

Alexandre Benois, who is president of the Fine Arts Commission, told me that the damage done to the Winter Palace is not as bad as people thought. It is confined to the theft of a few objects in the rooms of Alexander II and Nicholas I. The objects were mainly of sentimental value, as these rooms had remained in the state they were in at the time of the deaths of these two Emperors. They also slashed the portraits of the Empress's father and mother and that of a Prince Volkonsky who was Grand Marshal of the Court.

Neither were there any irreparable losses in Moscow, and the treasures from the Hermitage which had been moved to the Kremlin did not come to any harm. And yet, Polovtsov, who happened to be in Moscow at the time of the *coup d'état* and was staying in the Kharitonenko Palace just opposite the Kremlin, says that the bombardment was very heavy. Shells could be seen exploding on the crenellated towers and fires began to spring up on all sides among the cupolas and bell-turrets of the cathedrals. In the dark one had the impression that the whole Kremlin had been destroyed . . . but with the dawn it reappeared intact, and at a distance one could not even see any signs of the battle. To sum up, it is all confined to a few smashed cornices and some easily repaired damage to one of the cathedrals. What made the greatest impression on the Russians is the fact that an ancient ikon, which came unscathed through the fire of 1812, was ripped by a shell.

The inhabitants were terrified. . . . Part of the foreign colony left their hotel because it had been hit by shells and took refuge in a cellar, where they found some French officers. While they were down there, a shell fell quite nearby, fortunately without exploding . . . to the great despair of one of our officers, whose mission is connected with the manufacture of projectiles and who recognized that one of his latest models had failed to go off. . . . He would almost have preferred to be reduced to mincemeat together with all his companions, rather than suffer this humiliation.

Monday 26th November 1917

The diplomats are still refusing to recognize the new government, insisting that it is not the government of the whole of Russia . . . and dealing with current affairs through the intermediary of their consuls . . . which is just Jesuitical procedure.

Today Duchesne and Binet went to see Trotsky to ask him for visas for our compatriots who wish to leave, as the frontier is closed in theory. Trotsky received them courteously and gave them what they wanted. The Consul told him that he hoped that our nationals would not come to any harm because of current events, and that Russian hospitality would be worthy of that which Russians receive in France. Trotsky replied by assuring him vehemently that anyone attacking a foreigner would be severely punished: then he added with a smile, "As for French hospitality, I must tell you that I love France, her literature, her beauty and her climate . . . but I have had less enjoyment from her hospitality since, only too recently, I was taken back to the frontier between two of M. Malvy's policemen."

Tuesday 27th November 1917

The neutral diplomats also received a note from Trotsky, begging them to ask their governments to co-operate with Russia in putting an end to the war; they are adopting the same wait-and-see policy as the Allies. Nevertheless, they acknowledged receipt of the note which he had addressed to them (which we too should have done, out of the most elementary politeness). In the identical letter sent to him by them all, which was drawn up by M. Odier the Swiss Minister, they end by assuring him of "their civilities", which is an entirely new formula in diplomatic procedure. Trotsky's letter contained no such courtesy formalities.

M. Garrido, the Spanish *chargé d'affaires*, acted independently of his colleagues and sent a note assuring the government of Commissars of Spain's co-operation in its intended work for peace: he ended with the ordinary formalities, as though the note was addressed to a recognized government.

This move has been much censured not only by the Allies but by the other neutrals, who blame M. Garrido for having acted independently of them, without even having warned them during the meeting which they held for the purpose of agreeing on the proposed action.

Thursday 29th November 1917

Life is back to normal. . . . Yesterday M. Patouillet, director of the French Institute, gave a lecture on Bergson at which I found most of the friends of France. M. Oldenburg, former Minister of Public Instruction, presided and said a few charming words about the intellectual bonds between France and Russia.

Nevertheless, the reactionary parties seem to be preparing to take control again. I lunched today with the Kellers, where we ate oysters from the Black Sea, which makes me think that transport must be less disorganized than people say. There was a great deal of talk about a counter-revolutionary organization at Novo Cherkassk which has grouped a certain number of officers and Cossacks together. But none of this will come to anything because everybody chatters and this plot, which is no secret, can hardly worry those against whom it is directed; they are quite content to let it go on, and delighted to see the hostile elements assembling of their own accord in the one town, thereby putting themselves under easy surveillance.

In the evening, I dined with Alexandre Benois and there I found

Prince Argutinsky and Somov, with whom we spent a delightful evening looking at old drawings and engravings.

And meanwhile the French newspapers are making their readers shudder at the descriptions of Bolshevik atrocities. . . .

Friday 30th November 1917

Things are happening fast, and yesterday Trotsky was able to make a triumphant announcement to the Assembly of Soviets (which has been joined by the Council of Peasants, which up to now had remained with the opposition and had rejected all contact with the Bolsheviks). The announcement is to the effect that armistice negotiations have begun, that the parliamentary delegates sent by Krylenko have been received by the German military authorities, and that the opening of discussions with the object of concluding an armistice has been fixed for midday on Sunday, with the agreement of the Germans.

The Bolsheviks repeat that they do not want a *separate peace*: they are working for a *general peace* and they have invited the Allied governments to join in the discussions, which open on the day after tomorrow. But at the same time they have addressed a proclamation to the proletariats of the Allied countries informing them that, if they do not oblige their governments to participate in the discussions, the Russian people have decided to make peace on their own.

The Chancellor's recent speech to the Reichstag has had an important effect here and has produced considerable support for the Bolsheviks. In it he declared that Germany is ready to resume her neighbourly relationship with Russia, and that both countries would keep the territories they had before the war. They did not stop at restrictions concerning Poland, Lithuania and the Baltic States, which are cleverly disguised under the formula of the right of peoples to govern themselves . . . and they have not even noticed that the Chancellor condemned the revolution when he said that the German government was giving its special attention to "the events in the midst of which Russia is struggling", and that he hoped for the speedy return of order to that country.

But that is the German plan in a nutshell: to unleash revolution in Russia in order to force her into peace, and as soon as this peace is made, to work for the re-establishment of authority in order to

157

profit by the peace, and through it gain the support of a strong, pro-German government. This government would win the sympathy of all Russians, who would be grateful to it for having saved them from anarchy.

And judging by events, one might easily believe the Bolsheviks to be the executors of this plan, either consciously or subconsciously. And yet there are men amongst them who are sincerely dedicated, and enthusiastic spirits who pursue an ideal. Consequently, I absolutely refuse to accept the over-simple theory that they "have sold themselves to the Boche". That is an absurdity. . . . But one has to admit that appearances are sometimes against them and that at the moment they are literally playing the enemy's game. It is even possible that, without knowing it, they are being led into it by German agents.

So it is that, now that peace is practically a fact, one notices that the Commissars are taking measures which seem to encourage reaction. They have set free a large number of secret police agents of the old régime, who had been imprisoned since the beginning of the revolution. They are also credited with the intention of liberating the Tsar's former ministers. They are surrounded by men who served the old régime, and the military commandant of Smolny is said to be a former wrestling champion, well known as a reactionary and an Okhrana informer.

All this is strange, and if it goes on we might very well see things take a complete turn about . . . which would be less surprising than would seem on the face of it, because extremes meet in politics, and I would even say particularly in politics. It gives one a bit of hope concerning what is happening in France.

Saturday 1st December 1917

The Allies here continue to give an impression of complete confusion. The communications and moves of the Ambassadors and the Military Missions succeed and contradict each other. It's deplorable. On the same day, the American military attachés of Petrograd and of Stavka issued official proclamations flatly contradicting each other: one declared that the United States government will never recognize a government which does not honour its agreements, and the other assured the Russian people of American sympathy, recognizing its right "above all other, to work towards a general peace". Both of them, of course, are speaking "on the instructions of their government. . . ." What a bear-garden! and what it must be like with the rest of the Allies, judging by what happens in one mission alone, I can only leave to the imagination.

Meanwhile Trotsky keeps the score and no longer misses a single false move on the part of his adversaries. He has become very self-assured and has not hesitated to send a very firm note to Sir George asking for two Russian anarchists who are being held in England to be released immediately, and threatening to close the frontier to all English subjects by way of reprisal. People say that the Commissars even contemplated shutting up Sir George himself as a hostage in Peter-and-Paul. Anything is possible, and I am assured that in a discussion in the Soviet the day before yesterday, the idea was put forward that all Allied diplomats should be put in prison until their peoples had decided to make peace. . . . Perhaps it is the best method; if only they had applied it at the beginning of the war!

Tuesday 4th December 1917

The elections to the Constituent Assembly in Petrograd have produced a large Bolshevik majority. What is surprising is the relatively high number of votes obtained by the Kadets, whose list of adherents includes a concentration of all those who are in opposition to the present powers. The elections took place in perfect quiet and without any apparent pressure on the part of the Bolsheviks. The number of voters was considerable: almost eighty per cent of the register. This comes from the fact that a lot of people believe that they are forced to vote, just as they are forced to pay tax, and to them it is a compulsion rather than a right. In a lot of houses, the *starchi-dvorniks*[1] wanted to force the foreigners to put their names on the list, and threatened to withhold their ration-cards if they did not vote.

Wednesday 5th December 1917

Things are still going from bad to worse. The Bolsheviks have now

[1] Can perhaps best be translated as 'senior concierges'.

159

acquired the mentality of autocrats and are mercilessly breaking down all resistance. The Municipal Duma refused to obey their order of dissolution, so they have arrested the Mayor and the principal Councillors.

There is no more freedom of the press: all the newspapers (including even the socialist ones) who printed the appeal addressed to the Russian people by certain members of the former provisional government have been suspended, and a number of journalists put in prison. As for those signatories to the appeal who were unable to escape from Petrograd—they are in the Fortress. . . . Among them are some famous revolutionaries who have fought all their lives against the old régime and been sent to 'Tsarist' prisons in Siberia, and so on.

These proceedings have exasperated the revolutionary socialists and the other parties of the left who do not make common cause with the Bolsheviks: and the men of these parties, who so often before resorted to criminal attack, have let it be understood that they have not forgotten how they manufactured their bombs. So it is to be feared that Bolshevik tyranny will provoke the same excesses as did the Tsarist autocracy before it: murders, and the reprisals which result from them, which produce still more crimes. I still hope that the Bolsheviks, who are the apostles of peace abroad, will have the sense not to provoke civil war.

General Dukhonin has been murdered by the crowd in the railway carriage in which he had been shut up at Mohilev: this murder has certainly helped to provoke a surge of public opinion against the Bolsheviks, and the crocodile tears shed by Krylenko when he deplored this "appalling disaster which has stained the revolutionary flag with blood" have done nothing to quieten it. . . . Besides, nobody knows exactly what happened. General Dukhonin, who was in fact a man of rather advanced ideas, had apparently wished to defend Stavka against the troops sent by the Soviet under the command of Krylenko, and had started digging trenches to stop them. But at the last minute the Generalissimo gave up his plan and surrendered, in order to save shedding the blood of his soldiers in a civil war. He was locked up in his carriage without any further incidents. It was only a few hours later that some sailors succeeded in inciting the mob, which invaded the General's *coupé*. Krylenko claims to have saved him the first time by "shielding him with his own body" and to have got there too late the second time, but we

The Comtesse de Robien with Monsieur Gilbert

Comtesse de Robien and other members of the French colony in St.
Petersburg awaiting the arrival of the French President

Carriage escort of the French President in St. Petersburg

The Cossacks being reviewed at Krasnoe Selo, 1914

only have his word for it. The unfortunate general was torn to pieces by the mob.

The pretext which served to enrage the soldiers seems to have been the disappointment of the Bolsheviks at not finding Kornilov there. He had been imprisoned at Stavka after his famous attempted coup and had escaped, with four hundred Cossacks from the Savage Division who had been ordered to guard him, on the evening before the actual day when the Soviets arrived at Headquarters. The soldiers claim that this escape took place with the connivance of General Dukhonin, and they murdered him through hatred of Kornilov, who to them symbolized the counter-revolution and the continuation of the war.

And during all this time, the theatres of Petrograd are full and I found it impossible to get a seat for the ballet tonight, when they are doing *Eros*, *La Nuit d'Egypte*, and *Islamet*.

Thursday 6th December 1917

The territories of the Empire are being frittered away. . . . Finland has proclaimed its independence and has asked the foreign governments to recognize it.

In my view, one cannot deny that the Finns have the right to regain their freedom. They have nothing in common with Russia, neither race, language, religion nor customs. They were conquered by her and had to recognize the Tsar of Russia as Grand Duke of Finland, and I cannot see why we should deny this people the right to govern themselves, as our only excuse is that they tend to favour Germany. It is up to us to win the Finns over to our cause by hastening to give them the recognition which they are asking for before Germany does so, and to send a diplomatic mission composed of intelligent people to Helsingfors. . . .

This is the policy which we ought to pursue with regard to all those nationalities which are being born from the Russian corpse, without worrying about recriminations from our former allies.

Russia does not exist: a Russian Empire was the only thing which existed, and from the moment when the Imperial backbone became dislocated, there was no more Russia.

At this moment when the different nationalities which composed the Empire are regaining their independence and constituting themselves as countries, in the Western sense of the word, we must make friends for ourselves who will be bound to our cause by bonds of sympathy for our ideas, or by gratitude for the help which we give them. This bundle of young shoots will be far stronger than the enormous mouldy tree-stump which has finally rotted away, and which caused so much disillusionment after having raised so much wild hope in those people who turned a blind eye to its state of decomposition.

Friday 7th December 1917

The instructions which have just arrived from Paris prove that the Allies understand the situation better than one could have hoped for. The Paris conference has in fact approved the conduct of the Allied representatives in Petrograd. They should continue to abstain from all direct relations with Smolny; but they are authorized to let it be understood that, when Russia has given herself a regular government which is acceptable to the whole nation, the Allies are ready to recognize it and even to consider any proposals it might make on the subject of a fair and lasting peace. To sum up, it is the acceptance of that revision of war aims which we ought to have accepted long ago, in order to comply with public opinion in all the countries, and particularly with Russian opinion.

For my part, I would have preferred to enter into open relations with Smolny. But I realize that perhaps the policy decided on by the Allies is more cunning. By promising to take the same view as the Russian people on the subject of peace, as soon as they acquire a regular government, perhaps the Allies will succeed in detaching from the Bolsheviks a number of pacifists who only follow them, and with repugnance, because they have promised peace. Besides, the apparent failure up to now to start armistice negotiations could also cost the Bolsheviks the loss of some supporters. It is beginning to be realized, even among the people, that Germany is not anxious to treat with a government of this kind, and that if peace is to be obtained it will have to be proposed by a less advanced party, and one which can offer firmer guarantees to the country with whom it treats.

Peace is what the Russian people long for above everything, and the Bolsheviks have gained popularity by promising to end the war. . . . The surest way of overthrowing them would be to expose their inability to fulfil this promise, and to make peace without them. *Whoever they may be, it is the men who end the war who will be masters of Russia for a long time.* . . .

Saturday 8th December 1917

Horrible weather . . . this is hostile Petrograd: the bitter wind scatters the snow into a fine spray, like thin smoke rising from the polished ground. The white and dripping houses look like sucked barley sugar and it is difficult to walk on the slippery pavements, where sand is no longer spread.

The foreign colonies are getting more and more worried. I saw Charlier a few days ago at a little party given by the soldiers of the Belgian detachment; he is exasperated by the demands of his workmen, who extorted the sum of two million roubles from him in one day alone. He does not dare to shut down his factories, because it would cause disturbances, but he runs the risk of being ruined if he carries on under existing conditions. This is, moreover, the plight of all the foreigners who have set up concerns here which were so prosperous a short time ago. Mme Latilde came this morning to pour out her troubles to me; she is no longer mistress of the dressmaking establishment which she runs, and the workers have the right to control all her actions. She, on the other hand, has to pay them salaries which get higher every day, whereas the banks refuse to let her have any money, as they have been forbidden to pay out sums of over five hundred roubles. It is an inextricable situation.

Sunday 9th December 1917

Last night the *tovariches* looted the cellars of the Winter Palace, where there were thousands of bottles. Naturally, the drinkers expressed their joy by letting off their guns; all these people walk about with rifles and bayonets all day long, and these become rather dangerous toys when handled by drunkards. All the same, a few willing firemen were found to smash what remained of the bottles and flood the cellar, in order to prevent further attempts. A certain number of *tovariches* remained prostrate in the middle of this 'abundance', and perished there. It is sickening to see such good stuff thrown away: there were bottles of Tokay there of the time of Catherine the Great, and it has all been gulped down by these Vodka swiggers.

During yesterday, the *tovariches* having acquired the taste went on looting cellars and letting off their guns. Today they sacked the cellars of the English Club. The soldiers are enjoying this excuse to drink and make a lot of noise, and are reaping more practical advantages as well: they are running a more or less clandestine traffic in wine and brandy in the streets, and more than one bourgeois has fallen into the trap. Very high prices have been paid for bottles carefully hooded in champagne straw-cases and sold in secret by astute *tovariches*, who had taken good care to empty them of their original contents and replace them with water from the Neva.

There is the danger that the soldiers will take it into their heads to visit the Ochta depots, where formidable quantities of alcohol are stored, intended for the manufacture of explosives. Even though these soldiers are quite decent chaps when sober, they become wild beasts after drinking, and this mob of drunkards armed with rifles and machine-guns would be appallingly dangerous.

Monday 10th December 1917

The Commissars are supposed to have all sorts of plans. It is said that they are thinking of reorganizing the finances, and in view of this they are drawing up decrees cancelling all loans and seizing all private property. But the populace is only concerned with the armistice and thinks only about the peace. They hope that the town of Petrograd will be occupied by a German army which will put an end to the vagaries of Russia's present masters: the bourgeois make no secret of their wish to be protected by a *Schutzmann* standing guard at every street corner. And to think that these people, who today dream only of the Germans and a reliable police force, are the same ones who sacked the German Embassy, decried the *nemetski*,[1] insisted on changing the historical name of Saint Petersburg, cursed the police rule of the Tsar, and applauded the murders

[1] The Russian word for Germans, formerly the word for all foreigners, and meaning, literally, the 'mutes'.

of the 'pharaohs' and the burning of police-stations. . . . Oh! the fickleness of fortune here on earth!

Tuesday 11th December 1917

Today is another *prazdnik*, in honour of the so-called reunion of the Constituent Assembly . . . which is in fact not reassembling at all, and which will mean further *prazdniks* later on. Meanwhile all the shops are shut and the *tovariches* walk about in long processions with banners and red standards . . . but nobody looks at them now: they've seen too many of them.

During the evening the *tovariches* went on pillaging the cellars, and one could hear rifle-fire going off in all directions in the distance. This made the calm of the Scaveniuses' drawing-room all the more pleasant where, together with Gentil, we spent the evening sitting round the fire talking to our charming hosts and Countess Kleinmichel, while the two little Pekineses lay stretched out flat on the carpet, snoring through their little snub noses and gazing at the flames of the cheerful log fire with eyes as round as marbles.

Wednesday 12th December 1917

If one had to describe the régime which Russia is suffering from at the moment, one could call it a 'soldiers' dictatorship'. It was the soldiers who supported the Bolsheviks, because they promised peace: now they tend to go even further than them and to carry Lenin along with them, in the unleashed flood of their animal instincts.

These simple people, who for four years have been allowed to kill and be rewarded for it with crosses and decorations, now do it automatically. They know no other rule than that of the rifle and the bayonet . . . just as if they belonged to civilized States.

Yesterday, on the corner of the Liteiny Prospekt and Furchtadskaya Street, two soldiers were bargaining for apples with an old woman street vendor. Deciding that the price was too high, one of them shot her in the head while the other ran her through with his bayonet. Naturally, nobody dared to do anything to the two soldier murderers, who went quietly on their way watched by an indifferent crowd and munching the apples which they had acquired so cheaply, without giving a thought to the poor old woman whose body lay in the snow for part of the day, near her little stall of green apples.

At the moment, the Red Guards and the workers are almost a force for order compared to these soldiers, who are however fairly good-natured at heart; but they show no restraint, owe no allegiance, and are living in a state of anarchy, in the literal sense of the word. This anarchy is something into which the Slavs are easily led, and four years of lawless war-time life have further developed their taste for it.

In several factories, and in Charlier's in particular, the workers now form part of the managerial staff since they have the right to control the business, and they support the former owners against the soldiers and the unskilled labourers, and protect the stock and machines from sabotage.

They seem to have realized that the very foundations of the socialist system depend on increase of production, to allow of a wider distribution of wealth.

So, in this present phase of the crisis, we are witnessing a fight between the socialist and even communist worker elements, which represent order, against the anarchy of the all-powerful soldiery.

Thursday 13th December 1917

They are still plundering the wine-cellars: and in the morning the snow outside the ransacked shops is a purplish colour and smells of stale dregs. Raoult, Eliseiev, the big shop on the corner of the Liteiny Prospekt and Furchtadskaya Street, and Mme Serebryakov's cellar on the French Quay—they have all had to put up with it, since it started a week ago with the cellars of the Winter Palace.

Tonight it was the turn of Contant's restaurant: it happened exactly at the moment when Armand de Saint-Sauveur was giving a big dinner-party. In fact the *tovariches* were charming, and having heard that the French Ambassador was among the guests they left, saying that they would come back some other day. I wonder how much it can have cost Saint-Sauveur, who was warned before the dinner but too late to cancel it, although in time to prepare a convincing argument.

Amongst the cellar-wreckers there are also some men with good intentions who are trying to smash the bottles of wine to prevent drunkenness and disorder. There is inevitable conflict between these men and those who are bent on drinking, and this has degenerated into fighting, made worse by the fact that those who were content to smash soon got just as tipsy as those who drank, as the fumes went to their heads. At least this is what M. Croissant, the owner of the wine-cellars, told me: there, the sailors who had been ordered to smash the bottles behaved very correctly and did not drink a single bottle, and yet when they left they were all in a state of complete drunkenness.

Friday 14th December 1917

Finland has proclaimed its independence and asked the great powers for recognition. The Finnish manifesto is very well drawn up. It explains that the country is up against famine, and that it cannot ask for help from the foreign powers through the intermediary of the Russian Ministry for Foreign Affairs, since the foreign powers do not recognize the government of the Commissars: therefore Finland must have its own government. It adds that Finland needs order, and can no longer put up with the anarchy of Russian soldiers and sailors. Besides, from the legal point of view, the link which bound the two countries together was severed when the dynasty which was common to both countries fell, and therefore Finland has this right to regain its liberty. The manifesto ends with an appeal to the right of peoples to govern themselves, the principle which the *Entente* has so often proclaimed.

One cannot make any serious objection to these reasons, and it would be a mistake to once more refuse to act according to our principles, under pretext of not annoying Russia . . . who doesn't care a damn. Russia has not been all that polite to us: and, besides, does Russia really exist? I fear that here too, we are letting the Germans steal a march on us: they have built up the sympathetic feeling which the Finns already showed towards them into hatred of the Russians. I fear that we have missed the opportunity of ensuring the friendship of a people which is young, hard-working, and very open to progressive ideas, and which would be very willing to turn to us, now that Russia is no longer there to divide us and that they no longer need hate us as being the allies of the oppressor.

Relations between Smolny and the English had become very strained, following the imprisonment in England of some revolutionaries. Trotsky had insisted on their being set free and, by way of reprisals, had stopped the English couriers from leaving Russia. Relations had eased slightly following England's promise to release the individuals in question and a statement by Sir George, which was expressed in the most measured terms, and which certain people even interpret as a move towards the Commissars' government. But today the disagreement has entered a more acute phase: Trotsky has published a violent note in which he claims the right to send diplomatic couriers abroad, and in which he warns the ambassadors of the great powers in Petrograd that, if they refuse to grant visas to his couriers, he will have their couriers arrested.

The English Consul went to see the Peoples' Commissar for Foreign Affairs to protest to him that any such measure would be a violation of the rights of ambassadors accredited to this country. But Trotsky cut him short with: "Accredited! . . . To whom? Ambassadors mean nothing in Russia, since their governments refuse to recognize us. I don't give a damn for this recognition, which is just one of the monkey tricks of diplomacy, but I shall insist that the foreign governments really allow us all the advantages which we allow their representatives here. . . . And notably the right to correspond with our supporters abroad . . . even if they are working to overthrow established governments, like your embassies here are working to overthrow us." He added, not unreasonably, that the embassies recognized the Soviet government all right as soon as they needed it to get *laissez-passers*, rations, petrol and so on, and that it was inadmissible to use this recognition to obtain help and refuse to give it.

A decision will therefore have to be made. For my part, and contrary to the general view, I am in favour of a recognition which, when all's said and done, does not commit us in any way but which would let us know where we stand. By getting in contact with the Bolsheviks, we can make our opinions known. I cannot see why sentiment should play any part in this business. The recognition of a government does not mean that one is sympathetic towards this government. As the word implies, it is a question of *recognizing* a fact: it is simply an acknowledgement of that which exists. At present we are in the position of someone who goes for a walk in the rain and gets drenched, and keeps on saying "I refuse to admit that it is raining". Whether one wants them or not, the Bolsheviks are in power now, and all our 'monkey tricks', as Trotsky calls them, cannot alter the fact. People say that they will not hold their position for long. That is another matter, and there will be nothing to stop us, once they are overthrown, from recognizing in turn those who will have overthrown them.

Sunday 16th December 1917

A telephone call came yesterday evening warning us that the *tovariches* were pillaging a wine depot belonging to one of our compatriots who has been called up and is now serving on the French front. So I went there with Pingaud to try and safeguard the owner's interests, or at the very least to assess the damage. We arrived in the middle of heavy firing, but as our motorcar drove resolutely into the crowd of *tovariches*, with its headlights blazing, they drew back and made way for us.

Unfortunately there was nothing to be done: the cellar was occupied by about thirty soldiers who were already drunk, and was being besieged by about a hundred others, all wanting their share. The besieged didn't see things in this way, and were shooting through the door—in the air, most luckily for us. We therefore had to give up trying to get inside the cellar, but forced open the door of the house, where some panic-stricken passers-by had taken refuge in the halls and on the stairs. We got the manager and the head of the house-committee to sign an official report, although I doubt if it will be of much use. In spite of the shooting, we managed to get away again. The besiegers were answering the fire of the besieged, and rifle-fire at such close quarters really makes a very unpleasant noise. At each blast, there was a mad rush of *tovariches* inside the courtyard gates. Then the grey-capped heads would re-emerge and the gang of soldiers would go back to the cellar door until the next burst of fire, like a flock of sparrows which scatters when a carriage comes along and goes back as soon as it has driven past. Besides which, with great good nature, they got up and made themselves scarce as soon as we looked angry or shouted rather loudly at them.

I ended the evening at the Military Mission, where General Niessel very kindly made me stay for dinner. I had a long talk with Captain Sadoul, a socialist and a friend of Trotsky's. He told me that Trotsky receives quantities of love-letters, flowers and cakes, just like Kerensky used to. He would do well to be on his guard.

Monday 17th December 1917

I went to see the Destrées, who have moved into the Olive house and are delighted with it. The Belgian Minister feels just the same as I do about recognition of the Commissars' government, and I certainly hope that he will succeed in getting this policy adopted. But he is very depressed by events and is visibly upset at seeing the socialist doctrine, which he has always supported, discredited as a result of the deplorable experiments which have taken place here. It is always painful for a believer to lose his faith.

There is a lot of talk about the Caillaux business.[1] . . . When folly reigns it is a crime to be sensible, and Alcibiades himself was condemned by his compatriots for having tried to save Greece when it was rent by the Peloponnesian war. And yet Alcibiades was right, and because Greece wanted a 'fight to the finish' she ruined her civilization, to the advantage of another world. I fear, alas, that Europe too is heading for suicide, because of not having understood the people who think in the same way as M. Caillaux. . . .

Tuesday 18th December 1917

Today Trotsky made a new move towards us and, after having sent Captain Sadoul to inform us of his visit, he came to the Embassy, where he spent over an hour in conversation with M. Noulens.

This visit, which was purely a courtesy one, does not imply any recognition of the Soviet government on our part but it is a first attempt at contact, from which much can be expected. Besides,

[1] Former French Prime Minister and Minister of Finance. Arrested by Clemenceau in November 1917 on charges of treasonable defeatism. He favoured a compromise peace with Germany at the expense of Great Britain.

Trotsky is intelligent enough to understand the Allies' difficulties and their hesitation to recognize the Commissars' government, and he said so to the Ambassador.

They even tackled the irritating question of the couriers, which has reached an acute phase since Trotsky's last note: according to him, this note was mainly directed against the Swedish Legation as the result of a minor incident. A short talk sufficed to reach agreement, and it seems as though everything will turn out for the best.

Trotsky also asked for some enlightenment on the part played by our officers in the Ukraine, and he showed himself to be satisfied with the explanation. The Ambassador assured him that the attitude of the officers towards internal affairs is strictly neutral and that in the event of conflict between Russia and the new Ukrainian state, they would act as impartial military attachés like those whom the neutral countries have sent to the belligerent armies. Trotsky then talked of peace, as he sees it: a democratic peace, without annexations or war indemnities, conforming with the right of peoples to govern themselves. This peace must extend to all oppressed peoples, and the question of Alsace and Lorraine must therefore be settled by the inhabitants, of their own free will.

If Germany does not accept a peace conforming to this ideal . . . he will not yield, and Russia will carry on the war by all the means at her disposal. But he hopes that from now on Germany will treat on this basis, and he regrets that the Allies have not yet thought fit to associate themselves with the armistice talks; he is counting on prolonging these to some length, to give the Allies time to send representatives. Finally, he spoke of France in touching terms and there was even a tear in his eye when he mentioned the sacrifices which she has made. He said to M. Noulens: "As you see, I am moved because I am speaking of France, and the French people mean more to me than any other people. And by coming today to the French Embassy I wanted to prove to you that I feel that there is a difference between France and the other Allies."

The conversation then continued and took a more personal turn. Trotsky described his tribulations during the first year of the war when he was harried by the Tsar's ambassadors and deported at their demand from France to Spain, from Spain to the United States and from the United States to Canada. He finally got stranded in Halifax, where the English interned him in a concentration camp, while Mme Trotsky and her children were locked up in the house of a policeman. M. Trotsky seems to have been very much affected by this separation. He at once started to spread revolutionary propaganda among the three hundred Germans who were interned with him, and in a few weeks he had converted them all to the Bolshevik way of thinking. The camp commandant was furious and had the over-persuasive orator put into a cell, in spite of Trotsky's ironical protests that he was serving the Allied cause by deflecting "the Boches" from their duty. When the Revolution started, Trotsky was released at the request of the provisional government (who must surely have since regretted it) and when he took leave of the commandant he told him that he was going to Russia to become a deputy. The worthy Englishman who, like many of the Allies, judged things from a distance, replied: "Oh well! It's lucky that you won't be elected . . . so I needn't worry. . . ." And when Trotsky described this little anecdote to M. Noulens, he added with his subtle smile: "He must be feeling surprised now, that Halifax major."

To sum up, the interview was almost cordial and the Ambassador appears to be very satisfied. He even said to me that he appreciated the intelligence and the tact of his visitor.

Wednesday 19th December 1917

I heard from Sadoul that Trotsky on his part was delighted with his interview with M. Noulens. So I hope that this taking-up of contacts will ease relations. Unfortunately M. Trotsky is not the whole of the picture, and I fear that he too may be overwhelmed by this anarchy. The soldiers are masters, and they recognize no authority. All the officers whose powers are not renewed in the elections, which take place at every turn, are obliged to serve in the barracks and to perform the most abject tasks. Even those who are re-elected have no badges of rank and wear private soldiers' greatcoats.

The Bolshevik government is caught between this anarchy, which threatens to sweep everything away, and the intrigues of reactionaries who drive it into committing excesses in order to then exploit them to its detriment. It is surrounded by a host of more or less corrupt old régime agents. In this connection, I am told that General

Speredovich, the fierce *gradonachalnik*[1] of Yalta, is now at Smolny. And amongst the members of the delegation to the armistice talks there was a former secret police agent, Lieutenant Schnéour; there is a file on him in Paris, and our Military Mission has exposed him. It was a mistake not to have kept the information to ourselves in order to have the man in our power, and in trying to do the Bolsheviks a bad turn by discrediting their delegation we merely succeeded in proving their good faith, because they immediately arrested him and shut him up in the Fortress. The revolutionary socialists too are trying to undermine the present régime by spreading the silliest rumours, which the people accept with their usual credulity. A few days ago they even went so far as to publish a newspaper article stating that Lenin and Trotsky had had an interview with the Grand Duke Paul to arrange for the Tsar's return— they have even said that he has already left Tobolsk!!

Thursday 20th December 1917

The traditional institution of *dvorniks*, which one relied on to keep order in the houses and in the streets, has been hit too by the mania for disorganization and in the last few days these good people have been on strike, refusing to give their numerous services. Snow is piling up on the pavements, there is nobody to bring wood upstairs and at night one no longer sees the familiar shape of the *dvornik* sitting inside the courtyard gates, wrapped in his sheepskin *shuba*,[2] as still as a post in the falling snow. By order of the syndicates the *schveitzars*[3] have had to do the same, and they have been forbidden to open the front doors. The tenants have to come in by the back stairs, where anyone can get in, since there are no more *dvorniks* to guard the entrances. Happy days ahead for the burglars.

Luckily, in our building Baroness Korff's *schveitzar* is a good Balt, with a strong sense of tradition, who does not worship the fashion of the day and has not been infected by the Russian madness. He is content to make do with replacing his gold-braided cap with a fur bonnet, and he opens the door for me as in the past, casting a furtive glance to make sure that no one has seen him. I am there-

[1] The governor of a town.
[2] Fur coat or cloak.
[3] Porters, or door-keepers.

fore one of the few inhabitants of Petrograd who does not have to suffer the minor inconvenience of coming in oneself by a squalid back staircase and through the kitchen, and of having to ask one's visitors to do the same.

Friday 21st December 1917

I feel increasingly that Lenin and Trotsky are on the verge of being overwhelmed. But nothing will make them come down to earth, and in spite of everything and at the risk of being considered naïf, I have a certain sympathy for these visionaries who believe in the future of humanity. Instead of lolling about in the apartments of the Winter Palace like Kerensky, they lead a communal life at Smolny, and together they all eat a simple dish of gruel which is brought in every day for the Comrade Commissars' dinner.

Scavenius told me that when his Head of Chancery had to go and see Trotsky about something he received him most courteously, and after the interview he said: "The comrades in the Crimea have sent us some grapes, you must come and taste them." And he led him into the next room, where a hamper of grapes had been emptied on to the table, and there they sat, plucking at the bunches in brotherly fashion with the *tovariches*.

The Bolsheviks, or at least those among them who are dedicated, disarm one by this quality of naïvety. They have such a different mentality to ours that they cannot understand our reasoning. They live detached from reality, in a world of theory which they have fashioned for themselves. A few days ago Trotsky said to a journalist who was trying to explain to him what a disgrace it would be if Russia were to repudiate her foreign debts: "But after all, what can it matter, since all the countries are going to go bankrupt? . . ." The journalist rather aptly answered: "Well then, wait for the others and don't have a separate bankruptcy. . . ." But Trotsky made no answer, lost in his dreams which to him are reality and on which he bases all his actions.

Saturday 22nd December 1917

What must be prevented at all costs is that Russia, on concluding a separate peace, should give back to the Central Powers the prisoners taken during the course of the war, thereby providing our enemies with renewed strength to use against us on our front. But to achieve this it is important not to do what people are doing in France and elsewhere, telling everyone that the Russians are traitors because they are making peace. On the contrary, we must recognize their right to retire from the fight and accept their reasons for doing so: but on the other hand, we should ask them to fulfil their obligations of neutrality as laid down by international law, including the most universally accepted rule of keeping inside their own territory all belligerents who are already there. In a word, from now on we must treat them as friendly neutrals, and not as faithless and treacherous allies.

The newspaper campaign on this subject, which I have organized on the Ambassador's instructions, seems to have taken effect and I am hoping that the countless prisoners-of-war in Russia and Siberia will not be returned to their countries to reinforce those armies which are fighting against us.

Sunday 23rd December 1917

Prices have risen in a terrifying fashion during the last two weeks: a suit from Higgins costs between eight and nine hundred roubles; an *arshine*[1] of woollen material from the English shop ninety-five to one hundred and fifty roubles; a pair of made-to-measure boots at least four hundred roubles; and *valinkis*[2] three hundred roubles. If we turn to foodstuffs: a small chicken is twenty roubles; a thin turkey fifty roubles; pullets which used to cost seven-tenths of a rouble are now worth ten roubles; and a Russian pound (four hundred grammes) of pork costs five roubles. The *tovariches* continue to pillage the wine-cellars, but with less frenzy than a little while ago, and one hears rather less shooting. M. Juin has lost 36,000 bottles of brandy which were stored in the Duma cellars near the Stock Exchange, and yesterday they smashed three millions' worth of champagne at Doyen's. The Gorchakovs' wonderful cellar, which was so well looked-after by Abel, has been dispersed and given to the hospitals to prevent its being smashed

[1] 2.33 feet.
[2] Felt shoes or boots.

up. There were over four thousand bottles of wine and liqueur, which were worth a fortune.

Contant's restaurant is the only one which has been able to keep its wine-cellar safe up to now, by installing twenty or so hefty chaps provided with rifles, machine-guns and grenades, whom it pays, feeds, and supplies with drink in abundance. Up to now nobody has dared attack them, but the mere fact that one can organize *'forts Chabrol'* in the capital, who are able to resist all attack, shows the extent of the anarchy in which we are living. In the same way, a more or less bourgeois newspaper continues to appear under the protection of a guard of paid *tovariches*, and comes out every day under one title or another, without anyone being able to stop it. It's certainly an interesting situation—but it will end in war between the different quarters of the town, between the streets, and between the houses.

Meanwhile, we already have reached civil war, and ultimatums are being delivered between Smolny and the Ukraine *rada*, according to all the rules of the old diplomacy. In these conditions, it was not worth making peace with the Germans . . . though it's true that peace between Russians will be infinitely less dangerous!

Tuesday 25th December 1917

The question of the couriers, which appeared to have been settled after M. Trotsky's visit, has been aggravated by the English. This time Trotsky, in a great rage, took a firm stand and decided to arrest *all* the couriers until agreement is reached. He justifies this measure by saying that it matters little to him that his emissaries should have their French visas, if by not having the English visas they are unable to travel through English territory. As a matter of fact there is no question of retaliation, because the English would only have to entrust their bag to the French couriers to make sure of their communications, whereas the Commissars' government has not got the means to resort to a similar subterfuge to send its own courier on his way.

Wednesday 26th December 1917

Dinner at Contant's restaurant, the only one where one can still

176

get wine to drink. A lot of people. This evening all was quiet, but a few days ago some sailors came in brandishing revolvers, who forced the diners to empty their pockets, in order to satisfy themselves that these bourgeois were unarmed. In fact, they took nothing. Another time a solitary *tovarich* came in and sat down at one of the tables and from there he beckoned to the numerous officers in the room who, as they were not in the street, had kept on their epaulettes . . . he called them over to him . . . psst . . . psst . . . and then showed them the door. Those concerned quickly understood, obeyed, went out . . . and returned to their tables, having deposited their epaulettes and badges of rank in the hall. Not one of them even raised an eyebrow, and they went on with their dinner unabashed, while listening to Gulenko playing dashing tunes on the piano. . . .

If all these men had defended their Emperor better a year ago, they would not have come to this now.

This is what most of the French people here will not understand. They are exasperated with the Bolsheviks . . . but they welcomed the revolution and were indignant when some *gardavoys* shot down a dozen scoundrels in the Nevsky Prospekt at the time of the first demonstrations. Events are unfolding with implacable logic, and the bourgeois régime of the Milyukovs and the Guchkovs, founded on riots and supported by all well-disposed people, has had to end in anarchy while waiting for the return of the autocrat who will, I hope, subdue everyone by the rule of the knout. Our own bourgeois Revolution of 1789 lapsed into the excesses of the Terror, and ended with Bonaparte and his wars. But that was not enough to cure us.

Thursday 27th December 1917

The answer of the Central Empires to the Russian peace proposals became known yesterday evening. They accept a democratic peace 'without annexations or contributions' in theory and, to sum up, what they propose is a kind of profitless peace. In Russian circles it is considered that this note marks a 'turning-point' in the war, and people think that a general peace cannot now be very far off.

I think that the Russians are having illusions, because the note is full of reservations and restrictions which allow its meaning to be changed. Nevertheless, it appears to offer a basis for preliminary discussion. In spite of everything, it is a sign of great success for the Russian revolution to see its policy of democratic peace accepted by the Central Empires, after having been so much jeered at by nationalists of every country at first . . . . and after having been in fact sanctioned by the Pope's letter. The so-called liberal powers are the only ones to still rebel against the principle of generosity! Are not the Bolsheviks right when they say that it is the bourgeoisie who wanted the war and who want it to go on? It is certain that the nationalists in every country are recruited from this vain, selfish, grasping class of people; the aristocracy and the common people belong to the Internationale, up to a certain point. . . . Consequently, I can sympathize with the saying of a Bolshevik in Lenin's circle who said: "If we do not succeed, if Russia is not yet ready for socialist government, we would rather have the monarchy back again than have to come to terms with the bourgeois Kadets."

Friday 28th December 1917

Yesterday all the banks were occupied by detachments sent by the government, and they were all put under direct state control. At the Credit Lyonnais Lestrange, Beau and Castaigne were all arrested; but they were set free again at the end of the day.

This morning I went to Smolny to renew the '*propusk*'[1] for the Embassy motorcars, because it is important to have things in order. One is in fact stopped all the time by outposts of Red Guards or soldiers who check car-licences, and one has got into the habit of sticking them inside one of the headlights for convenience. At night one gets a picturesque glimpse of a ragged *tovarich* emerging from the darkness, sharply lit up by the harsh glare of the headlights as he bends over them to decipher the '*propusk*'.

At Smolny there is the usual beehive activity. One has to deal with comrade soldiers and sailors who receive one—politely, in fact—at wooden tables, sitting on period furniture which seems to have got left high and dry amongst the reek of stale tobacco smoke. Everyone keeps their hats on, they all shout, smoke and throw fag-ends and bits of paper on the floor, which is never swept.

[1] A pass.

178

I also went this afternoon to a session of the revolutionary tribunal which holds court in the palace of the Grand Duke Nicholas Nikolaievich on the quay at the far side of the Neva, facing the *Jardin d'Eté*. This tribunal consists of half a dozen elected judges who are changed almost every day. They are usually soldiers or sailors. There is no public prosecutor and no defence, and the public are asked to produce someone to make the prosecution, and someone to conduct the defence. This sometimes provokes incidents and a few days ago, when a Bolshevik police commissar who was accused of theft during a search was being tried, his improvised defending counsel shouted out: "What right have you to sentence a thief . . . you, who are sitting in a palace which was stolen in the name of a usurped power. . . ." His pleading went no further than that!

Nevertheless, the judgements usually comply with common sense and equity, although they are passed without either legal code, rules or correct procedure.

The revolution, however, willingly practises a more summary kind of justice, and a few days ago some soldiers quite simply shot three thieves they had just caught, on the Red Bridge over the Moïka Canal. It was obviously less trouble than taking them to the police station as they had been ordered to do . . . but what would have been said if the *gardavoys* of the old régime had done the same? In fact, in spite of this drastic procedure, thefts are now frequent. In Princess Shahovskoy's house part of the silver was removed, and Lieutenant Renard, who has an apartment in the building, never heard a sound. Some more or less drunk *tovariches* broke into the Mordvinovs' palace, after having pillaged the wine-cellar, and took everything within convenient reach in spite of the efforts of Taliani, who is the First Secretary in the Italian Embassy and occupies an apartment in the palace. The Swiss guard and the *dvornik* tried to stop them and received bayonet wounds in the process.

Saturday 29th December 1917

The Central Empires accept the principle of 'no annexations or contributions' in their reply, while at the same time introducing certain restrictions; they refuse to recognize the right of peoples

179

to govern themselves, and consider that this right cannot be the aim of any international legislation.

It is certainly true that historical experience is hardly encouraging and it is regrettable that Europe has acquired the tiresome habit of intervening on behalf of every Balkan country during the last hundred years: it was very much better for world peace when they were under Turkish domination.

Besides, one should not exaggerate these supposedly nationalist aspirations. The so-called oppressed nations are only oppressed in the imagination of a few ideologists, lawyers or agitated professors who are out of touch with reality. These people usually live abroad, where they frequent the universities, found newspapers and give lectures: they no more represent the bulk of their compatriots who remain in their own country, than the intellectual Kadets represent the mass of the Russian people. Besides, even supposing that these aspirations really existed, it would be impossible to give satisfaction to them because the races of Eastern Europe are such a complicated tangle that anything which was done for one would be to the detriment of the others. No matter what was done, it could always be said that part of the population was still 'oppressed'. This is what is happening in the Balkans, where it is impossible to disentangle the inextricable confusion which exists between Turks, Greeks, Serbs, Bulgars and Albanians. The best example of this mix-up is Macedonia, to the extent that it has given its name to a mixture of different ingredients: the results are enjoyable when applied to a dish of fruit surrounded by ice-cream, but deplorable where different races are concerned, which cannot be blended together with a champagne sauce.

The gratification of the natural instinct for nationalism, that is to say a feeling for provincialism, would only be possible if one could go back to the system of the Middle Ages, when each town and each small plot of land had its own identity and when each person's idea of his country was confined to the small village he knew, within the shadow of the church tower which had witnessed his birth. It is true that there were frequent wars, but they only cost a few human lives. Besides, the supremacy of the Pope's religious power united all these small places into a society which obeyed the communal rules and was subject to the restrictions of the religious authority. Perhaps that was the real solution to the problem of the society of nations, which is so difficult to solve with the powers constituted as they are today. One can certainly build a wall with bricks, no matter how small they may be, but one cannot build it with fragments composed of disparate elements.

But all this is still far removed from reality, given the present state of affairs, and there will always be malcontents: all one can hope for is that the constitutions and internal legislation of each state will grant the maximum freedom and autonomy to the diverse races of which this state is composed. The answer of the Central Empires seems to me very wise: they say that this question "must be resolved by each State, in agreement with its peoples and according to the methods suggested by its Constitution."

I might add that from the French point of view it would be in our interest too to stick to this way of thinking. France will gain every advantage by preserving Austria, which would disappear if all the nationalities of which it is composed were to be emancipated. The German part would come over to swell the Teutonic bloc and reinforce Germany, whereas the rest would break up into small states which would be all the weaker because most of them would be Slav ones. During the course of history France has lost too much through the crumbling of Turkey, our traditional ally, for us to make the same mistake over Austria. "If Austria did not exist, it would have to be invented."

The more I think about it the more I believe that we must avoid getting excited about 'the right of peoples to govern themselves', which can only be a snare and is against the interests of our country. I like the first part of the democratic peace policy—'no annexations or contributions'—because it answers to one's ideas of justice and because it brings into the international field the theory that to steal property is a crime. But the second part—'the right of peoples'— strikes me as dangerous. In any case it is hardly for the Allies, who all possess immense colonial territories, to invoke this principle which can so easily be turned against them; and particularly not for England, where the question of Ireland poses a problem.

Whatever the case may be, the German proposals undoubtedly mark an important stage in the direction of peace . . . because, taken as a whole, they do not differ essentially from the programme laid before the Chamber of Deputies a short time ago by M. Painlevé. After all, if France gets back Alsace and Lorraine, what right would we have to cause the deaths of French soldiers by delivering people whom they have never heard of from 'oppression'?

Sunday 30th December 1917

The question of the couriers seems to have been definitely settled, and our courier has at last been able to leave.

People are demonstrating in the streets to celebrate the conclusion of the armistice, while a German delegation of thirty officers led by Admiral Kayserling, former Naval Attaché to Pourtalès, has moved into the Bristol Hotel in order to settle the practical details in Petrograd itself.

I came back this evening from the Vassily Ostrov in a sledge accompanied by Pingaud and we entered into conversation with the driver. He was bemoaning the present hard times: he has to bring in twenty roubles at the end of the day, which is barely enough to live on, whereas before four or five roubles were ample to provide for his needs. Pingaud asked him what he thought of the Allies and the enemies, and which nation he preferred; to which he gave the admirable reply, worthy of Tolstoy: "It doesn't make any difference, they all eat bread like we do." And this good man in his worn *armiak* made me feel all the poetry of the Russian soul, while the snow crackled beneath the horses' hooves and the runners of the sledge, on this bright, cold night. And yet he had been to the war and returned with three German bullets in him, one of which had almost immobilized his arm, but he felt no hatred: allies or enemies, it matters little to him, they are men who "all eat bread like we do".

What a lesson for the people who think they rule the world, and how these words of an illiterate peasant driving me home on a moonlight night in savage, remote Russia seemed beautiful and profound to me compared with the bombastic proclamations we have become accustomed to through the eloquence of statesmen.

Monday 31st December 1917

Trotsky has informed all the Allies of the German peace proposals and invited them to take part in the negotiations. In spite of everything, and no matter what afterthoughts our enemies may have, the fact that the Central Empires have stopped making use of the map of the war allows one to hope that the end is in sight, and that the year which is about to begin will bring peace at last.

Unfortunately people in France seem to be hypnotized by the question of the rights of peoples, which is so much against our interests. In his last speech, Pichon exalts the policy of nationalities which is the 'glory of France'. He forgets that this policy actually created Germany and established Italy, who only happens to be on our side by a miracle instead of with our enemies. In his speech he only talks about Poland, about Syria, and about the Lebanon.... this must all seem very far away, to our poor peasants in the trenches....

I couldn't help being reminded of some examples of a dictation which I read some time ago in a primary school. The subject was the Cedars of Lebanon.... A short questionnaire followed, to see whether the boys had understood what they had written. The word '*Liban*' had been interpreted in some very different ways: one of them saw it as 'a heap of earth'; another as 'a sort of plough'; and finally a third one as 'a woman of loose living'. But I am sure that it could not have entered the head of any one of them that some day he would have to fight for this unknown thing.

Wednesday 2nd January 1918

The Bolsheviks recently seized the banks and have now definitely taken them over and have decreed that they are nationalized. All the banks will be incorporated in one State bank, of which all the others will be branches. From now on, all operations are suspended. The safes will be opened in the presence of their owners, but there is no mention of what will be done with the contents. The decree certainly promises to safeguard the interests of the small depositor, but naturally this promise has not reassured anyone and there are long queues of anxious people besieging the doors of the banks, which are kept firmly closed and guarded by *tovariches*.

Heartrending scenes take place. I was told that outside one of the Nevsky banks an old lady took a sentry to task, at the risk of getting shot point blank: "You scoundrel! It's thanks to you and the likes of you that they've been able to commit all these hideous crimes.... You are responsible for my children dying of hunger because I cannot give them the bread which I have saved up for

183

them. . . . In the name of God who is in the Kazan Cathedral, right next to you, I curse you . . ." The soldier went pale, threw his rifle on the ground, and fled.

The natural goodness of the Russian still sometimes comes out in these rough characters, who are good at heart. But nevertheless what scenes of savagery there are when these brutes are let loose. At Tashkent, the soldiers struck down a general who was trying to restore order añd put him on view in a room where, for thirty kopeks, people could buy the right to watch his dying agonies and spit at him.

The Russians have even lost their traditional respect for the dead. During one of the recent strikes, some undertaker's employees fought over a hearse which was being taken to the cemetery, dragging the corpse out of its cutlet-papers and throwing it into the street. Murders are increasing every day. Old Goremykin and his wife have had their throats cut by a gang of thieves in their villa at Sochi on the Black Sea, and I have been told this evening that several Frenchmen have been massacred at Irkutsk.

Thursday 3rd January 1918

A few days ago at the Ministry of Foreign Affairs an auction was held, and all the objects which had been sent in the latest diplomatic bags and confiscated for the benefit of 'the people' were sold. Apparently the crowd mainly consisted of soldiers, who squabbled over a mass of incongruous objects: silk stockings, corsets, dresses, hats, scent, cameras, and even a gramophone. A louse-ridden soldier bought half a dozen silver forks and spoons for six hundred roubles.

The most simple-minded people have realized that money no longer has any value and they buy absolutely anything to use up their paper notes, as their purchasing power decreases all the time.

Dinner at the Belgian Legation. M. Destrées deplores the fact that the Allies refuse to recognize the Commissars' government because by doing so they are depriving themselves of an advantage: they are represented in Russia by men of value, whose personal authority would obtain results which cannot be hoped for from the official agents whose services one has to resort to at present.

Friday 4th January 1918

Trotsky has sent an angry note to the Military Mission asking for an explanation of a press communiqué concerning the peace conditions which the Central Empires are supposed to be imposing on Russia. Trotsky accuses our officers of being *agents provocateurs* and of spreading lying rumours which are causing 'counter-revolutionary' agitation, and he is threatening to expel the entire Mission.

And, in fact, just what are the army doing, sending communiqués to the press?

This mania which General Staffs have of abandoning their true role and setting themselves up as governments is involving us in the risk of serious trouble in the Ukraine, where the officers of General Tabouis' entourage are playing at high politics. Whereas they should be behaving with the greatest caution, they insist on special trains, display flags on their motorcars, and make themselves objectionable to the population, who are fed up with everything military after four years of war. . . .

We ought to be using very different methods to counteract 'German militarism' effectively, and we ought not to show ourselves to be more militarist than our enemy. Let us occasionally re-read Nietzsche, even though he is a 'boche', and let us remember his advice: "When fighting against monsters, let us beware of becoming monsters ourselves."

Saturday 5th January 1918

A delegation of about twenty officers' wives came to the Embassy to ask the Allies for help. It was pathetic to see these unfortunate women, who have been used to a certain comfort, still wearing fur coats and decent clothes, but reduced to begging as most of them have no knowledge of any profession. Their husbands are prisoners in the barracks, where they lead the life of convicts and only get a private soldier's pay of about fifteen roubles, and the soldiers prevent them from working outside and earning more money. One of these ladies told me that her husband, who is a Guards officer, had managed to escape and had spent the night unloading sacks of coal at the station: but the *tovariches* found out, and confiscated the few roubles which he had earned with such difficulty. . . . The Ambassador received these poor women and said a few words of comfort to them. . . . But there were tears in his eyes as he talked about it.

The fate of other middle-class Russians is hardly more enviable. The University professors only get a ludicrous salary and have had to turn themselves into an '*artel*', that is to say a kind of syndicate, and accept any kind of manual work. They must be really sorry for having so thoughtlessly contributed to the revolution by rebelling against the old régime.

One wonders how the 'bourgeois' can live at all. All property has been confiscated in actual fact, all bank deposits seized, and salaries and pensions stopped. It means utter destitution. A few days ago near the Cinizelli Circus I saw an old general and a priest—the old Russia itself—clearing the streets of snow in order not to die of starvation. A gang of soldiers, in the prime of life, stood and mocked them.

Monday 7th January 1918

Sir George Buchanan left this morning. This departure has made a strong impression on the town, and people are trying to interpret it as the sign of a coming rupture. There is nothing in it, and although it seems to me unlikely that Sir George will come back to Petrograd, for the moment it is only a question of a holiday, made really necessary by the state of his health. He even said in an interview that he was so tired that "at certain moments he no longer knew what he was saying or doing". Needless to say, this statement called forth a kindly-disposed remark from Bezak.

Scavenius, whom I saw this evening, talked to me about the feelings of the members of the Austrian delegation, who have come here to settle the details of the armistice. Like the Germans, they are 'horrified' at what is happening here and cannot believe their eyes. They seem very cold in their attitude towards the *tovariches*. The sessions of the commissions are a real farce, and have degenerated into political meetings. The other day when one of the Germans wanted to bring a worthy 'comrade' down to earth again out of an eloquent digression, the comrade lost his temper: "What, in Petrograd itself . . . if a Russian citizen is not allowed to say what he thinks . . . ." and so on, and the 'good' Boche had to listen, stupefied by the torrent of words and shrugging his shoulders in resignation. But I am beginning to think that the peace negotiations will not go as smoothly as people believe and that the Germans will very soon realize that in spite of our trenches, our guns, our English friends, and our American ones(?), the most dangerous enemy, for them, is not in the West. In point of fact, the Russian revolution presents the most formidable peril for Germany: it is the poison which will paralyse her. People say that the disease has already made its presence felt in some German regiments and that machine-guns have had to be used in several places to force the troops to obey. There are also supposed to have been mutinies in some Hungarian regiments, notably at Kovno, and to anyone who knows the value of those troops this must appear particularly serious. All this could have good results by obliging our enemies to make concessions to us, in order to be able to face the Russian danger. But the epidemic must not spread because, for us too, revolution is the great danger. If peace-loving people of all countries mean to maintain the present state of affairs, it is high time that they faced up to the situation. It will soon be necessary for everyone to unite if we want to stem the flood which is rising in the East.

Wednesday 9th January 1918

The cold is very severe, and I have never seen so much snow. The Highways Department is disorganized because nobody wants to work, and wood is too dear and too scarce to be able to use it for melting the snow, as is usually done. The *izvozchiks* demand fantastic prices (ten roubles for the shortest trip) and follow each other in Indian file along the paths which have been cleared and which snake their way through the banks of snow. And as for the trams, they stopped completely a few days ago. Walking is difficult because of the shortage of galoshes. One has first of all to get a certificate from the house committee in order to be able to buy a pair in the shops at exorbitant prices. As the number of these certificates allotted to each house has been greatly reduced, the custom is for all the tenants to draw lots for them once a month. The winners re-sell the certificates if they do not need to make use of them.

It is said that the government is going to take measures to get the traffic going again, and that the inhabitants themselves will be forced to work at clearing the snow from the streets, with the exception, naturally, of Red Guards and soldiers.

Thursday 10th January 1918

The Brest-Litovsk talks are making no progress and there are obviously some difficulties. Consequently, the populace is discontented because peace has not yet been signed. It is rumoured that a movement against the Bolsheviks is starting and that it may come to a head on the occasion of the Russian first of January.

What is more serious is the conflict between the Commissars' government and Rumania. The Rumanian authorities took steps to suppress the intolerable excesses committed by Russian troops, and the Russians are threatening to arrest M. Diamandy and the members of the Legation by way of reprisal. M. Diamandy is expecting the Legation to be occupied from one day to the next, and has had his codes and his secret archives moved to our Embassy.

This incident, coming so soon after the one concerning the English couriers, shows what a false position we are in and how precarious it is. To my mind, there are only two courses of action: either to recognize the Peoples' Commissars and live in harmony with them, or else to fight against them. To do the latter would mean making peace with Germany because as long as we are at war we are absolutely helpless against them, whereas they are all-powerful against us because of their propaganda. I am beginning to believe that in spite of everything it is this second solution which will win, and that the countries of civilized Europe with their bourgeois society will end by forming a bloc against Russian anarchy. Germany would be quite ready, and it is being said here that the Germans even made peace proposals to France last spring by offering her Alsace and Lorraine, on condition that they could take it out of Russia. The Russians are far from being grateful to us for having turned down these proposals: they accuse us of being the cause of all their present troubles by refusing to make peace, which they wanted above all else and were ready to pay for with the heaviest sacrifices. To a great many of them, it is the obstinacy of the Allies which has landed Russia in Bolshevism, with all its horrors.

Perhaps the Russians exaggerate, but it is certainly true that we should have made a fair peace a very long time ago. The French and the Germans would have profited by it. . . . And as for the Russians . . . they would have been delighted.

Friday 11th January 1918

M. Dumas, a socialist who has been sent on a mission by the Ministry of Foreign Affairs, brings good news from France. The state of mind is excellent, and people are much reassured by the hope of American reinforcements.

But they have got delusions about Russia. The French are imbued with the spirit of the *Marseillaise* and still believe that the Russian revolution was caused by patriotism. Nobody has yet understood that from the very beginning the revolution was just as much against the war as against the régime.

Saturday 12th January 1918

Massacres are still going on in the provinces: at Sebastopol in particular, a number of naval officers have been murdered by the sailors. According to the (very old) newspapers which have just arrived from France, I see that people are greatly counting on Kaledin, Kornilov, and Alexeiev. . . . What a hope! Perhaps all these generals mean well, but they have always proved themselves incapable of organizing anything or of making a success of anything. Besides, they have only got a few old Cossacks, some officers and some *junkers* with them. However, they are holding their own against the Red Guards who have been sent to fight them, but they have not got the wherewithal to make an advance. Their attempts only aggravate the exasperation of the populace against former officers and they are the cause of the latest massacres.

Sunday 13th January 1918

Disturbances continue. In the wake of Finland, the Ukraine, the Don, the Caucasus, Siberia and many others whose names I forget, we now have the Republic of Archangel which has just proclaimed its independence.

It is the end of a world. And on the last day of the old year, as I crossed the Troitsky Bridge I gazed at the Imperial city in the rays of the setting sun: it is already dead, and its magnificence will soon be only a memory. The outline of the historic Fortress, now just a prison, stood out against a green sky which graduated into tones of orange. In contrast to the luminous sky, the snow on the Neva seemed blue, and as far as one could see a violet-coloured mist wrapped itself round the palaces like a crepe scarf. . . . High above, there was a star which was green too, like the flames of the flares which people put on hearses.

I was getting ready to go and have supper with Claude Anet, to 'see the New Year in', when someone came to tell me that the Bolsheviks had invaded the Rumanian Legation and arrested the Minister M. Diamandy, together with those of his colleagues whom he had invited to his New Year party, and with whom he was about to sit down at table.

The news was brought by a Rumanian soldier who managed to escape, and it has provoked general indignation. It is an unprecedented violation of international law. Even among savages, the person of a diplomatic representative is sacred. Alas! diplomats are today paying for their leniency in the past, when they thought it wonderful that the German Embassy was looted, or that the German consul from Kovno was shut up in the Fortress. Those were the days when we talked about the 'enlightened Slavs' fighting at our side for *civilization* against the German barbarism. . . . At least the Bolsheviks deserve the credit for having put things right again.

M. Destrées, together with General Niessel, Colonel Lavergne, the Dupierreux and others who were all at the supper-party given by Claude Anet, reckons that in order to obtain some redress we ought not to flinch at the thought of a breaking-off of relations and the departure of all the diplomatic missions. I agree with him, but will the Bolsheviks let us go?

Monday 14th January 1918

All the chiefs of the Allied and neutral missions met at mid-day in the United States Embassy, as Mr. Francis is the *doyen* since the departure of Sir George Buchanan. They unanimously decided to make common cause with their Rumanian colleague and to go in a body to protest to the Peoples' Commissars, while at the same time making it quite clear that this move in no way affects the establishment of diplomatic relations between their countries and the Smolny government. An appointment was made by telephone with Lenin and at four o'clock all the Ambassadors and Ministers, twenty strong, left in a procession for the Smolny Institute: between them they represented, apart from enemy countries, *all* the civilized States of Europe, America, and even Asia. When I think that last year on the same date (it is now the Russian first of January) the Diplomatic Corps went to Tsarskoye Selo to present its good wishes to the Tsar, and that today the long procession of carriages, with their gold-braided *chasseurs* on the front seats, drove to Smolny to make a protest to Lenin!

Lenin was waiting for the Diplomatic Corps on the doorstep of his Cabinet Room, a small, very simple room. Mr. Francis went in first and called out the names of his colleagues as they entered one by one. Lenin looked slightly disconcerted as he heard the names of almost every world power announced in this way. He had with him two secretaries and M. Zalkind, who studied in Paris and obtained his science degree there. Mr. Francis presented Lenin with the text of the joint protest and owing to his difficulty in expressing himself in French, he then called upon M. Noulens to speak: M. Noulens declared in the strongest terms that if the Commissars did not immediately set M. Diamandy free, the representatives of all the countries would leave Petrograd.

Lenin answered by maintaining that the arrest of M. Diamandy was justified by the necessity to prevent war between Russia and Rumania! He added: "Is it not better that M. Diamandy should be in prison, and that Russian and Rumanian soldiers should not start killing each other?"

Mr. Francis replied with a great deal of common sense that the Commissars' conduct towards the Rumanian Minister, far from preventing war and the shedding of blood, was much more likely to provoke it. This remark seemed to impress Lenin, who then asked the *doyen* of the Diplomatic Corps if he could guarantee that war would be avoided if the Soviet government set M. Diamandy free again. M. Noulens replied that he and his colleagues could give no assurance whatever of this kind, and that besides, as it was a question of *principle*, that is to say of the privilege of diplomatic immunity which has been recognized by all civilized peoples for centuries, they could not continue to argue about a question of *fact*. Consequently, the Diplomatic Corps refused to take cognisance of the reasons which the Soviet government gives in justification of this arrest, and demanded that M. Diamandy be immediately released, by tonight.

M. Destrées also intervened in the discussion, thereby provoking the rage of Zalkind, who addressed him as "citizen Minister" although he behaved correctly towards the other diplomats. He was obviously furious at being confronted by a socialist who sided with the bourgeois in their defence of the rights of peoples. Moreover, throughout the interview Zalkind's unfairness and his tone of hatred and arrogance were noticeable, and it was clearly he who was urging Lenin towards intransigence and suggesting lines of argument to him.

Finally M. Spalaikovich, the Serbian Minister, who had restrained himself with difficulty from the start, rushed forward with clenched fists vehemently upbraiding Lenin and his acolytes and accusing them in strong terms of having betrayed Serbia. . . . This forceful language impressed Lenin, and seeing that certain of the diplomats tried to hold back their Serbian colleague, he said to them: "Let him be: I prefer M. Spalaikovich's insults to the eternal rhetoric of the other diplomats. . . . At least he says what he thinks."

The interview ended with Lenin's promise to ask the Commissars' Council to release M. Diamandy and his staff that same evening. . . .

But at midnight nothing had yet been done. Things don't happen all that quickly here. During the interview one of the Ministers asked Lenin where M. Diamandy had been sent. Lenin seemed taken aback, hesitated a second, and ended by answering: "But . . . he's at Peter-and-Paul . . . probably . . ." This "probably" is Russia in a nutshell. And I am neither surprised nor indignant that Lenin has not yet fulfilled his promise. . . . First of all we must find M. Diamandy . . . and then it will be a question of palavering with all the Soviets and under-Soviets to finally get the agreement of the *tovariches* who are guarding him who, as good Comrades, will only take orders from themselves. . . .

Besides, "*sichiaz*", which is Russian for "at once", at the most hopeful means "*zavtra*", or "tomorrow", especially on a New Year's Day.

In fact, everything is in the greatest disorder. There is no electric light, the excuse being that it is the 1st of January, and we had to give up all idea of dinner as all the restaurants we went to with Saint-Sauveur were closed. There was not a single servant in the Hôtel de l'Europe!

Tuesday 15th January 1918

We heard this morning that before they will release M. Diamandy, the Council of Commissars insists on his promising in the name of his government to set free the *tovariches* who were arrested at Jassy.

M. Diamandy replied with great dignity that he would not discuss his country's affairs in prison, and that he refused to be set free under such conditions. The diplomatic representatives are in complete agreement with their colleague's point of view and have decided to meet again at two o'clock in the *doyen*'s house, to discuss what measures shall be taken. They appear to have even decided to leave Petrograd if M. Diamandy is not immediately and unconditionally released.

The Commissars had doubtless been informed of this decision because when M. Noulens was leaving for the meeting at a few minutes to two, he received a telephone call from the Fortress informing him that M. Diamandy was free and that he had asked him to send a car for him. The Ambassador insisted on going himself to fetch his colleague. He saw the cell in Peter-and-Paul in which M. Diamandy had been locked up. It was number fifty-nine, a foul hovel: cold, dark and damp, a bed with no bedclothes, a wooden stool, and a filthy bowl containing some *kasha* and a chipped wooden spoon. Luckily M. Diamandy's neighbour was M. Tereschenko, who was able to give him a candle and a tin of sardines. At first M. Diamandy did not recognize him, as his hair and beard have grown so long since being in prison.

The formalities for the order of release took rather a long time as M. Diamandy did not want to leave prison until an official report had been drawn up in French and Russian, to say that he was leaving prison unconditionally, so that his government would not be committed in any way. The report was witnessed by the director of the prison (a kind of student) and two *tovariches*, a soldier and a sailor. These formalities were not over until about four o'clock: then M. Diamandy came back to the Embassy with M. Noulens, where his secretaries and Mr. Francis were waiting for him.

It is said that yesterday evening there was an attempt on Lenin's life after a meeting in the Mikhail Riding School which he had attended in order to report on his interview with the Diplomatic Corps. Someone fired several shots at his car at the corner of Karavannaya Street. It is not known whether the attempt was directed against him, or whether some *tovariches* were shooting at the car because they thought it belonged to '*burjuis*'. Whatever the facts may be, he was within an inch of being killed because apparently his secretary, who was sitting beside him, pushed Lenin's head down to make him duck, and got a bullet in his hand.

Wednesday 16th January 1918

The Commissars, having released M. Diamandy, have sent an ultimatum to the Rumanian government and have ordered all Russian soldiers to proceed to the arrest of the King of Rumania.[1] This time they are within their rights . . . but I think the order will be more difficult to carry out, and the *tovariches* will not show much eagerness to obey.

The Diplomatic Corps met today again at three o'clock to hear M. Diamandy and congratulate him, and to draw up an official report on the affair, which M. Destrées has been asked to edit.

Thursday 17th January 1918

According to what I have been told by an officer who has just come from Kiev, it appears that our Military Mission in the Ukraine has not been at all a success, in spite of the fighting qualities of its chief, General Tabouis, who is one of the heroes of the war. The officers of his staff have not behaved tactfully enough towards this difficult people and in less than two months they have put everyone against us, Ukrainians and Poles alike. One of the leaders of the Ukrainian government who was very friendly towards us has not concealed his displeasure and said to someone, who repeated it directly to me,

[1] King Ferdinand, who came to the throne in October 1914.

194

that "his compatriots are fed up with being treated like Zulus by the French officers". As for the Poles, they have discovered a way of exploiting the situation: whenever they want a five-hundred-rouble note to go on a spree, all they need do is to go to the Military Mission and denounce somebody, anybody will do. This is how the unlimited funds so freely distributed to the army are used. . . . When I think of what we could have done with a few of those bank-notes which are being so foolishly wasted now; if they had been put to good use in time, the whole course of events here could have been changed! . . . Anyhow, let us hope that after the war it will not only be in Germany that we will destroy militarism.

Meanwhile, the Germans are making the most of the situation. They are dangling one or two Ruthenian cantons of Austria-Hungary in front of the Ukrainians, to lead them into a peace which would allow Germany to dispose of the considerable natural resources of the Ukraine.

Friday 18th January 1918

There has been a bit of trouble at the opening of the Constituent Assembly but on the whole it came to hardly anything, and the big demonstrations against the Bolsheviks which had been promised were a lamentable failure. It must be admitted that these Peoples' Commissars know how to bring the people to heel and in the same way that ex-poachers make the best gamekeepers, these revolutionaries know exactly how one stamps out revolutions. If last year we had had a Lenin or a Trotsky to defend the Tsar order would soon have been restored, and they wouldn't have put the machine-guns on the rooftops, where they were no use at all.

While walking to the Embassy this morning I saw a column of demonstrators coming from the Vyborg district, crossing the Liteiny Bridge with a great unfurling of banners, flags and standards. The head of the bridge was occupied by an outpost of soldiers, sailors and Red Guards who ordered the demonstrators to about turn, and backed up the order with a good salvo in the air. No time was lost and it was comic to see those heroes running as fast as their legs would carry them. There was a sudden falling-back of the red surge formed by the flags fluttering above the dark mass of people. In order to run faster many of them were throwing away their banners which the pursuing Red Guards were trying to snatch from them, and one could see the flags falling from the bridge and fluttering down on to the glittering, frozen surface of the Neva, like great scarlet butterflies.

Towards midday there was a second attempt during the course of which a Bolshevik aeroplane dropped a bomb, making a large hole in the ice. In the afternoon I had several telephone calls from different places, to say that people were fighting in the streets. M. Dumas, a French socialist on a mission (who is not used to revolutions), had sent word to say that people were dropping like flies so I went to Liteiny Street to fetch Pingaud from the *Pension* Choisey, to do the rounds of the town and see what was happening.

They were indeed shooting in Liteiny Street, on the corner of Kirochnaya and Pantelemonskaya Streets but as always happens here, there was more noise than damage. Nevertheless, I waited inside the *Pension* Choisey until the battle was over, and it was an interesting sight from there: the passers-by, and especially the soldiers, fled panic-stricken at each burst of fire while a squad of women sweeping snow off the street went stoically on with their work without taking any notice of the shooting. Courage, unconcern, or resignation? Whatever it was, I admired them.

After a few minutes we went out. In fact everything was quiet again and the traffic was back to normal. Only the numerous groups of people clustered in the doorways and the entrances to the court-yards showed that it was a big day. At each burst of fire these groups vanish into the courtyards, where everyone falls flat on their faces. This explains how the good M. Dumas saw so many corpses. But at the first sign of calm, curiosity triumphs over fear, the gates half open, the corpses are resurrected and the groups re-form, until the next fusillade.

Spalernaya Street, which leads to the Taurid Palace where the Constituent Assembly meets, was blocked by an enormous barricade made of logs and bundles of firewood; the *tovariches* in charge were borrowing freely from it to keep up the roaring fire round which they huddled. The flickering light of the flames lit up their doll-like faces, which contrasted strangely with their brigand's equipment: rifles slung on bandoliers and tied up with bits of string, revolvers, cartridge-belts and fur hats. Nevertheless, the cases of ammunition piled up beside the barricade show that they have decided to use convincing arguments to stop people getting past.

We let ourselves off the rest of our tour at Zakharevskaya Street, at the end of which a horseman was calmly exercising two shaggy, bear-like horses on a leading-rein; they were trotting sedately one behind the other in a circle, their big hooves sinking into the snow.

There were several barriers with Red Guards and sailors guarding the entrance to the Palace, but we only needed to show our French Embassy '*proputsk*' and they let us through immediately. In fact I must admit that up to now the Bolsheviks have always shown me the greatest courtesy in the streets and I have never had any reason to complain. Declaring my occupation has been enough to ensure my being treated with respect.

Precautions have been taken by a master-mind for the defence of the Palace approaches, and at several ground-floor windows I saw sailors beside their machine-guns, which are aimed to take in the full length of the street. This time they are not in the attics.

In front of the Palace itself, there are batteries of field guns with their caissons open, surrounded by sailors and Red Guards, who are warming themselves while awaiting events. The gates are locked and I did not try to get in, which I could have done without any difficulty: but I did not want to take it upon myself to attend the Assembly without instructions from the Ambassador. Pingaud questions the *tovariches*, who tell us that all is quiet in the district and that the deputies have met in the Palace.

The Bolsheviks have gone back on their previous aims and have agreed that the Constituent Assembly shall open, without reaching the number of four hundred deputies which had formerly been agreed upon. They have also given up the rule that each deputy has to be approved by his Commissar before taking his seat.

The Bolshevik deputies are in the minority: about a quarter of the Assembly. The Revolutionary Socialists form the biggest party in the Assembly: they go through all the shades from right to left of centre.

Saturday 19th January 1918

The Constituent Assembly will not have lasted long. . . . When the

197

deputies belonging to the Bolshevik minority left the hall, the government considered that the Assembly no longer represented national opinion, and decided purely and simply to forbid it to assemble from then on. It is being said that the Revolutionary Socialists intend to organize big demonstrations the day after tomorrow, but I doubt if they will take place after yesterday evening's incidents. While we were near the Taurid Palace, the Red Guards did in fact open fire in the Liteiny Prospekt in order to stop a column of demonstrators which was trying to reach the Palace of the Constituent Assembly. Several people were killed and many wounded, especially among the musicians and standard-bearers who were marching at the head.

It seems therefore that the Constituent Assembly will not re-assemble. The first session, moreover, has proved that this Assembly is powerless and cannot be relied on in any case. The Revolutionary Socialists, on whom we pin our hopes for the continuation of the war, joined with their Bolshevik enemies in chanting the *Internationale*, and the Constituent Assembly opened to the sound of this hymn. This is significant. Afterwards they listened to a declaration of the rights of "the exploited working proletariat". Then they tried to elect a president. There were two candidates, or rather a candidate and a candidatess: M. Chernov, supported by the Revolutionary Socialists and Mlle Spiridonova, put forward by the Bolshevik minority. Chernov was elected, with a rather weak majority. The session continued until rather late into the night with palavering. The military had taken charge of the hall and towards two o'clock in the morning one of the sailors on guard having had enough of it, beckoned to the Comrade President that it was time to stop, and at his injunction everyone had to clear out.

So that was the famous Constituent Assembly, which people in France were relying on to force Lenin and Trotsky to go on with the war!!

In consequence, we should have no illusions: whether the policy of 'All power to the Soviets' or 'All power to the Assembly' wins, the result will be exactly the same from our point of view, that is to say from the point of view of the war. . . .

The Japanese have sent some battleships to Vladivostok, which has called forth a protest from the Bolshevik government. Let's hope it will not create a fresh Diamandy incident.

Monday 21st January 1918

Although the town is quiet, the people are showing a certain amount of resentment towards the Bolsheviks. People are comparing the recent events with the bloody repressions of 1905 and are beginning to say that the Bolsheviks are using "old régime methods" and "shedding the blood of their brothers".

People have been particularly shocked by the murder of two former Kadet ministers, Chingarev and Kokoshkyn who, because of the state of their health, had been moved from the Fortress to a hospital in the Liteiny Prospekt, near Jukovskaya Street. At night a gang of fanatics broke into the room where they were being held under guard, and killed them with revolver shots in the mouth. Of course it is dreadful: but the executive power of the Peoples' Commissars are the first to condemn these excesses, and one cannot hold them responsible. For my part, I would feel much more inclined to look on it as an attempt by *agents provocateurs*. "*Is fecit cui prodest*." Besides, the government had nothing to gain from this abominable murder, whereas the opposition finds it a useful means of exploitation. The Revolutionary Socialist party, which is leading the campaign against Lenin and Trotsky, is capable of anything. We have them to thank for Kerensky: one need say no more!

As regards this sinister character, it appears that nearly two million roubles were found in his safe in the bank. He was very near to becoming a thief, and one must be somewhat grateful to the Bolsheviks for having finally exposed him.

The inspection of safes has started in several banks. Up to now, this operation of brigandage has been carried out most systematically. Gold coins or ingots are confiscated and delivered to the State Bank, but a receipt is issued for them. . . . Securities, silver, papers and jewellery are checked and then left "at the disposal of their owners"! . . .

Tuesday 22nd January 1918

The burial of the people killed during last Friday's demonstrations took place without incident. . . .

The weather in fact was favourable to the Bolsheviks. The temperature suddenly rose to two degrees below zero, and there was a frightful thaw. The snow had been accumulating for weeks and had turned into a *sorbet* in which one sank up to the knees, while the pavements became real skating-rinks and one had to perform prodigious balancing acts in order to walk. It was most difficult to demonstrate under such conditions.

In order to appeal to people's imagination, last week's dead have been buried next to those who were killed in the 1905 shooting outside the Winter Palace. There were a few speeches in which the victims of 'Bolshevik' tyranny were likened to those of 'Tsarist' tyranny. But it takes more than eloquence to move the men of Smolny.

The Commissars, moreover, have taken every possible measure to prevent any effective campaign against their authority. All newspapers except the Bolshevik mouthpieces *Pravda* and *Izvestia* have been suppressed since the latest events, and most of the editors are in prison. However, a few pages seem to get published clandestinely; but janissaries keep watch to see that they are not sold and snatch them out of the hands of readers, even threatening them with death. A Frenchman described a scene to me which he witnessed a few days ago: at the corner of the Suvorovsky Prospekt a shabby old general stopped to ask a paper-boy if he had either *Dien* or *Viek*. The lad replied that he only had *Pravda* and *Izvestia*, whereupon the general said to him grumpily: "It's a pity you haven't got a single decent newspaper." A passing sailor had heard the conversation and with one shot from his rifle he laid the poor general low in the snow, where he lay, quite dead.

It is not healthy to be a counter-revolutionary, and specially not to say so. Excesses like these infuriate the people, who are already very upset by the food shortage. And yet the Smolny leaders very strongly disapprove of such excesses, just as they disapproved of the murders of the former Kadet ministers in the Mariinsky Hospital. But the revolution was bound to lead to horrors like these, by letting instincts run loose and by removing all restraint from the soldiers. The fact that such cases are not more frequent and that they are still being discussed, shows that there is a basic kindheartedness in every Russian, which is not found in any other people.

If one thinks that for nearly a year the soldiers have not had to submit to any discipline and that they go about armed all day long, one is surprised that there have not been more atrocities . . . or more accidents. During the last few days, as if it were not enough to carry rifles with fixed bayonets, the soldiers have devised a way of hanging strings of grenades on to their belts, like rosaries. One trembles to think of the number of victims there could be in a crowd, with drunk or careless soldiers throwing these contraptions around. In this case one can no longer rely on the singular clumsiness of Russian marksmen, whose rifle shots are of little danger. One has got used to hearing random shots, caused by *tovariches* dropping their guns when they slip on the icy ground. Usually no harm is done . . . but with grenades, things could be much more serious.

Wednesday 23rd January 1918

An order was given out some time ago from Smolny forbidding the inhabitants to clear snow from outside their houses, and yesterday one could see professors from the Law School armed with rakes, spades and pick-axes, clearing Sergevskaya Street under the cynical eyes of the *tovariches*. Amongst them was a Frenchman, M. Loustalou, whose official title is Professor of Boxing and Gymnastics at the national school of Law. . . . In Russia the uppercut is a necessary adjunct to the study of the Law, and one can foresee the kind of case in which right will need to depend on might. For having ignored this one of the *tovariches*, who had jeered too loudly and too near to one of our legal experts in pursuit of his new occupation, got his ears boxed by M. Loustalou in the most splendid fashion in spite of his status a Red Guard. M. Loustalou's normally fiery blood had boiled as a result of working in the fresh air, and he had never had such a wonderful chance to fulfil his function as Professor of Boxing in a school of Law. The *tovarich* fled, yelling, but soon returned with about thirty of his own kind: Red Guards, soldiers and sailors, all armed to the teeth. In spite of our compatriot's exploits they hustled him and arrested him and, with heavy blows from a rifle-butt, they took him off to the police station, having previously removed from him everything which was worth removing. Naturally his companions were panic-stricken by the row, and by the gunfire which is obligatory on such occasions, and they rapidly dispersed: but when all was quiet again they hurried to the

Embassy. I was busy working when Leonid came to announce a delegation of professors from the school of Law. I rushed to the drawing-room in order not to keep such important personages waiting: from my memories of the past I visualized them dressed in scarlet robes trimmed with ermine, presiding over the torturing of candidates sitting for the Law degree. . . . The professors who were waiting for me presented a far less solemn appearance . . . since they had just come in from sweeping the streets. They told me of their anxiety as to the fate of their colleague, and I informed the Ambassador. He was highly indignant that professors of Law had been set to shovelling snow, and he instructed Pingaud to go to the police station and try to get our compatriot released. The Commissar, a huge devil of a Caucasian in an immense fur hat, welcomed Pingaud all the better for having seen that he was very determined. Besides, a pleasant state of drunkenness had made him amiably disposed, and when my friend sat down his foot knocked against a supply of bottles which had somehow escaped from the recent looting and found a last resting-place under the Commissar's desk. It was therefore not difficult to come to an agreement, and Pingaud had hardly raised his voice when, with a conciliatory "*pajalst*",[1] the ferocious Caucasian had our compatriot released and, as proof of his goodwill, had the *tovarich* Red Guard locked up in his place. The *tovarich*, with a black eye as the result of his juridical arguments with our Professor of Law, had made the fatal mistake of attending the interview. This end to the affair seems to me very 'old régime' and I am delighted to see that there are still some traditions left, in spite of everything! All is not lost in Russia and, as with the '*pristav*'[2] of former days, the Bolshevik Commissar is sometimes a good chap.

But in spite of the *ukazes* of Smolny the streets are in a state of indescribable filth. The snow has accumulated and it is impossible to drive out on the days when it is actually snowing. The carcass of a horse has been lying on the pavement outside the *Jardin d'Eté* for nearly a fortnight, half buried in the snow, with a blown-up stomach and stiff legs. Today one of the legs is missing: a butcher must have 'lifted' one of the haunches, which will be bought by some *burjui* tomorrow as beefsteak at eight roubles the pound!

There is no more petrol, and when one does find some one has

[1] Please, or, if you please, allow me.
[2] An inspector.

to pay fifty roubles the *poud* (which cost one-fifth of a rouble before the war). In consequence, one hardly sees any cars except government ones. Besides, Smolny has issued a decree requisitioning all private cars, and Red Guards stop cars at every street corner, even those of the ambassadors, to check if they are in order. A few days ago the Ambassador and his Japanese colleague had to enter into a long argument with some sailors who wanted to take them to Smolny on the pretext that their car-licence was out of date. The *chasseur* tried to cut short the discussion by ordering the chauffeur to drive on, but the sailors aimed their guns at him and he had to continue the argument until he had convinced the *tovariches*.

Thursday 24th January 1918

The preliminary armistice talks seem to have come to a halt. Trotsky is doing his best to oppose the claims of General Hoffmann. His latest statements seem to have disconcerted the Germans, and one must truthfully admit that they are real little masterpieces. This behaviour certainly proves that the Bolsheviks are not German agents, as people have tried to make us believe. It is more likely that they have been taken in, than that they are accomplices.

It is more than probable that the Germans, having obtained an armistice on the Russian front which has enabled them to move troops to the French front, have broken off negotiations in order to play the easy part of restoring order in Petrograd, where they will be acclaimed as saviours by almost all Russians. By this means they will make sure of getting a magnificent colony right next to their own country, which will enable them to sacrifice a great deal to the Allies in order to obtain peace.

This policy involves only one hazard, but it is a terrible one: the contagion of Bolshevism may infect the German masses! And it also constitutes a danger for us as, if the revolution breaks out tomorrow in Germany, it will reverberate very close to our own frontiers.

So it is Russia which is the stake in the peace: in any case we will have to come and re-establish order in this country, either to prevent the Germans doing it to their own advantage, or even in collaboration with our present enemies to stop the revolution destroying our civilization.

203

Perhaps the Bolsheviks are precursors like the disciples of Christ, but it is our duty to fight against them, just as it was the duty of Roman society to fight against the newly-born Christianity which carried in itself the leaven which was to cause disruption to rise in the Empire.

In order to save established society and civilization, one should never hesitate to stifle any sympathy one may feel towards certain generous ideas, because the fulfilment of these ideas can only be achieved at the cost of ruin and sorrow. And if a new idea does not succeed, then it is a criminal one. Therefore it is our duty to oppose Bolshevism with all our strength: it will probably anyhow end in asserting itself, just as Christ's subversive doctrines finally did. Let us hope that it does not bring several centuries of barbarism and fanaticism with it, like Christianity did.

Friday 25th January 1918

The hardships of life are increasing. The shops are empty and the trains always several hours late: they are full to bursting point with *tovariches* hanging on like bunches of grapes from the buffers to the roofs, on which people are found every day, frozen to death and clinging on with stiffened hands.

Under these conditions it is impossible to keep up the town's food supplies. A pound (four hundred grammes) of pork meat costs nine to ten roubles, and a sack of grey flour which was worth three hundred and fifty roubles a week ago, today costs six hundred and twenty roubles. Nearly all the restaurants are closed, and Donon's is the only one where one can still get a decent dinner, at a price. The German delegates take their meals there and thanks to this, the restaurant is given a specially privileged food allowance by Smolny. There is even some wine still left. . . .

I had lunch there, sitting at the next table to Count Mirbach and Admiral Kayserling. Their behaviour was perfectly correct and after casting a discreet glance around, they continued to speak in their own language, not too pointedly. They had with them two delegates from the Peoples' Commissariat for Foreign Affairs: two little young men who looked much too smart: clean-shaven, dressed in well-cut long jackets . . . smooth hair with impeccable partings. . . . One could easily have mistaken them for under-secretaries in

Sazonov's Cabinet, rather than Bolsheviks. . . . Decidedly, we shall soon be able to recognize the Commissars' government . . . whose future diplomats are already preparing to follow all the Russian diplomatic traditions . . . including even the least manly ones!

In the streets one sees a lot of Austrian soldiers and officers going about in uniform: they are prisoners-of-war, and nobody takes any notice of them. In fact I must admit that they behave very well and do not draw attention to themselves.

Meanwhile, the Brest talks are making no progress and it is said that they are to be broken off for a couple of weeks. It is greatly to be feared that the Germans will profit from this delay to treat with the Ukraine: it is much more to their advantage to come to an agreement with the Ukraine, because they will find everything they need in that district and it will save them from the danger of having to negotiate with the Bolsheviks.

They must realize that Bolshevism is the biggest peril threatening Europe and that it is time for all civilized countries to unite in an *Internationale* of order, against the *Internationale* of disorder. We must take from the Soviets the sublime idea of a Society of Nations and make it into a weapon against the revolution. This society of bourgeois nations must, through its principles, recall the Holy Alliance of old, and it must be a mutual uniting of governments against the revolutionary scourge which Russia is spreading throughout the world. It is a strange repetition of history to see an association of this kind being revived during an era of bloodshed, coming after a century's interval of such striking contrast. Russia, in whose name Alexander formed the Holy Alliance, would now find the future 'Society of Order' against her; and France, who in 1815 was the home of revolution, would today be at the head of those countries who are trying to overcome it. A radical change has swept through Europe, from the West to the East. Central Europe alone has not altered during the century and has remained level-headed. It is the central balancing point of the scales, from which each side has taken up diametrically opposed positions. Perhaps that is the secret of its strength.

Saturday 26th January 1918

Finland is once again devastated by civil war. The Russians had recognized the stable government of that country: it answered to the wishes of the majority of its populations, which consist of orderly people who want to live and work in peace. The unrest is the fault of the Russian soldiers who remained in the country and are a real plague, and who commit the worst atrocities against the civilian population and make war against the bourgeois government under the pretext of propaganda. The exasperated Finns have formed a White Guard to protect their government and to suppress the activities of these fanatics. An appeal was sent to the Red Guards of Petrograd for help, and in defiance of all the rules the Red Guards crossed the frontier to go to the support of agitators in an independent state. There has been fighting in the outskirts of Vyborg. The Reds opened fire on trains coming from Helsingfors and several passengers were hit: at present they occupy the station and have cut the rails, so that communication with Europe is once more interrupted.

In fact, the whole Empire has been plunged into bloodshed by civil war. In the Crimea there is fighting between the Tartars and the Bolsheviks. The Cossacks and the Bolsheviks are fighting savagely in the Caucasus and on the Don. A few days ago three sealed wagons with the inscription 'fresh meat, destination Petrograd' arrived at one of the Petrograd stations. When the wagons were opened they were found to be filled with piles of the stiffened corpses of Red Guards, covered with frozen blood, with grimacing faces, placed in obscene positions. . . . I certainly no longer have any sympathy for the Bolsheviks and I have no pity for those who go and get themselves killed fighting against Kaledin, but I cannot find words to describe this ghoulish farce. The Cossack who thought up such a horror must have the mind of a brute, as also the men who carried it out. . . . And to think that in 1914 Europe was civilized and believed that it had the right to impose its civilization on the negroes!

Under the present conditions it is impossible to travel in the interior of the country. One of our couriers only managed to get to Jassy by assuring the *tovariches* that he was the French Ambassador on his way to Brest-Litovsk for the peace talks. It was a great success, and during part of the journey he actually had a Red guard-of-honour on his coach. From a distance it must seem like a pantomime, but on the spot it's not so funny, and the fact that one has to rely on expedients such as these shows what we are reduced to!

Sunday 27th January 1918

I spent my whole day arguing with some delegates from the Revolutionary Tribunal who are attempting to arrest a French business-woman,[1] and to confiscate all the merchandise in her house, on a charge of 'criminal speculation'. As if it were a crime to do the Russians a service by bringing merchandise from abroad, which is destined to be sold in this country where there is a shortage of everything!

In front of me were three delegates of the Revolutionary Tribunal, looking like bandits and armed with large Colt revolvers. Their chief in particular, *tovarich* Borissenok, looked a real brute: he had an emaciated face with evil little eyes and bat ears and he was dressed in a sailor's jacket, with a yellow muffler round his neck and a plate-like cap on his shaved head. In answer to all my protests he replied that the people no longer recognized the treaties made by 'Nicholas' with the bourgeois people of France, and he wanted at all costs to have our compatriot taken off to prison. Finally, I telephoned to the Foreign Affairs Commissariat where at first they answered that "the Law must win" and that in Russia, as in "all civilized countries", an Embassy representative could not be allowed to obstruct the course of justice, even if it concerned one of his fellow nationals. . . . I answered that in France justice gave certain guarantees whereas here I was up against a gang of fanatics; and I added that under these conditions the only thing I could do was to share the fate of my compatriot. . . . At least this made the Commissar stop and think, and then he promised to send me one of his assistants, adding: "Just see how conciliatory we can be. . . . You wouldn't do as much in France." So I changed my tone and thanked him as politely as possible. I then suggested sending the Embassy car to fetch the Commissars' representative, who in fact was brought there in a few minutes. I must say that the assistant in question, in spite of his soldier's cap, his black nails, his worn-out shoes and the general shabbiness of his appearance, was an intelligent and cultured young man who spoke very good French and

[1] *Author's note:* the lady concerned is Mme Langlois, a relation of Colonel Langlois who was liaison officer between French General Headquarters and Russian General Headquarters!

who at once sized up the situation, agreeing with me in principle. . . .
But all his arguments were of no avail against the *tovarich*, whose
obstinacy had been increased by the arrival of a reinforcement of
twenty-five soldiers which he had sent for, who were already starting
to unload the goods into the lorries and sledges which they had
brought with them. They clearly did not want to relinquish this
booty, consisting of woollen clothes, rugs and jerseys, and all my
efforts were frustrated by their covetousness.

On the other hand they did not put too many difficulties in the
way of granting the legitimate owner of the goods provisional
liberty, and the 'delegate' was satisfied with the guarantee which I
had to make out, promising that she would appear at the convocation
of the Revolutionary Tribunal.

There was nothing else to do, and we had to bow to superior
force . . . at the price of an official report of protest signed by the
representative of the Foreign Affairs Commissariat and myself and
bearing the seals of the Soviet and of the Embassy. . . . It is the
first document to carry both seals: but it is not worth any more
because of this, and I doubt whether our compatriot will ever get
anything for the goods which they 'requisitioned' from her in this
manner.

Monday 28th January 1918

M. Diamandy has for several days been expecting to be conducted
to the frontier, and today he received a blunt order telling him to
leave the country within eight hours. No diplomatic mission has
ever been treated like this before and, even in the case of a declaration of war, diplomats have always been allowed time to put their
affairs in order and to hand over their country's interests to a neutral
mission.

The United States ambassador, in his capacity as *doyen*, has made
a demand for the time-limit to be extended, at least until tomorrow;
but this evening he had still received no reply.

So M. Diamandy is expecting to leave tonight. He came to the
Embassy to give us his instructions for putting a guard on his
legation and for the evacuation of his colony. It will be a very
difficult situation: France is the ally of both of the opposing parties
at the same time, and the Embassy will have to represent the interests

of one in relation to the government of the other . . . with which we have no official contact. . . . The Bolsheviks for their part maintain that they are not at war with the Rumanian *people* (of whom they claim to be the most faithful allies), but with the Rumanian *bourgeois* and their government. Meanwhile, they have seized the Rumanian treasure, which those in charge were foolish enough to send to Moscow . . . to rescue it from the Germans!

Tuesday 29th January 1918

The Bolsheviks have shown themselves to be intractable and have insisted on M. Diamandy leaving within the fixed time-limit. The United States Ambassador was only warned an hour before the departure, which took place at three o'clock in the morning, and he was the only one of the diplomatic corps who was able to go to the station. Saint-Sauveur went too, and drove M. Diamandy there in his car (M. Paléologue's old one). Of course the Bolsheviks wanted to prevent any collective demonstration by the Diplomatic Corps at the station, in which they succeeded by keeping the departure time secret until the last moment. Everything went off in more or less correct fashion. M. Diamandy left in a special train, with a saloon car and a restaurant car. A member of the government has to accompany him as far as the Swedish frontier.

Because of the anarchy in the interior of the country, the Bolsheviks have in fact decided to send the Rumanian mission by way of Finland, but I am wondering how it will get through, because of the fighting between Reds and Whites. According to the latest news, the Reds have cut the railway in several places and blown up the bridges.

Wednesday 30th January 1918

The Brest negotiations seem doomed to failure, and the Bolsheviks are now talking of proclaiming a holy war. . . . One wonders how they will be able to do it. The front is in a state of the most incredible confusion and in certain places the *tovariches*, who have been given the rank of officer by election, have sold their batteries complete with guns, horses and harness. There is one story of a

Jew having bought sixty-three horses for one hundred and twenty roubles!

Anything seems credible in this state of things. I myself saw a gang of soldiers with two sledges filled with greatcoats and military equipment which they were putting up for sale near the Nicholas station. In fact it is through the soldiers that one can best obtain food. They steal it from the barracks and re-sell it for its weight in gold.

For some time violence in the streets, which up to now had been rare, has increased alarmingly and there is nothing but murder and robbery. The Fontanka is one of the most dangerous places, and several people we know have been attacked. A lady and her daughters were robbed near Sergevskaya Street and had to walk home barefoot as even their shoes had been taken from them. General Niessel came home at eleven o'clock one night to find a man on his doorstep who had been killed with revolver shots and stripped.

And yet it seems that in spite of the inertia of people here, they have decided to take things in hand. . . . A few days ago some thieves tried to break into the building of the English Shop and into a jeweller's: they were spotted in time and the house committees of their own accord passed judgement on them then and there, condemned them to death and executed them on the spot. . . . If everyone showed the same strength of purpose, there would soon be an end to all this violence . . . because the *tovarich* does not like danger, and he would still rather have an empty stomach than risk getting a bullet in it.

Thursday 31st January 1918

The Embassy has taken over the care of the Rumanians until such time as the Norwegians definitely agree to accept the responsibility. . . . It is no easy task to represent the interests of an allied state, in a country which is also our ally but with whose government we have no official relations.

The Peoples' Commissars know only too well how to profit by the situation, and they evade all requests with sly little looks of astonishment. Trotsky's assistant, Zalkind, plays this little game for all it is worth: "The Rumanian subjects? . . . but we don't want anything to happen to them. . . . Under the protection of the French

Embassy? ... But I'm delighted ... except that the French Embassy has broken off relations with us. ... Indeed, I am sorry about it, and it is not our fault. ... We ought to fly the French flag on the Rumanian Legation? ... What an excellent idea. ... In Russia we have learnt to love your three colours, and we cannot see enough of them ...", and so on.

It is most difficult to get the last word with this Commissar, who has decidedly benefited far too much from his stay in France, where he made all his studies and from where he even brought back the spirit of repartee. And it is becoming increasingly difficult to protect our own compatriots against the excesses of the *tovariches*.

The situation of the French industrialists here is untenable. M. Beaupied, the director of the Renault factories, has been forced to close them down because of the impossibility of supplying them with fuel and raw material. He has had to give the workmen a month's pay in advance, a matter of a million and a half roubles, and as all the banks are shut he sent a cheque for this amount to the Workers' Committee of the factory. But the workers insist on being paid in cash and today at about mid-day a gang of Red Guards invaded the former Laguiche mansion, which houses the administration, to arrest M. Beaupied. Most fortunately, he was in the Embassy at that moment, lunching with M. Noulens. He and I left immediately and went to the Peoples' Commissariat for Labour, which is in the Marble Palace. The Palace is in a sickening state, with its painted ceilings and its walls still hung with valuable pictures; gangs of *tovariches* were sprawled over the brocade-covered chairs, chucking their cigarette-ends on the Oriental carpets and the wonderful parquetry floors.

We saw the *tovarich* assistant to the Peoples' Commissar, who behaved correctly and quite understood that M. Beaupied has done everything possible to give satisfaction to his workmen and could not pay them in cash since the banks are closed. He has arranged a meeting of workers' delegates for tomorrow, in order to settle the business. ...

But until then M. Beaupied is at their mercy. ...

Friday 1st February 1918

The Peoples' Commissars have issued a decree forbidding diplomats to dispose of sums in current accounts in Petrograd banking establishments: this is by way of reprisals, the pretext being that foreign governments do not allow Soviet envoys to draw from funds deposited in foreign banks by the former Russian government. We are therefore outside the common law and are being treated even worse than the ordinary bourgeois, who is authorized to draw one hundred and fifty roubles a week.

Very varying decrees are being issued one after the other. One lays down that there should be no jewellery in a democratic republic. It gives a certain time-limit in which all jewellery and gold objects weighing more than seventy grammes must be deposited; they will be paid for at the uniform rate of forty roubles the *zolotnik*.[1] . . . After the expiry of the time-limit, they will be purely and simply "confiscated for the benefit of the people". Another decree orders the seizure by requisitioning of all reserve food supplies . . . which serves as an excuse for the *tovariches* to break into houses at any hour of the day or night and to take whatever they fancy.

It cannot last much longer: the Bolsheviks themselves are being overwhelmed by the anarchists. The sailors' delegates have forced the Commissars to immediately put a stop to the enquiry into the murder of the Kadet ministers, and nobody has dared arrest the murderers, who are well-known. The anarchists have established their official headquarters on board the *Polar Star*, the Emperor's former yacht, which is at Helsingfors. They have a seal and writing-paper with a printed heading, on which they wrote a letter to the United States ambassador, summarily ordering him to release a *tovarich* imprisoned somewhere in America. Having naturally received no answer, they sent another letter through the Ministry of Foreign Affairs making Mr. Francis personally responsible for anything which might happen to the *tovarich*, and threatening him with reprisals! (It sounds incredible, but I have it from the Counsellor himself at the U.S.A. Embassy.)

The excess of confusion might itself bring a reaction: the word revolution, by its very name, implies a revolving wheel and we must be approaching the moment when the wheel begins to come up again, having reached the lowest point of its course. . . . Let us hope so. . . .

---

[1] Equals 2.40 drams.

Saturday 2nd February 1918

We have heard the news of the German air-raid on Paris. . . . It seems a thoroughly ill-chosen moment for the Germans to revive hatred . . . at a time when all civilized nations ought to unite to combat disorder and famine. The situation here has greatly worsened during the last few days: the *tovariches* take no notice of anything and obey nobody. Everything depends on those with whom one has to deal. There are still some in whom the basically good Russian character comes out on top, and with them one can make arrangements: but many others have become real bandits, from whom the worst is to be feared.

At eleven o'clock last night M. Beaupied was warned that the workers of the Renault factory had met and condemned him to death, in spite of the arrangement concluded that same morning with the Peoples' Commissar for Labour. Before he was able to get out of his house, a gang of workmen arrived to inform him of the sentence, which did however allow him a time-limit of twenty-four hours in which to pay. . . . After a great deal of difficulty, this morning we were able to obtain authorization from the Peoples' Commissar to draw the sum from the bank. M. Beaupied, full of courage and still spick and span, came with us this evening to the Michael Theatre, to applaud Mme Roggers in *Le Demi-Monde*.

During the morning, the Danish Legation was invaded by about twenty people who went into all the rooms and tried to remove reserves of food, ignoring the protests of M. Scavenius. In spite of showing them documents from Smolny and even red seals, which up to now have produced such a good effect, they would not listen and said that they didn't care a damn for embassies or Smolny either. A delegate from the Peoples' Commissariat for Foreign Affairs, who was sent for in a hurry, was himself very ill-received and had the greatest difficulty in persuading them to go and pillage further away, after endless discussion.

Trouble is expected tomorrow, as the Patriarch Tikhon has ordered an expiatory procession in protest against the occupation of the Alexander Nevsky monastery by the Bolsheviks. They broke into the venerated sanctuary of the capital's founder by force and evicted the Metropolitan and the monks, who defended themselves with sticks. The Red Guards fired and used their bayonets: some of the crowd were wounded and a monk was killed. The Bolsheviks have seized the monastery's treasure and intend to use the buildings for their administration. The Patriarch pronounced an anathema against them and declared them unworthy to approach the sacraments. For several days the priests have been spreading very active propaganda among the people and even inside the barracks, and it would seem that Russia's traditional religious feeling has been re-awakened by the Bolsheviks' sacrilegious attack. Tomorrow's procession has been banned, but people say that it will take place in spite of the ban: this is sure to provoke conflict which could end in bloodshed, because of the tension of feeling.

Sunday 3rd February 1918

The night was somewhat disturbed. There have been pogroms and looting in the Sadovaya area, and near the Alexander Market and the Catherine Canal. Several shops were ransacked by the famished crowd who, having found a few bottles of vodka, were then seized with real destructive mania. The Red Guards had to send for motorized machine-guns to disperse these frenzied agitators.

On the other hand, and in spite of forebodings, the day went off quietly as the Bolsheviks had given in at the last moment and authorized the procession. I went to the Nevsky Prospekt to watch it. There was an enormous crowd, in which a lot of men were walking about bare-headed, carrying ikons and singing hymns. The weather was superb, with that yellow light which is peculiar to this country, and which lights up everything with flashes of gold. As I watched the procession passing, I had a vision of the old Russia of the past. The solemn chanting of the hymns, sung in several parts by the choirs, was a rest from the revolutionary tunes to which we have become accustomed. Banners with a mellow patina and gleams of tarnished gold floated above the heads of the crowd and were a change from the vivid red standards, whose startling colour has for the last year proclaimed itself stridently above the dark mass of the demonstrators and the whiteness of the snow. A lot of people were carrying big Orthodox crosses like those which one sees on graves, and at times they were so numerous and so serried that it seemed like a walking graveyard, a dream graveyard with crosses of gold.

All this created an impression of strength, the strength of ancient, ignorant Russia, superstitious and formidable. It is the first time since the revolution that I have felt that this Russia still exists, dormant, but ready to be awakened. The Bolsheviks know this well, and that is why they gave in. There were no incidents and as the procession went past, Red Guards and soldiers observed a respectful silence and uncovered their heads.

Monday 4th February 1918

In the Ukraine, the relatively moderate government of the Kiev *rada* has been overthrown by the partisans of the dissident Kharkov *rada*, which is supported by the Bolsheviks. In fact, some time ago this *rada* sent plenipotentiaries to Brest-Litovsk, along with those of the Kiev *rada*. Of course, both the one and the other claim to be the only one qualified to speak in the name of the 'Ukrainian Republic', and naturally their points-of-view are entirely different. I am sorry for the Germans having to face these escaped lunatics, and I hope that they will realize that there is only one way of dealing with them: to pitch into the whole pack of them, and I only hope that we will not hesitate to follow their example.

Meanwhile, people are fighting, pillaging and burning more or less all over the place. The position of foreigners amongst all this is sometimes desperate. Some time ago, a Frenchman who is the director of a mine in the Donetz Basin, was at his house when a horde of Cossacks arrived one morning. They forced him to hand over all his supplies of fodder, leaving his own horses to starve to death. That same evening, a gang of Red Guards arrived and when they heard that he had given all his hay to the Cossacks, they stood the director and four of his engineers up against a wall, and were about to shoot them. Luckily for our compatriot, a group of loyal workmen managed to persuade the Red Guards that there might be 'trouble' if they put a Frenchman to death. Thanks to them, his life was saved but the four Russian engineers were mercilessly murdered.

In Finland, on the other hand, it appears that the White Guard, which had retreated to the North, has renewed the offensive with a certain amount of success. It is said that they are receiving help and arms from Sweden, and possibly from Germany. It is a step towards the only possible solution: the re-establishment of order by the foreigner, as it has been proved that the Russians only know how to destroy. They must be treated like the Boxers were, who had done far less harm. . . .

Tuesday 5th February 1918

There has been no news of Brest and the peace talks for three days. People are taking advantage of it to spread the most extraordinary false reports throughout the town. The least of these is that peace has been signed, and that M. Balin, director of the Hamburg-Amerika line, is being sent here as ambassador. But a few minutes later there is a telephone call to say that everything has been broken off, that Trotsky has proclaimed the holy war . . . and that he has been arrested by the Germans. *Peace*, or *war*, against Germany can only be a matter of words now, not of facts . . . and it is only facts which count.

Wednesday 6th February 1918

A journalist told me that Burtsev, the former revolutionary, who had been put in prison first by the Tsar and then by the Bolsheviks, found himself shut up with Brelerzky, the former chief of the secret police, in the Kresty prison. These two implacable enemies became the best friends in the world. They have managed to get put into the same cell, and never stop talking about the time when they were both fighting; they each relate anecdotes, completing their stories by comparing each other's versions, recalling their impressions of revolutionaries or policemen . . . who, moreover, were sometimes one and the same. . . . They ought to write their memoirs in collaboration!

Thursday 7th February 1918

Attacks at night are increasing alarmingly, and it has become dangerous to go out in the evening. Princess Paley's brother, who was known by the pseudonym of Valois, was murdered a few days ago when driving past the Fontanka in a sledge. The day after, M. Batyuchkov, who has replaced Teliakovsky as Director of Theatres, was robbed and left unconscious near the Preobrajensky church. More recently Captain Sadoul saw two civilians killed by revolver shots on the Simeonsky Bridge as they were walking home about one in the morning: he was unable to intervene as he was unarmed and there were about ten of the aggressors, who were soldiers. And then yesterday Major Castel was in uniform going home to Princess Shachovskoy's house where he lives, when he was attacked on the Fontanka Quay just by the Nevsky Prospekt. A soldier who was walking in front of him tripped him up with a kick on the knee just as he was overtaking him, and two *tovariches* who were a bit further ahead immediately turned back and flung themselves upon him. A Browning was pressed to his forehead and he heard the click of the trigger. . . . The bullet was probably not in the barrel and luckily the gun did not go off; but he was knocked out and robbed. His clothes were slashed from top to bottom with a sword in order to strip him to the skin, and he was seriously wounded in the hand while trying to grasp the sword. He is now in hospital and has a good chance of escaping with his life.

General Niessel has ordered his officers not to go out at night unarmed, and the Ambassador has given us similar instructions.

Meanwhile, Countess Kleinmichel continues to go out at night with the most amazing courage, in her two-horse carriage which is all the more noticeable because it is one of the few which are still to be seen. When I scolded her for her imprudence, she answered most jauntily: "I am seventy-five and I have lived longer than a lot of other people. . . . I've lived too long, since I see what we see now. Whether I'm murdered in the street or murdered in my own house makes no difference, and I shall have no regrets. So I would rather go on visiting my friends than sit alone at home waiting for death. . . ." What a lesson in courage to all the people who have shown themselves to be so feeble . . . from this great lady, who is old and ill.

Friday 8th February 1918

We are living in a madhouse, and in the last few days there has been an avalanche of decrees which by their arbitrariness remind one of those of Paul I banning round hats, but are far more dangerous. First comes a decree cancelling all banking transactions, then comes another one confiscating houses. A law is being made to take away even their children from the bourgeois: from the age of three they will be brought up in establishments where their parents will always be able to go and see them a certain number of times in the year. In this way, differences in education which are contrary to the sacred dogma of equality will be avoided, by degrading them all to the same level, that is to say the lowest level of all.

I have made no mention yet of the taxes which continue to hit people from whom all source of income has been removed: five hundred roubles for a servant, five hundred roubles for a bathroom, six hundred roubles for a dog, and as much for a piano.

All inhabitants under the age of fifty are forced to join the 'personal labour corps'. Princess Obolensky has been ordered to go and clear snow off the Fontanka Quay. Others have to sweep the tramlines at night. Only the *tovariches* do nothing.

The delegates of the house committee came to enlist me for work of this kind too. I received them correctly, and then told them that if I cleaned anything for the Russians it would be something which doesn't often get cleaned, and that I would do it with kicks . . . they understood perfectly and did not insist any further.

Saturday 9th February 1918

We have been assured that Count Mirbach told a delegation of compatriots who had come to tell him of their anxiety, that they would not lose a single kopek and that he was only asking them to be patient for a few more days. It certainly seems that the Germans are getting worn out by the claims of the Bolsheviks at Brest-Litovsk, and that they want to speed things up. . . . Whether they come here as conquerors or whether they come after peace has been made, they will see to it that order is dinned into people's heads . . . with a few bullets if necessary. Let us hope that Russia's allies will not be any worse treated than her enemies, and that it will be possible for our compatriots to benefit from the advantages which the Russians will be forced to hand to the Germans.

It is high time that all nations should understand that the greatest enemy of civilization is the Russian revolution . . . and that they must join together in this crusade. When a house catches fire it doesn't much matter if there are some poachers among the firemen although, as Chevilly quite rightly points out, one must avoid letting the poachers put it out *alone*.

I fear, alas, that we are making this mistake and that we are allowing the Germans (or poachers) to be the only firemen to put out the blaze which has started in Russia and to reap all the profits. . . .

But in spite of everything, I would still be able to get over this . . . provided the fire is put out.

Sunday 10th February 1918

In Finland, the White Guard seems to be getting the upper hand. Apparently the Reds are very demoralized and are refusing to fight people who when they shoot are not content to just make a noise, according to the rules of the game which the *tovariches* are used to in Petrograd.

In the Ukraine, too, the *rada* troops have recovered. The Polish legions which had been dissolved by the new government seem to be resisting. Alexeiev, in spite of his disagreement with Kaledin, has managed to group together a fairly important nucleus. Apart from this, the religious movement also seems to be being reorganized and to be gaining in importance. Today, the Patriarch Tikhon's anathema against the Bolsheviks was proclaimed in all the churches in Russia. The Bolsheviks took no action against this demonstration. They even ended by giving in to the priests of the Alexander Nevsky monastery, and did not dare occupy the premises they had seized. They seem worried about the situation, and the hurry they are in to destroy everything which remains and . . . to fill their pockets is perhaps a sign that they feel their end to be approaching. . . .

I spent the afternoon with Alexandre Benois, who is still bravely working on the scenery for Petroushka. Naturally, there is no longer any question of producing this ballet at the Mariinsky Theatre, but they hope to give it in Stockholm. He is also very busy with the Commission on historical monuments. Up to now, the treasures of the Imperial Palaces have been saved, but it is harder to save the rich collections in certain private houses. The sailors have installed a club in the Stroganov Palace on the corner of the Nevsky

219

Prospekt and the Moïka Canal, and they smoke their cigarettes and spit out their sunflower seeds beneath the Claud Lorrains and the Poussins. . . . They want to make openings in the wonderful panelling in the ballroom, and turn it into a cinema!

Monday 11th February 1918

Today we heard the sensational news of the breaking-off of the Brest negotiations. Trotsky has solemnly declared that Russia cannot sign a peace which would alienate Russian territory . . . but that the state of war between Russia and her enemies has ceased to exist. Let him understand who may! Only a Slav mentality could have thought up this bastard combination of an intermediary state between peace and war, which is inconceivable to a European mind. If German divisions march into Petrograd gun in hand it will still be war, no matter how M. Trotsky may describe this action. If, on the contrary, German nationals come and settle here under the protection of a representative of their country and start trading, and if prisoners are exchanged, then it will be peace—with or without the signature of those *tovariches* who claim to represent Russia at Brest-Litovsk.

The news of the 'end of the war' was at first acclaimed with enthusiasm by the crowds. But after a few hours, when they realized that the magic word 'peace' had not been mentioned, this enthusiasm gave way to a state of uneasiness and anxiety. The Bolsheviks' popularity is going to take a terrible knock, because their strength comes from the fact that they promised peace, whereas they have not carried out their plan in effect. The iniquitous measures which they have taken lately with such real fiendishness, their fight against the Orthodox Church and their struggle against international finance, which endangers Jewish interests, have raised up redoubtable adversaries against them. They are now losing their strongest means of support in not allowing the people to acclaim that peace which they long for with all their might. . . . If we were clever we would be able to organize a reaction which would surely be to our advantage, instead of letting the Germans reap all the profits. But it seems to be in our nature to support a power only when that power has ceased to exist: and I am sure that, having refused to recognize the Bolsheviks when they were all-powerful, and could have been useful to us, we will now decide to do so at the very moment when they are on the point of disappearing.

Tuesday 12th February 1918

The Allied ambassadors and ministers met this afternoon to draw up a protest against the latest measures taken by the Peoples' Commissars. They have declared that they consider all actions taken against their own nationals, in which loans have been annulled or in which private property is affected, to be null and void. They reserve the right to insist in due course on complete reparations for damages suffered by their nationals, in the name of their governments.

It is undoubtedly the first time that the resident Diplomatic Corps of any country has intervened so definitely in the affairs of that country, and has gone so far as to declare government action null and void. But in spite of the forceful language used by the diplomatic representatives, I doubt whether they will succeed in making any impression on the People's Commissars, who only recognize the rights of the strongest as law.

Wednesday 13th February 1918

We are still without any communications with France because of what is happening in Finland. Nevertheless we are going to try and get a courier off by sea. Apparently one can get to Sweden without too much risk, there being just one possible crossing by a narrow channel driven through the frozen sea and kept open by ice-breakers. In this way one is safe from attack by German submarines.

The economic situation is getting worse every day. The bread ration has again been reduced, and I am really thankful for the army biscuits which the Military Mission has got for us from France: they are a real delicacy compared to the gluey paste which is sold here as bread. At Smolny they are very worried by the situation, and it is said that the great man Trotsky is going to take advantage of the leisure which their foreign policy has allowed him since the end of the Brest talks to apply himself to solving the apparently insoluble problem of food supplies for Petrograd. It is a fact that the peasants are refusing to sell their produce and would rather let it go to waste. Besides, the railways are in such a state of decay that one wonders how they can get everything here which is needed to feed the population. The distress among the members of the former bourgeois class is sickening. At the Hôtel de l'Europe a Guards colonel, who was half dead from hunger, came to ask the head waiter if he would give him a bowl of soup, as he had been a former client. . . . On the Nevsky Prospekt middle-class women are selling newspapers or queuing up at tobacconists in the hopes of re-selling cigarettes to the troops for a small profit.

Thursday 14th February 1918

The Marchese de la Torretta, the Italian chargé d'affaires, was robbed last night at eleven o'clock on the corner of the Mikhail Square on his way back to the Hôtel de l'Europe, where he lives. It is one of the most frequented spots in town, and at that hour many trams had come to a halt at their terminus, only a few steps from the place where he was attacked. They took everything: fur-lined coat, note-case, rings, tie-pin, keys . . . and even his snow-boots. The previous evening one of our friends, M. Hartong, was also attacked by three soldiers outside the little chapel of the *Jardin d'Eté*. He defended himself courageously, but a revolver bullet went right through his hand.

In order to put an end to these attacks, which have become a real danger, the People's Commissar for the Interior can think of nothing better than an 'appeal to the criminal elements of the capital's population', in which he calls upon them to stop their activities . . . or to leave the town within twenty-four hours! . . . This appeal, signed by Commissar Bronch Bronchevich, has been published in the newspapers!

In the same spirit, the Revolutionary Tribunal has decided to pursue the murderers of the Kadet ministers by publishing an appeal to the guilty parties expressing the hope that they will agree to go and present themselves to the Law Court of their own free will.

In this manner too the murderers of the Goremykins, who slaughtered these two old people and their servants, have been sentenced . . . to give their word of honour in writing, that they will not kill anyone else. . . . They probably don't know how to write, and have certainly never heard of a word of honour!

Oh, the incredible naïvety of the Slav soul, lost in the pursuit of mirages, without any sense of practical reality! Trotsky at Brest-Litovsk, with his formula 'neither peace nor war', and Bronch Bronchevich with his 'appeal to the criminal elements of the population', are the incarnation of this mentality. It is typical of careless, charming, infuriating Russia, where women who have nothing to eat wear necklaces of priceless pearls, where the railways don't run, where the ballet is a state institution, and where the capital city of Petrograd has no drains. . . . This is Russia in a nutshell, where the cold reaches twenty degrees and there are no covered cabs!

Friday 15th February 1918

This morning, at the People's Commissariat for Foreign Affairs, I had an interview with the Chief of the Department·of Law (what a title, at a time like the present!). The Ambassador had sent me to talk to him about the violations of this same law which he is supposed to uphold which have been perpetrated against the French. Like all his Bolshevik colleagues, he was extremely pleasant and seems to have been flattered by this approach. We parted the best of friends and at least I came away with some splendid promises. . . . I have practically no illusions as to their fulfilment, but I believe it is still the best way to get our claims listened to, rather than to enter into direct contact with the present custodians of power.

Besides, the Bolshevik leaders are very sensitive about any contacts made personally by members of embassies, and the more 'burjui' we are, the more sensitive are they. Consequently, the man they hate the most is M. Destrées who, they say, is a 'false brother'. They were raiding the house of a Belgian, and when he upheld his Minister as a 'socialist *tovarich*', the Bolshevik Commissar answered: "We love Belgium and we respect King Albert, but as for your socialist Minister. . . . You can keep him!" . . .

I think therefore that in our contacts with the Bolshevik authorities, which to my mind are a necessity, we should remain on our dignity at the same time as being very courteous; in similar circumstances I always make a point of having myself announced with my full titles.

Saturday 16th February 1918

The Bolsheviks, and the Russians in general, have been much more impressed than I thought by the recent protest of the Diplomatic Corps against the latest decrees. The newspapers have commented indignantly on this intervention and, moved by Russian pride, they complain that "their country is being treated in a way in which one does not even treat Siam". . . . I brought this matter up in my daily meeting with the journalists at the Embassy, and I told them that Russia was being treated as she deserved to be. Siam has not failed in its obligations like Russia has, and in that country they do not rob ambassadors in the principal street of the capital.

It is high time to stop putting up with so much from these people, and since they can only understand the knout . . . the knout is what they must get. Alas, it is still not possible to see who is going to apply this salutary treatment. The situation in the provinces seems to be extremely bad, as far as one can judge from the very rare and very uncertain news which reaches us.

Alexeiev's movement appears to be compromised. It is said that Novo Cherkassk, which is the centre of the Cossack administration, is on the point of being taken. But as all this news comes from Bolshevik sources it must be treated with caution; it is just as likely, on the contrary, that it is the Cossacks who have beaten the Red Guards. I doubt it, however, as I have never had any faith in these hordes who are only good for raiding and pillaging.

On the other hand I take a fairly good view of what is happening in Finland, and it seems possible that the White Guard may be capable of defeating anarchy in that country. The Finns are a stable people, who set about things slowly but surely, do not risk anything lightly, do not get over-excited, and rely more on methodical organization than on the too familiar method of 'getting out of the muddle'.

These are good conditions for getting the better of the gangs of Red soldiers who, like all good *tovariches*, will flee as soon as they are up against people who are methodical, determined, and who know what they want.

Monday 18th February 1918

I went out to Tsarskoye Selo to have lunch with the Grand Duke Paul, on a most wonderful fine day: it is a real pleasure to get out into the pure air after leaving this misty town, and to enjoy the sharp contrast between brilliant snow and blue sky. It was quite cold, but it was that nice sort of cold which makes you feel alive, with beautiful sunshine lighting everything up in dazzling colours. Along the railway line abandoned goods wagons made splashes of a magnificent red in the blue shadows of the snow, and everything was a fairyland of bright colour . . . the kind of scene which certain Russian painters know so well how to paint.

I found the Grand Duke and Princess Paley living in a small *dacha* which is part of the Grand Duke Boris's palace. They could not stay on in the palace, which was anyhow impossible to heat. It is quite a nice little cottage, but not at all luxurious. The furniture is covered in light-coloured cretonnes, and it seems odd to step out of one's sledge into this summery setting. It is all very simple: no Swiss, not even a servant at the front door, and Vladimir Paley himself helped me off with my coat.

The Grand Duke and the Princess welcomed me with their usual kindness to their family meal with the children and the governess. They had made some brown bread in my honour, which we ate with relish. The bread which they get there, which is rationed to one hundred grammes per person, is even worse than what we get here. We seem far removed from the beautiful etiquette of former days, and the Princess got up several times to cut some bread and to pour out a bottle of marvellous Mouton-Rothschild which they had decided to drink with me: it was one of the few bottles left to them, as the whole of their cellar containing treasures like this was smashed up.

They have no money and in order to live they are obliged to sell pictures and works of art. All these trials, particularly the murder of her brother, seem to have affected Princess Paley's health. The Grand Duke, on the other hand, seems to bear it all with a rare greatness of spirit. He has not lost his optimism and still has hope; he says that good may come out of this excess of evil, some day. Nevertheless, he keeps out of everything and rumours which are circulating about his participation in a monarchist plot, with the connivance of certain Bolsheviks, are completely without foundation. He is too high-minded to agree to a surrender of certain principles.

I have the impression that if a restoration were possible, he would favour the succession of the little Grand Duke, the heir, with Nikolai Nikolaievich as Regent. When I remarked that the latter is considered a dangerous madman by a lot of people, the Grand Duke answered that he has prestige and was a short time ago much loved by the soldiers, as was little Alexei. I agree that this combination is the kind of thing which would appeal to the sentimental imagination of the Slavs, and I am sure that this delicate child making his entry into the capital at the side of the romantic old giant would be acclaimed by the people. . . . I can almost see it as an opera or as the finale of a review at the Folies Bergère, but I fear that the present drama will have a more tragic ending. The Grand Duke did not mention the Grand Duke Dmitry as a candidate: it is said here that he is supported by the English, who have given him shelter in the Embassy in Teheran since the revolution.

Vladimir Paley is trying to find some distraction from the present events by introducing the schoolgirls of the Tsarskoye Selo *lycée* to play-acting. He has written a great fairy-tale piece called *Cinderella* which is to be performed next week, and in which there will be over fifty parts. He has done everything himself, verses, music and scenery. The star turn is a ballet of violets and glow-worms: it is a pretty idea . . . if not very original.

There was also talk of what has happened to various friends of the family. Many members of the aristocracy are at Kislovodsk, including the Grand Duchess Vladimir and her sons Andrew and Boris. They appear to be safe there. They say that the big oil merchant Mantachev is the real king of the town. He entertains gypsies and gives parties there, but above all he pays for a Caucasian guard to protect the region against the Reds. On the other hand, people are rather worried about the numerous refugees who were in the Crimea. There has been serious trouble at Yalta, forcing them to leave the town and hide in the mountains, where many of them are said to have been massacred.

According to news received this evening, Diamandy has arrived safe and sound in Sweden. The story is being told here that the Bolsheviks had sent an order to the Commissar who accompanied him, telling him to shoot Diamandy before arriving at the frontier:

the telegram containing the order was seized by the White Guard, who took over the station at Torneo just in time. Apparently it was the Bolshevik Commissar who was shot by the Whites as soon as the train arrived, and in spite of the entreaties of Diamandy. But . . . is all this true?

Tuesday 19th February 1918

The Germans have informed the Commissars' government that they cannot accept the declaration of 'neither peace nor war'. They are therefore preparing to resume hostilities. The Prince of Bavaria has said quite openly that he intends to come and restore order in Russia, in a proclamation in which he announces that talks have been broken off and that hostilities will be resumed.

The *tovariches* have learnt with dismay that their splendid scheme whereby the state of war was ended without signing peace has not been accepted. But the Prince of Bavaria's proclamation has unleashed their fury, and in the press it has provoked a torrent of insults against the bourgeois of all countries . . . but specially against those of the Allied countries, because for the moment they are less dangerous than the Central Powers. The Bolsheviks fill the columns of their newspapers with indignation against the bourgeois of France and England "who have instructed Germany to be their police-man". . . . After having branded them so infamously they got together countless soviets, committees, commissions, central or executive councils, committee councils or council committees, plenary assemblies, and general assemblies. During these sessions remarkable speeches were made and interminable palavers were held by the Bolsheviks, Mensheviks, majorities, minorities, Social Democrats of the Left and Right, and social revolutionaries of all colours, during which dissidents and partisans alike exalted socialist doctrine, branded the bourgeoisie, and saved the revolution with fine phrases. And after having discussed a great deal, talked a great deal, weighed for and against a great deal . . . nothing was decided. *Razgavors!*

It is generally thought that the Germans have decided to put an end to the revolution . . . and for performing such a service they should be forgiven many of the crimes of which they are accused. . . . But fortunately I don't believe we will have to thank them for this, because the revolution is going to come to an end of its own accord. . . . In fact, today we received a telegram from Paris urging us to make an approach to the Bolsheviks. It must be their *de profundis*, because whenever we have supported a party in Russia it has immediately fallen from power.

Wednesday 20th February 1918

In spite of all the splendid meetings and all the speeches Smolny has not found any solution, and in face of the imminent danger the Council of Commissars took it upon itself to telegraph during the night to the German General Staff, submitting to the conditions and accepting the peace terms which Comrade Trotsky refused to sign at Brest-Litovsk. For further safety he sent a courier at the same time, to confirm the telegram and bring back an answer.

There is a rumour that the German General Staff, before ceasing hostilities, is insisting on the annexation of Lithuania, a contribution of eight milliards in gold (not Kerensky's notes), the retreat of Russian troops in Finland, and the cessation of all propaganda in Europe. These conditions have horrified everyone: the Bolsheviks because they feel that their cause is lost . . . but much more so the bourgeois, who fear that Smolny will accept and that the Germans, for whom they have prepared triumphal arches as though for the coming of the Messiah, will not come to Petrograd to deliver them from the Bolshevik yoke after all.

Thursday 21st February 1918

The courier sent to the German General Staff returned this morning with an answer which Smolny did not consider suitable for submission to public opinion, no doubt on the strength of the principle 'no more secret diplomacy'. The Bolsheviks have even tried to spread a rumour that the Germans have not sent any reply.

In any case, the mysterious answer has had the effect of radically changing the mood of the great masters of Smolny, and those sheep who were bleating yesterday have been transformed into roaring lions. They have, naturally, issued a proclamation calling on all peoples to join in a holy war against the capitalists. The docu-

228

ment begins, of course, with a vehement diatribe against the Allied bourgeois who "have stabbed the Russian revolution in the back" by raising up enemies in the Ukraine, the Don, Rumania—Kaledin, Alexeiev and so on. The proclamation rejects all sacred alliances and calls upon the proletarians to arm against the bourgeois of the interior as much as against those of Germany. In short, this famous declaration of holy war is directed in particular against the law-abiding parties of all countries. In my view, it fully justifies the work of cleansing and hygiene which the Germans undertook by coming to sweep away this horde of brigands. Moreover, things are happening fast. It was announced this morning that having taken Dvinsk they are approaching Pskov . . . it is said that the advance is being made by train. The train stops at each station, leaving four men and a corporal there and then goes on its way, this being fully sufficient to occupy the country. The few *tovariches* who have ventured into these parts flee faster still: they do not even stop at the stations. As for the population, they are so pleased to see the Germans coming that they would beat up anyone who took it into their heads to slow up the advance by cutting the lines or blowing up a bridge.

. . . Here, everyone is radiant with joy and on the Nevsky Prospekt people greet each other with beaming faces. The optimists believe that 'they' will be here in three days . . . at last! . . .

I rather understand the feelings of our Russian friends; they have suffered too much for me not to forgive them. But they really are a little lacking in shame and ought to show their pleasure in a less demonstrative way. . . . It's really quite embarrassing.

Meanwhile, the embassies are upside-down. . . . The Americans in particular are panic-stricken, and Francis is running round all the stations trying to find a train. Here, there is a continual coming and going. We are preparing for departure, but God knows for what place, and God knows by what means, for I doubt whether the *tovariches* will allow us any room in the few trains which are still able to run. But what a splendid excuse for holding confabulations, getting up meetings, and shaking the dust off the files. M. Destrées alone remains calm: I went to see him to inform him of the 'measures'(?) taken. He said to me: "If the Germans want to take us over, together with our colonies, no good will come of getting upset. Given the numbers of their prisoners-of-war who are at liberty everywhere, they can cut off all the exits. Besides, the

Germans have no cause for hurry: they will doubtless be able to avoid having to come and restore order themselves, which could be inconvenient for them from the internal point of view. They have only got to establish themselves somewhere near and after having cut off all access, wait until the Russians eat each other up: all this at the small cost of sending aeroplanes when there's a fine day to take a little flight over the town. They will intervene when the right moment arrives, and will impose a government of their own choosing, from which they will extract all the advantages they could want."

This opinion, which seems to me so sensible, is not that of most of the augurers, who prefer to see things at their worst and evoke visions of concentration camps in Germany and forced labour in the enemy trenches. . . . There are long discussions as to whether we should 'evacuate', as it is called in military language, to Finland, Murmansk, Vologda, Moscow, or even Vladivostok, at the risk of embarking on an adventure which may end in disaster. It is not the moment to leave: more than ever before, we ought to remain here.

The zeal of these agitators has found another objective during the evening, and they are now talking of organizing Bolshevik resistance to the Germans! Captain Sadoul, who is our usual intermediary with Smolny, in fact came at about five o'clock to say that Trotsky is asking for our help. . . . The Ambassador at once telephoned to Trotsky . . . which was really rather more to offer our help than to grant it. M. Trotsky thanked him and said that he would mention it to the Council of Commissars this evening.

All this seems to me highly suspicious and I fear some intrigue on the part of the army, who are trying to have a hand in it! And indeed it is not very clever, with a view to the Russia of the future, to support the Bolsheviks at the moment when they are about to fall, let alone the fact that it is hardly encouraging to have to give more money to these brigands, when they have shown what small regard they have for Russia's obligations.

Friday 22nd February 1918

I went back to Tsarskoye Selo today with Chevilly. The Grand Duke cannot conceal his joy at the approach of the Germans, in spite of his great loyalty to the Allies. . . . It is only too understandable, because for him and his family it means salvation. Besides, he told me that as soon as order is restored, Russia will be able to shake off German domination, and that she counts on France to help her. It is therefore important for us to keep in contact with the real Russia, that is to say the Russia of the old days, and it is madness to help the Bolsheviks against the Germans. One could still agree with this policy if one could hope for any action from the Bolsheviks against our enemies. But it will only amount to a lot of talk: and all the speeches of the orators of Smolny on the holy war will not succeed in making a single German division retreat from the French front. This being the case, I cannot see that any good will come from compromising our future in Russia . . . for love of the Bolsheviks.

At the moment, and I was well aware of it at Tsarskoye, people are annoyed with us for having set ourselves up as the champions of anarchy . . . and simply because anarchy makes *speeches* against Germany. One cannot expect anything else. The soldiers do not want to fight, and they are not going to fight.

Meanwhile, Smolny has issued some fine proclamations and once again declared a state of siege and announced general mobilization. A decree has come out ordering all workmen's organizations to force all the bourgeois, men and women alike, to go and dig trenches for the defence of the revolution. All that the *tovariches* will have to do is to supervise, smoke cigarettes, and shoot the people who in their opinion do not work with enough zeal. I cannot understand how French officers can rely on these Red Guards and soldiers, to whom no one dares give the order to work and who are only fit to keep watch on the galley-slaves, which is what the unfortunate bourgeois condemned to forced labour by the all-powerful rabble have become.

On thinking over what M. Destrées said to me, I believe in fact that the Germans will not get as far as this. There is no glory attaching to a solemn entry into the capital of the *tovariches*, and I doubt whether it can haunt the dreams of Emperor William. They will stop before reaching Petrograd and will make peace, with conditions which Smolny will hasten to accept, and they will settle down in the country as neutrals. It will be easy for them, once they are installed, to undermine the power of the Bolsheviks and to weave around them a network of intrigues, until they disintegrate while seeming to disappear by the will of the Russian people. When that happens, the Germans will be faced with a government planned by themselves, which will ensure for them all the economic advantages which they seized from the Bolsheviks.

This is why I am very sceptical of all the rumours which are running round this evening about the German conditions. It is said that they are insisting on the military occupation of the capital, that they are refusing to treat with the present government, and that they will only agree to receive envoys of the Constituent Assembly or of the four old Duma administrations as plenipotentiaries. It is even being said that they insist on the restoration of little Alexei to the throne with the Empress's brother, the Grand Duke of Hesse, as Regent. These are the lucubrations of Slav imaginations.

Saturday 23rd February 1918

General Niessel came this morning to announce that the Bolsheviks have definitely 'accepted' the help of our Military Mission. . . . If they have accepted it, then they have not asked for it. . . . So here we have a French general who is 'the Bolsheviks' War Minister', as he himself says jokingly. Fortunately it will not be for long. According to information which Lindley has had from a good source, the Commissars have tonight already heard the conditions on which Germany will cease hostilities. We still do not know what these conditions are, but what one can be sure of is, that whatever they are, Smolny will accept them.

The most varying rumours about the German conditions were going round the town all the afternoon. People said that Lenin was giving in, whereas Trotsky claimed to be fighting a holy war, and for that there was a complete split between the two Bolshevik leaders. People were talking of the occupation of Petrograd and of the restoration of the monarchy, and so on.

I lunched with the Scaveniuses, who cannot understand why the Allied embassies want to leave at this moment.

Sunday 24th February 1918

This morning, at the same time as hearing the German conditions,

232

we learnt about the note sent by the Central Committee: as was to be expected, they have decided to submit and to send plenipotentiaries to sign the peace.

So we shall not see the officers of our Military Mission making their entry into Berlin at the head of a gang of apaches, Red Guards, and ragged soldiers. . . . All the better, as I hope that if we ever enter Berlin it will be in a more dignified manner.

Meanwhile, the Germans are taking everything which it suits them to take. Their frontier will in actual fact be pushed forward as far as Dvinsk. They are making sure of a commercial treaty which will allow them to exploit Russia at their will until 1925. They demand the withdrawal of Russian troops from Finland and the Ukraine, the demobilization of all forces including the Red Guard, and the cessation of all revolutionary propaganda. The Baltic provinces will be occupied militarily by German troops.

If these conditions are fulfilled, the German General Staff will give up its plan to enter its own town of Petrograd, to the great disappointment of all the bourgeois, who are thus condemned to remain there for some time still, and still in the clutches of the fanatics of Smolny. I do not believe it will be for long though, because the treaty gives the Germans numerous pretexts for intervention, particularly in the clause forbidding revolutionary propaganda. It would have been much wiser on their part, instead of banning this propaganda, to have come here and nipped it in the bud.

Besides, in the provinces order is being restored as if by magic in all the places where the populace were able to believe in the coming of the Germans. The peasants are giving back land, bringing back furniture and silver, and calling all the bourgeois "My Lord" . . . it is the return of the golden age. It was enough for them to know that the Germans would mercilessly shoot all Red Guards caught armed—which is indeed consistent with the rules of war. The only thing I am afraid of is that the Germans will not have time to apply this salutary rule, because at the news of their approach the Red Guards transform themselves into good, docile peasants, devoted and hard-working, respectful of persons and of property, and who are only too ready to sing "*Boje Tsarya Krani*" and to proffer their backs to the wholesome knout!

In Petrograd itself one no longer sees *tovariches* in the street dragging guns along tied up with bits of string, and miraculous to relate, today I was able to get into a tram without having to stand on the step.

Could this be the reaction? . . . It is up to us to manœuvre cleverly and prevent the new régime from giving in to the Germans. Alas, we have not been able to contribute towards the cleansing operation which our enemies have undertaken and by which they are ensuring the gratitude of all of the real Russia. It is now a question of our counterbalancing this influence and trying to maintain the position in this country to which France is entitled by reason of all the money which she has poured in, and because she has so many interests here and so many possibilities for the future. . . .

But to achieve this, one must be on the spot . . . and all the talk is of leaving!

Monday 25th February 1918

During the night we learnt that Pskov has been taken by the Germans: the factory sirens called the workers to arms, as the Petrograd soviet, in opposition to the central pan-Russian soviet and the Commissars' Council, has decided to defend the revolution. Since the early hours motorcars have been driving through the streets, scattering proclamations calling on the proletarians to fight against the 'international bourgeoisie'. The passers-by, as inquisitive as usual, rushed forward each time a shower of papers fell from a car and fluttered down into outstretched hands . . . but as soon as they saw what it was about, they threw away the pages with expressions of indifference. The people who are not actually hoping for the coming of the Germans at least look forward to their arrival without the slightest emotion, and it is only the unruly elements in fear of punishment who are worried about the enemy's entry into what was once the capital of Russia.

In fact, as the day wore on, the idea of defending the revolution lost ground. At the Charlier factory, only nineteen out of four thousand workmen volunteered, in spite of sirens and proclamations. It's the same in all the other factories. In the recruiting offices which have been opened in each quarter of the town (in each 'department', as they call it here), the result has been even more piteous.

In the embassies everyone is determined to leave, and they are busy trying to get a train ready for the Allied diplomats; but they are having the greatest difficulty collecting the necessary coaches and getting them put into working order.

Tuesday 26th February 1918

The news is better this morning. The Germans seem to be advancing less fast and it is not known for certain whether they have occupied Pskov, or whether they have evacuated the town after merely making a reconnaissance. A lot of people are even asserting that it is only some German prisoners-of-war who have armed themselves and taken possession of the town.

Naturally the most fantastic rumours never stop going round. At one moment it was announced that the *tovariches* had retaken Pskov at bayonet point, and that sixty thousand Red Guards had left Moscow to repel the invader. Then we were told that the Germans had already seized Luga and that they were approaching Gachina. People also said that a cavalry section had reached the Moscow railway and had cut the line at Bologoy and occupied the station at Dno.

The Russian imagination, which is usually so fertile, is definitely no good at giving geographical identification to its easily invented romances. Dno, Bologoy and Gachina are the three names which crop up at every crisis. This is where they said the Emperor's train had been stopped, and where Kornilov's Cossacks were supposed to have arrived and to have fought heroically against Kerensky's troops. So it was enough for someone to mention one of these three names for me to become sceptical.

The embassies are taking things more seriously and the Americans, who have shown more panic than anyone else over this business, suddenly decided to leave yesterday evening in the direction of the East, taking the Chinese and, I believe, the Siamese Ministers as part of their luggage.

The departure of the other powers' representatives has been provisionally arranged for tomorrow. The Ambassador, who up to now seemed anxious to stay here, has suddenly decided to leave. The arrival of a telegram from Tokyo, sent on from Paris 'for information', has had a lot to do with this decision: in it there is talk of the possibility of Japanese intervention against the Bolsheviks. Coinciding with the departure of the Japanese mission, this has been cleverly exploited by the alarmists, who visualized themselves being kept here as hostages.

Among the Ambassador's friends, people keep on saying that we must leave Russia because we cannot continue to put up with the insults and the snubs. . . . I fail to understand how a measure which has been decided on in principle in order to avoid falling into the hands of the Germans can become a demonstration against Russia.

Our departure is therefore provisionally arranged for tomorrow. We are to go to Helsingfors, where we will await instructions from the Allied governments. I hope that they will realize that at all costs we must stay in Russia, and not leave it entirely to the Germans.

Whatever the outcome of the war, it would be fruitful for our enemies if they could be sure of their predominance in this rich country, where there are so many future possibilities. Whatever else happens, this would be an immense victory for Germany and I cannot see what we could ask for to counterbalance such a big advantage, even if we were in a position to ask for what we wanted or to impose our demands. . . . Alas, we are far from it, and I tremble to think what the Germans will do to the Russian giant, when I see what they have done to little Bulgaria and the sick man of Constantinople. . . .

I wonder if anyone really thought of all this when they decided to take the train tomorrow, and are we sure that this abandoning of everything will not have terrible repercussions on our front . . . and perhaps on the whole issue of the war!

Petrograd, Wednesday 27th February 1918

I talked at length about the departure plans of the diplomatic missions to General Niessel. He is basically not sorry to be rid of Embassy supervision, but nevertheless he seems worried by this venture, and thinks that we are acting too hastily. He deplores our departure for Finland and would have preferred us to remain on Russian territory.

The Military Mission will not leave Petrograd, at least not for the moment. This clearly shows that the excuse which is being given for our departure is not a valid one, and that we do not envisage the immediate entry of the Germans into the capital. Besides, if we did, it would be the military who would have to be got out first, as they are the ones who run the greatest risk of being taken prisoner.

The Military Mission's position from the legal point of view will in fact be rather peculiar, because this belligerent Military Mission will more or less depend on a neutral legation, the Danish Legation, as it is Scavenius who will be in charge of French interests.

What would happen if, at some future time, the Military Mission wanted to leave against the wish of the Russians? Could not the Russians maintain that as France has broken off diplomatic relations with Russia, they are relieved of all obligations towards a military mission which has no legal status and cannot claim any privileges?

Petrograd, Thursday 28th February 1918

A very agitated morning, spent in making the final preparations for our departure. All day long we were burning papers, dragging luggage about, nailing up packing-cases or sealing trunks, thinking that the Bolsheviks would show respect for the seals.

Many of the French colony, on hearing the news, came to the Embassy: they were panic-stricken at our departure and thought that all was lost, as did some of the old régime Russians who were quite justifiably worried at losing their last means of support. I did my best to reassure both the one and the other.

It was rather sad leaving the house. Old Anna cried like a child, and good Friquet came and rubbed his dear head against me, gazing at me with his limpid eyes. But I had no time for emotion; after eating a hasty lunch and tying up my last personal parcels, I rushed to the Embassy to pack up the codes and then dashed to the station to make arrangements for the train, which the Ambassador had ordered me to do.

It was no easy matter as of course there were far more passengers than seats, not to mention the mountains of luggage, which Marchand was coping with most skilfully.

Besides our own Embassy, it was a question of finding seats for the English Embassy and part of its Military Mission, the Italian Embassy, and the Legations of Belgium, Greece, Serbia and Portugal. We only had six coaches and four vans at our disposal for all these people.

Luckily the Bolsheviks made our task easier. As they look very much askance at our departure for Finland and consider it an insult, they started by turning out of the train all the English who were not in any official capacity: these people had arrived ahead and had occupied all the best seats. The Commissar let it be known that only the holders of valid diplomatic passports would be allowed on the train, and that he had orders to stop the departure of anyone who was found to be cheating.

Having made us wait for over two hours and having exacted payment for the hire of coaches and vans and a fee for the Red Guard who is to accompany the convoy, the Commissar locked us into our coaches while he proceeded to check our passports. Among the Italian diplomatic passports he discovered one belonging to Count Frasso, whom the Bolsheviks had accused of spreading counter-revolutionary propaganda in this country: the Commissar protested against the fact that he carried a diplomatic passport and made him get out of the train, together with all the other Italians, the Marchese de la Torretta at their head.

All this made a bit more room in the carriages, and the people who were left found places. I made a plan of the coaches, just like a sleeping-car attendant, and we settled ourselves as best we could into the compartments, which in fact were quite clean.

On the platform there were a lot of people who had come to see off . . . their friends. Princess Urusov was with Gentil, Karsavina with Bruce, Countess Beckendorff with Cunard, Countess Nostitz with Lalaing, and the steel king Saint-Sauveur . . . was with all the important people. He thinks our departure is premature and has refused to come with us, as suggested by the Ambassador.

Everyone disappeared towards half past eight to go and have dinner . . . and we were left alone in our train, which still had not moved. It was not until about half past ten that the Bolsheviks authorized our departure, after fresh vexations of every kind and nearly five hours delay.

Helsingfors, Friday 1st March 1918

We have settled down in Helsingfors . . . while awaiting events.

The journey was rich in incidents. The frontier authorities were not satisfied with the check carried out in the train before our departure, and as soon as we arrived at Byelo-Ostrov they made us get out and fill in control forms, and so on. At first it all seemed to go very well, but when everything appeared to have been settled the Soviet Commissars, a soldier and a sailor, began to make difficulties and tried to make out that the seals on our passports were false ones.

The soldier, a sickly-looking little man with a nasty look in his eye, egged on the disagreeable and envious-looking sailor, who was delighted to exercise his authority over ambassadors. They went as far as to consider arresting the heads of missions but did not quite dare to put this plan into practice: they telephoned to Smolny, who told them to keep the train at the frontier and, if necessary, to bring it back to Petrograd.

After having struggled with them for some time, I went to inform the Ambassador, who protested most vigorously and demanded to be put into communication with the Foreign Affairs Commissariat . . . which, it being this country, surprised no one although it was nearly two o'clock in the morning.

The station-master, M. Savitsky, tried in vain to settle the matter: the Commissars remained inflexible and went on insisting that our passports carried false visas sealed with a round seal whereas, according to them, it should have been a square one.

Finally, the station-master suggested driving the engine back to Petrograd, taking all the passports with him. About two hours later the engine returned, bringing the Assistant Commissar for Foreign Affairs himself, *tovarich* Petrov. This man had been interned for a long time in England and harboured a hatred for all foreigners, and for diplomats in particular. He began by upholding the point of view of the Soviet Commissars, and accused us of having knowingly obtained our visas from a department which had no qualifications to issue them. Then, realizing that his attitude must seem ridiculous, he tried to make us believe that he did not doubt the good faith of the missions: he said that it was his duty to open an enquiry to find out who had authorized the irregular visas, and thus uncover a counter-revolutionary plot in his own Ministry. After half an hour's discussion I made him see that if there was a plot, we had nothing to do with it and that we could not be made responsible for the mistakes of his subordinates. I got him to give us our exit visas himself: like this, the matter would be beyond dispute. . . . He then pulled out from the pocket of his leather jacket the famous square seal, which was attached to a heavy iron chain round his waist.

There was very soon further chicanery when he started examining the passports of our staff: he categorically refused to stamp them with the square seal, and wanted to send them all back to Petrograd.

The discussion continued in the Ambassador's compartment and very soon became acrimonious. Petrov spoke in bad English and M. Noulens answered in French, which the Commissar can understand but not speak. Finally, he had to give in and issue visas for all the passports.

At half past six everything was finished at last, and the train crossed the frontier. The Finnish guard who had replaced the Russians, while condoling with me on what had happened, added: "Now we are going to a good country . . . the Reds will soon be finished . . ." and he made a gesture as though squashing a bug with his thumbnail.

For this good man's prophecy to be fulfilled, the Whites will have to make a big effort, because the Red Guards whom we saw in Vyborg and at stations along the line seem very different to the Russian ones. At one of these stations, Kuvola, the Red Guard was lined up along the platform and M. Noulens inspected them, accompanied by Destrées, Batalha Reis and Lindley.[1] They are magnificent peasants, wearing *valinkis*, varying forms of headgear trimmed with red ribbons, homespun coats or short fur-lined jackets, cartridge-belts round their waists and haversacks slung across their shoulders. These people have never done any military service, but they did the honours like the Imperial Guard of old: there is certainly no training like the wish to fight for producing good soldiers, and no need for a long life in the barracks. Knowing that we were without provisions, they sent us fifty kilos of bread without accepting the smallest payment, and when we left they gave us the customary three cheers.

As one gradually gets further away from Russia the country, although monotonous, becomes more pleasing. There are hills covered with pine trees which stand out purplish-grey against the white plain on which one can see the palisades dividing the land,

[1] Sir Francis Lindley, Counsellor to the Embassy in Petrograd in 1915. Left in charge of the mission in January 1918 after the withdrawal of Sir George Buchanan. In May he was transferred to Archangel as Commissioner, and in June became Consul-General in Russia.

looking like hatchings drawn in Chinese ink. The houses are bright red or brilliant yellow, with the window-panes painted blue, and it is a landscape of supple lines and elementary colours which stand out clearly: under the grey of the sky, it is not lacking in charm. Sometimes the villages are built high up in terraces, and the houses are grouped together in an amusing way. Everywhere one has an impression of cleanliness and activity.

We stopped at several very clean stations which were a contrast to the Russian ones, and where the train waited for us to go to the refreshment rooms and drink milk, which tasted delicious to me. At Rejmaki we even found that dinner had been ordered by telephone by the Commandant of the Red Guard at Kuvola: it was served Swedish fashion on a big table from which everyone helped themselves. . . . Unfortunately there are some English people on the train, who are so selfish and pushing that it is almost impossible to get to the buffet. . . .

We arrived at Helsingfors towards nine o'clock in the evening. The consul was waiting for us at the station and told us that the Reds were well-disposed towards us, and had even requisitioned and opened up a hotel which had been closed, for us to settle into. But it was too late for us to go there because of the state of siege existing at present, which makes it difficult to move in the town after nine o'clock. We therefore decided to spend the night in the train, and I went to get the necessary authorization from the station-master. I found an extremely courteous man, well installed in a very clean room painted in bright blue Ripolin and comfortably furnished, which bore no resemblance to Russian Bolshevik offices. He agreed to everything we wanted, and even had a station engine attached to our train to provide our carriages with heating, and had the train surrounded by a detachment of Red Guards to watch over our safety.

(Here follows a long interval of six weeks in the Diary.)

Vologda, Monday 15th April 1918

This morning the Russian papers published the text of the Emperor Charles' letter which was handed to Poincaré in March 1917 by Prince Sixte. It is scandalous that a document such as this should have been kept secret for so long. I think that they must have answered the Emperor Charles like they did the Emperor Joseph in November 1914, when he made peace offers which were so acceptable that the French government had to send a telegram to Paléologue saying: "Decipher yourself", in order to prevent the Russian government from replying.

What a lot of blood has been shed since these two peace attempts . . . may it fall on the heads of those who are guilty. I am horrified at Europe's progress towards the abyss, when I relate all this to so many other incidents, which I try to snatch from my memories. There was the occasion when that officer[1] on Poincaré's staff drank a toast "To the War!" in the Embassy a fortnight before the catastrophe: the protests which were raised against the use of the word 'peaceful' in connection with the allusion to "the strength of the armies of land and sea" in Poincaré's speech: the nightmare days of July 1914, and the admissions which Sukhomlinov made during his trial. One is forced to wonder whether this war does not represent the wrath of God, as is believed by simple souls: for one cannot believe in the folly and the crimes committed by both sides— and premeditation is just as evident with the Germans.

All the same it is surprising that such an important document should be published on the occasion of a purely formal argument to prove that Clemenceau did not make advances to Austria, and that it was Czernin 'who was lying'. The question which is brought up by this letter is far more important than the present argument. It is now a matter of the government having to point out the trap, if trap there be, and to state what has been done to take advantage of the chance it was given to detach Austria from the Quadruple Alliance. I fear, alas, that it did absolutely nothing, and that it was because of yet another stupid sentimental scruple about Russia that we missed the opportunity. The Emperor of Austria's letter, *which was written a fortnight after the Russian revolution*, must of course have hinted that Russia would pay the piper.

And it was the moment when people in France were having illusions about the 'young democracy', and about the 'national' revolution which had overthrown the 'German' régime of the Empress, of Stürmer, and of Rasputin! Milyukov was Minister of Foreign Affairs and dreamed of what his pan-Slav friends called 'The Russia of Ugor', which extended as far as Kassa, in the heart

---

[1] *Author's note:* Colonel Aldebert.

of Hungary. Albert Thomas had left Paris to guide the sister democracy towards victory, evoking memories of the French Revolution. The great spring offensive on the French front was in preparation, Hindenburg had evacuated the regions which he has now once more occupied, and it was several weeks since Doumergue had returned from his journey to Petrograd, where he had talked to the Tsar about the left bank of the Rhine, about Syria, Palestine and Constantinople, and where he had divided up the map of the world on Paléologue's desk. It was a moment of the maddest illusions, and nobody wanted to listen to the warning voices of General Janin or of M. Paléologue, who had lost all their former illusions about the revolution and who had uttered cries of alarm in face of the optimism of Albert Thomas.

Under these conditions, what did the Emperor's letter matter? He was Emperor of a country which everyone in France considered about to be divided by imminent revolution and crushed by the Cossack armies who, stirred by the breath of patriotism and democracy like their 'great ancestors' of the French Revolution, would shortly enter Vienna and Berlin.

I quite understand why Poincaré did not answer the Emperor Charles directly: it was because of our Allies, and the Italians in particular, whose help had to be paid for, not to use a harsher term. But why did he not make parliament give an indirect answer, by repeating the terms of the letter and declaring our war aims, which people still ignore today? This would have been enough reason for announcing negotiations, which would have enabled us to know whether there was anything in the Emperor Charles' proposals, or whether they really were nothing but a trap. . . .

I am sure that the socialist party throughout the world will feel the same as I do at this moment. I immediately realized this when I saw the effect that this publication had on M. Destrées, with whom I had a long talk this morning.

Vologda, Tuesday 16th April 1918

A telegram was received this morning announcing my promotion to the rank of Third Secretary. Everyone here greeted the news in the most friendly fashion and the Destrées, thanks to the unfailing Charlier, managed to get a bottle of excellent Pommery brought to the restaurant-car, in which my health was drunk, following a few charming words from the Ambassador and the Belgian Minister.

In fact, the department seems to be in luck at the moment and has given each of us an indemnity of six hundred francs for the duration of our stay outside Petrograd. This will allow me to keep on our flat in Petrograd, because I persist in believing that we will end in going back there.

Meanwhile, people have been fighting in the streets and even at the station, and Soviet troops have arrested a group of anarchists who had taken refuge in some houses and in some railway trucks.

Vologda, Wednesday 17th April 1918

The operation against the anarchists which we witnessed here has also taken place in other Russian towns, notably in Moscow, where there were real battles between government troops and anarchists. The anarchists were disarmed and many have been killed.

It was time something was done as the anarchists had been terrorizing the population, taking over houses and turning out the occupants and helping themselves to everything they wanted. Princess Gorchakov wrote and told me that two or three times gangs had invaded the Kharitonenko palace and taken over the bedrooms and drawing-rooms, in spite of the presence of French and American officers who are living in the house, and in spite of the intervention of Soviet delegates who were unable to impose their authority. Force had to be used to evict the gangs.

These isolated incidents made the Commissars decide to take sides against the anarchists and proceed to concerted police action. In acting thus, whether consciously or not, they have steered hard over to the right. People here say that it is the Germans who encouraged them and gave them the necessary moral support.

But in spite of it all, their situation seems precarious. The various parties of the opposition, Kadets, Social-revolutionaries and so on, are getting up great confabulations. For the moment it is all only 'razgavors', and it is probable that these people who are incapable of agreeing among themselves, will accomplish nothing. The only régime which can be imposed on Russia is autocracy or dictatorship which, if necessary, will be supported by German bayonets.

I would therefore not be surprised if we were to witness a restoration under these conditions, because Count Mirbach would not have agreed to represent the German Emperor with the *tovariches* if he did not secretly intend to establish a régime which is more suited to his tastes. This will be the moment for us to seize upon, and it would be a right and proper task for a diplomat to give the new Russian autocracy a distaste for those to whom they will owe everything . . . and whom they will perhaps be disposed to hate precisely because of that . . . which is only human . . . and in any case very Russian.

Vologda, Thursday 18th April 1918

Major Gallaud arrived yesterday evening from Petrograd, bringing with him some impressions of his stay in the capital. Everything is quiet, but it is practically a dead city. Prices have continued to rise, and the population is dying of hunger. A pound of potatoes costs ten roubles and it is practically impossible to find any. To remove the snow from the Embassy courtyard as far as the Quay where it is thrown into the Neva, you have to pay fifty roubles for the journey by sledge. It seems unbelievable. In truth, money no longer has any purchasing power.

In the Nevsky and Liteiny Prospekts so-called commission shops have been opened, where society women sell every kind of object belonging to people who have been ruined. One can find jewellery, pictures, silver, and china at very reasonable prices which will not allow the unfortunate owners to postpone for long the moment when they will die of hunger.

On his return journey, Major Gallaud saw a group of *moujiks* at a station not very far from here: three men and three women, with their faces and hands covered with blood, who were trying to get into the train. As there was no room, which is always the case nowadays as Russian trains are full up from the roofs to the steps, he opened the door of his sleeping-car to them. These unfortunate people had been attacked by a pack of wolves, who had literally devoured them alive. One man no longer had a human face: his nose and lips had been torn away, and another had a large part of his hands missing. The ones who could still speak told Major Gallaud that several of their companions had succumbed to their wounds. Their courage was indeed wonderful, and their resignation; they remained stoically in the corridor, without dressings on their wounds. . . . What a country!

Vologda, Friday 19th April 1918

There is a lot of talk about Japanese intervention from which, for my part, I do not expect anything much, contrary to general opinion.

The Japanese are only considering their own interests in this operation, and to try and make the French public believe that a descent on Vladivostok would worry the Germans and force them to remove troops from our front, is to stuff their heads with false ideas. People forget that it used to take *twelve days by express train in peace-time* to cross Siberia, and army corps do not travel by express: they will probably not even be able to travel by train if, as seems likely, the Russians oppose their passage.

I tremble when I think that the French are being hoaxed with the Japanese mirage, just as they were with the Russian steam-roller mirage, the English mirage, and the American mirage, and that people are losing sight of the appalling reality: the German offensive, whose progress we follow with anguish. What butchery it must be.

Jean de Saint-Sauveur left today for France. During his absence I shall carry out the duties of Commercial Attaché.

Vologda, Monday 22nd April 1918

Today I saw Chevilly, on his return from Moscow and on his way to Petrograd. He thinks as I do that the Bolsheviks have not got much longer. Besides, there is no folly which they have not committed and they seem to be making a point of letting their reign sink into absurdity.

The plan for a decree ordering the 'nationalization of women' has appeared in *Izvestia*, and it is so extraordinary that the Ambassador could not resist sending the full text to Paris by telegram, to be communicated to the press. All young girls of over eighteen will have to inscribe their names in offices of free love, under the Commissar for Public Health. Each of these offices will make up a list of 'eligible men', from which the young girls will have the right to choose a 'concubine'. Anywhere else this regulation would seem like a joke out of *La Vie Parisienne*, but it is apparently already in force in certain districts, such as Saratov, Luga, Kolpino. . . . The red lamp, which a short time ago burned in front of the ikons in all the frontier stations of Russia, can never have been as symbolic as at present.

The Bolsheviks believe that they can count on the Germans, who are indeed supporting them, at least in appearance. The Germans will play this game until the moment when the régime will have wrecked itself and will fall of its own accord. This is clever on the part of our enemies, who will thus ensure the gratitude of the future government without incurring the odium of having imposed it, and while appearing to allow the country to remain master of its fate.

The Germans are credited with the intention of installing themselves in Petrograd when the Bolshevik government is about to fall, and of supporting a government based on the former Duma and the former Senate. The régime which the Germans would thus give Russia would have all the appearance of a régime issuing from the former national representation.

As from now, German propaganda is becoming very active. It is done mostly by means of the cinemas, which have almost all been bought by the Germans, so that in many cases this propaganda costs nothing and even sometimes brings in something to the people who spread it. Instead of showing, as we do, guns, aeroplanes, trenches, and reviews in which General Joffre decorates and embraces '*poilus*' in the presence of King Albert and the inevitable Poincaré in his gaiters and his chauffeur's cap, they show amusing scenes which take place in markets, in restaurants, and in shops filled with food and other goods, all of which calls forth a picture of an existence which is free, easy and cheap. They had the good idea of showing Russians in these settings: Russian actors were engaged for this purpose, and the films have been such a success that our own have been lamentable failures in comparison.

Vologda, Tuesday 23rd April 1918

After long hesitation, the Belgians have decided to go from Russia and are due to leave tomorrow for Vladivostok. In fact, nobody can understand why they are leaving, nor why they do not take the Murmansk route which is always used by people going to Europe. . . . But at Murmansk there is no Fujiyama, and no avenues of cherry trees!

However that may be, their departure is arranged for tomorrow and the Destrées have invited the Ambassador and Mme Noulens, Gentil, Taliani and myself to a farewell dinner in their restaurant-car.

Claude Anet was among the guests, and I sat at his table. He has come from Moscow, where he was very struck by the growing difficulties which the government of Peoples' Commissars is encountering, and which the Bolsheviks themselves admit. The Director of the Commissariat of Finance, Gukovsky, admits that Russia is facing bankruptcy, and he has given figures which show that it is impossible to make a budget. Expenses are mounting, and there is no revenue. Taxes are not being paid and there can be no thought of a loan because, by denouncing former borrowing, the Bolsheviks have denied themselves recourse to this resource. The railways are in a still worse state than can be imagined from what we see here: the cost price per kilometre has multiplied almost a hundred times. Because of lack of discipline among the railway workers and because of the so-called social laws, repairs to the lines and maintenance of rolling stock have become impossible.

For this reason, the Bolsheviks are thinking of going back on some of their decisions. They have had to revoke the decree nationalizing petrol transport companies on the Volga: not a single ship has put in to Astrakhan since the reopening of navigation, and if this continues Russia runs the risk of being without petrol.

In the country districts the sowing of crops has not been carried out, or else has been done under deplorable conditions: the harvest will be execrable, and the present food shortage will turn into real famine in a few months. The peasants are discouraged and are beginning to think of the 'Little Father'.

The Germans have discovered the only remedy for famine, and have decided that in the provinces which they occupy all the land which is being badly cultivated by its present custodians shall be given back to its former owners. With civilization as it is at present, only the régime of big estates can develop the land in Russia, because capital and ample means are needed to obtain good returns. The 'unions', or peasant co-operatives, seem purely Utopian in a country where the primitive mentality of the *moujiks* cannot adapt itself to a complicated organization. As for small holdings, which give such good results in France where everyone cultivates his plot like a real garden, they are quite impracticable in the vast stretches of land you get here, and impossible as long as the country is not more thickly populated and is not served by a widespread network of communications, and until the population is more enlightened and, above all, less lazy.

It therefore seems certain that the fundamental dogma of the revolution, 'The land for the peasants', is fated—and the revolution itself is therefore fated too. Secret organizations are being formed everywhere, which tend towards a restoration . . . the only thing is that nobody can agree on the candidate: there is a lot of talk of a Prince of Hesse who is supposed to be favoured by the Germans.

Destrées, Claude Anet and the Marchese de la Torretta discussed the Russian problem the whole evening. The first two think that Russia as a state is fated to disappear, and they cite the lack of patriotism and national conscience as their reason. According to them, Peter the Great's achievement was all artificial.

But according to the Marchese de la Torretta, on the contrary, Peter the Great's achievement was one of the landmarks of Russian history, as is the present revolution. He thinks that after passing through this crisis Russia will recover her self-awareness and will return to her traditional aspirations: the Baltic and Constantinople. In his view, it is the old régime which is the principal cause of the lack of national conscience, for by concentrating the whole state in the person of the Tsar, it left no room for the idea of patriotism. . . .

Vologda, Wednesday 24th April 1918

The Belgians left this morning. They will arrive in Japan in time to see the cherry trees flowering.

During the last few days one has felt a certain movement of dissatisfaction forming against the Germans, but this movement is in danger of being turned into a wave of xenophobia against all foreigners.

Today there was a rather serious incident at our station, provoked by the passage of a train-load of corn destined for the Germans who are occupying Finland. The railwaymen went on strike, uncoupled the engine and unbolted one of the rails. But on orders by telegram from Moscow, the local Soviet insisted on the departure of the train: there was a fight, and after several shots had been fired the train left. The angry workmen tried to manhandle the members of the Soviet, and things would have gone badly had not some Bolshevik speakers arrived from Moscow during the evening. In this country fine words are all that is needed to rouse the masses.

In the Embassy people are exaggerating this incident, and they think that it means there is a reaction against the Germans. This, I believe, is a profound error. The people here are no more angry with the Germans than with anyone else: the only feeling which moves them is selfishness. They are quite rightly annoyed at seeing a trainload of provisions slip through their hands when they are short of everything: it matters little to them whether these provisions are meant for the Germans, or anyone else. The wife of the bell-ringer in the Kremlin, who was showing me round the tower one day, mistook me for a German and had in fact been most agreeable. As I tried to point out her mistake, she answered: "It's all the same to us: we don't understand what it's all about! As long as we have bread."

And yet it is not quite the same thing on the confines of the occupied regions, doubtless because one only sees Germans there, and not other foreigners. In several places, Red Guards and peasants still attack isolated detachments, and the authorities have tried in vain to establish a neutral zone between the occupied regions and those which are still under Soviet direction.

The Germans are masters in the Ukraine. And in fact they have behaved with perfect correctness towards those of our officers who are still in the country and have done everything possible to facilitate their departure, even sending German officers to accompany them as far as the other side of the lines. Unfortunately the countryside is still infested with gangs of sailors and *tovariches* who do nothing but get drunk, pillage and murder. The officers of the Donop Mission have several times almost been in trouble because of these savages, who have no respect for anything.

In Finland the Whites are advancing, and today it has been announced that they have reached Byelo-Ostrov, from where they will be able to take Vyborg in the rear: it is the last resistance centre of the Reds.

Vologda, Thursday 25th April 1918

Chicherin, People's Commissar for Foreign Affairs, yesterday presented the Ambassador with a request for a denial of the statements which he had made a few days ago to the press representatives of Vologda on the landing of the Japanese at Vladivostok and the possibility of Allied intervention against the Germans on the Eastern front, *in agreement with Russian public opinion.*

The government of People's Commissars at the same time made a statement to the Moscow newspapers announcing that it had asked for the recall of M. Noulens, in a wireless communication addressed directly to the French government. As a matter of fact the Bolsheviks have no great illusions and one senses their impotence behind all this bluster, as they conclude by recognizing that "the working people of Russia can do nothing for the moment, but they will remember when their hour comes". . . . It ends rather unexpectedly with recriminations against "the harsh treaty of Brest-Litovsk"! The document is therefore not inspired by Mirbach, as over-simple people believe . . . unless it is a trick to allay suspicion.

This incident is most inopportune just at the moment when the Ambassador and his family are about to settle into the girls' high school, which has been requisitioned for him.

Vologda, Friday 26th April 1918

The incident between Chicherin and M. Noulens has aroused strong feeling . . . but as everything ends in *razgavors* in this country, I feel sure that it will sort itself out.

And yet the situation now is somewhat strained, the more so because on top of this business, there now comes the discovery of suspected relations between the 'counter-revolutionaries' of Siberia and certain Allied consuls. Reports on the subject have been published by the Peoples' Commissariat, who have sent a note to the Allied powers demanding the recall of the consuls in question.

The arrival of the German representative in Moscow has perhaps got something to do with the arrogant attitude of the People's Commissariat, but I feel it is largely our fault. The Allies have a whole gang of officious agents in Moscow—Sadoul for us, Robins for the Americans, Lockhart for the English—who flatter the Soviets too much, and make them believe that the Allies are ready to recognize them. The Bolsheviks think they are supported by the Military Missions, and they have gone so far as to state in print that M. Noulens' statements were disapproved of by the French officers. Their plan is to divide the Allies, and even the Missions of the same power: it would be a mistake for us to let them have their way!

We have had a few details of Mirbach's establishment: he has been in Moscow for a week with the title of 'Head of Mission and German Minister to the Republics of Russia, the Ukraine and Finland'. The presenting of his credentials has raised several problems of procedure which no previous 'precedent' has helped to solve.

At first M. de Mirbach wanted to present them to Lenin as head of the government, but it was decided that Lenin is not qualified and that the President of the Executive Committee of the Soviets, *tovarich* Sverdlov, is the person to be approached. At first Count Mirbach was supposed to go in uniform ... then in evening dress. ... After having discarded both the frock coat and the morning coat, he ended by agreeing to the request of the *tovariches* and going in a suit, and was thankful not to have to wear overalls or a mechanic's blue dungarees. Sverdlov had prepared a beautiful propaganda speech lasting for an hour, but apparently Mirbach did not give him time to extract this literature from his pocket and left after the first introductory part, taking his leave in a few brief words.

The Turkish representative, Kiamil Pasha, has arrived too, as part of Count Mirbach's luggage. The Bolsheviks were rather surprised to see him, as they have had no news of the peace having been ratified by Turkey. They took advantage of his presence to raise a few protests against the continuing operations in the Caucasus. But Kiamil got out of it by saying that he represented his country with the Republics of Russia, the Ukraine and Finland ... but that he was not in any way delegated to the Republic of the Caucasus and that it was for them to settle matters with Turkey.

The Austrian representative has not yet been appointed, though Count Forgach is being mentioned. As for Bulgaria, it is likely to be old Mandjarov, who was formerly Bulgarian Minister to the Tsar: he showed himself to be so favourable towards the Allies at the beginning of the war that there was a rumour that he had been shot by order of King Ferdinand on his country's entry into the war.

We have also had news of Petrograd from various travellers who report that everything is quiet there. A lot of German prisoners are to be seen, mostly officers. They are carefully selected, and any suspected of contamination by the Bolsheviks are immediately repatriated. They are all dressed in new uniforms, and thus are all the more impressive, and more protected against the revolutionary fever. Apparently there are only a few Austrians, who are much less reliable and are not kept in Petrograd.

In spite of difficulties between the Peoples' Commissars and the Ambassador, the Soviet here continues to be very agreeable and it has invited the Ambassador to a performance tonight, in aid of the refugees. He did not want to go, so I represented him. The theatre is a very strange building, with its huge gable of carved wood and its façade made of logs. But the play, a tragedy, was terribly boring, and the audience did not make up for the boredom of the play!

Vologda, Saturday 27th April 1918

Today I spent a long time visiting the Grand Duke Nicholas Michael. He is living in two rooms on the first floor of a wooden house at one end of a courtyard, and he received me in a small room furnished most modestly, with a plain white cloth on the table. As I sat in a shabby armchair in this miserable place I thought of the vast palace on the Court Quay . . . the drawing-rooms filled with works of art and historical souvenirs . . . and the panelling of the council chamber of the Five Hundred which covered the walls of his study.

The Grand Duke has practically no illusions: he is fully aware that everyone has had enough of the Bolsheviks but feels that there is nobody to give them the final push. As one of the Commissars himself said: "We are dead, it's quite true, but I can't see the grave-digger yet."

After having reviewed all the possible candidates for the Empire, he discarded them all as being incompetent: the Grand Duke Sandro of Leuchtenberg, whom certain people have mentioned as a possible Emperor and the Grand Duke Paul, in particular, most provoked his sarcasm. He took advantage of it to recite the usual tirade against "the Paley", whom he detests: he maintains that she is very proud of the fact that her son Vladimir has been included in the banishment list of the real Grand Dukes.

He considers Japanese intervention to be Utopian because he says that they will never involve themselves far enough inside Siberia to be any danger to the Germans. Talking of the difficulties they would encounter, he recalled those which he had met during the Russo-Japanese war, when at least the transport of Russian troops was being carried out in their own country and everything was organized, as much as there ever can be any organization in Russia.

The Grand Duke told me that, for the moment, they are leaving him more or less in peace, as well as the Grand Duke George who is also at Vologda; but he is afraid for the future. The Bolsheviks take no notice of the local Soviet, which is moderate, like all the governments of the North. It is for this very reason that they have not left the Grand Duke Serge and the Constantinovich princes at Viatka, but have transferred them to Alachevsky in the Urals, a centre where the workers are in the majority and have a very different spirit to that of the good *moujiks* of Viatka.

The Grand Duke Paul is still at Tsarskoye and is the only one to have escaped banishment thanks, people say, to Princess Paley's efforts, which fact has contributed not a little to the Grand Duke Nicholas' bitterness towards them.

Vologda, Sunday 28th April 1918

Lubersac has arrived from Moscow, in a superb drawing-room compartment which must have been part of some Grand Duke's train. He quite simply appropriated it about two months ago, and travels in it on all the railway lines of Russia.

He has become infatuated with the Red Army and believes that there is something to be done. . . . True that he is such a liar that one never knows whether what he says corresponds to what he thinks . . . unless, since he has found the way to get into Trotsky's good books, he is under the spell of his charm: the fascination of the serpent.

According to him, Red Guards are fighting the Germans in many places, and if they were supported they could seriously worry our enemies. René Marchand, whom I have also seen, has the same illusions; he has always been a fanatic.

The news from France seems better. The realization of unity of command on our front will alter things considerably. But it is nevertheless unfortunate that it should have taken four years of so many failures and so many deaths to realize that one cannot make war in a state of anarchy, and that there must be someone in command whose decisions apply to everyone. . . . What a lesson to the democracies!

Vologda, Monday 29th April 1918

Our life at Vologda continues, a little monotonous but full of charm. The new-born spring clothes everything in light and colour, and I enormously enjoy my strolls through this big village, where one feels so far away from what is known as civilization. One can already go out without an overcoat, the 'white nights' will soon begin, and after dinner the sky already starts to take on that wan green light which is peculiar to the countries of the North.

The scene in the station, which is always picturesque, is changing: in place of the *tulups* or sheepskin coats, and fur hats, notes of bright colour appear, orange or purple skirts and red or blue or striped head-scarves. Yesterday I saw a wonderful group of gypsy women, with dull dark skins and enormous shining eyes. They were dressed in sordid rags, but were so picturesque, with a kind of turban of a yellowish olive green wound tightly round the head over faded blue veils, and oriental sashes marking the waist-line under their rags. They were sitting, hieratic and immobile, nibbling sunflower seeds without even moving their heads when speaking. Beside them stood superb, dishevelled men, dragging cast-off soldiers' clothes as though they were state robes. A gang of filthy brats with fuzzy hair crawled all round them.

Trains full of French and Belgians from the Donetz Basin have been passing through here all the time. All these unfortunate people are packed into *tepliuchkas*, or goods vans, in which stoves have been installed: but the interiors of these vans are very different to those occupied by Russians. Everything has been arranged as well as possible, with straw mattresses and bunks to sleep on, and so on. Nevertheless, the journey from the Donetz Basin to Murmansk, which lasts several weeks by 'slow train', must be very trying for the women and children. For food, drinking water and fuel, they depend on what can be found at the stations. These people are wonderful and manage to keep their good spirits in the midst of their trials: they seem delighted when the Ambassador goes to see them in their train, which he does with a very good grace.

Without even being forewarned we know at once when there are French people in the station, just from seeing little short men appearing, smoking pipes and with caps on their heads—Frenchmen always wear caps for travelling. They run to the buffet, or queue up with the *tovariches* by the urns from which hot water is distributed. . . . They are so different to the people here, and one can see at a glance what distinguishes the two races from each other!

Vologda, Tuesday 30th April 1918

The incident between M. Noulens and Chicherin is far from settled, and it could easily end in our departure . . . unless the Bolsheviks put us inside, instead of putting us out. But it would surprise me if they did, because Russians always do more talking than acting. So I am not unduly disturbed by the Peoples' Commissars' announcement that "if in three days the French government has not complied with the demand addressed to it by radio and recalled M. Noulens, they will take the measures which the situation calls for."

At the same time as publishing this ultimatum, the newspapers give lengthy details of the Embassy's move to Vologda and of all the alterations which are being made to the girls' high school to house it! What incoherence!

The Bolsheviks' position seems to be getting more and more precarious: the workers themselves are beginning to have had enough. The railwaymen, and the workmen who are at work on the future Embassy, do not hide their feelings about the régime. One of them said to me: "We were happier under the Tsar: then, there were judges who sent one to Siberia. Now, one is shot without trial. . . ." In Petrograd itself during the last elections of the Soviet, the Bolsheviks suffered a setback, although the elections were conducted under public scrutiny and barefaced pressure.

It is said that the Social Revolutionaries are counting on tomorrow, the 1st of May, to demonstrate against the present powers.

It seems in fact that there is some attempt among the opposition parties to come to an agreement and fight together against the common enemy, to establish a coalition government until a Constituent Assembly can meet.

Our support could crystallize these attempts and end in the overthrowing of the Bolsheviks, but we would have to act quickly to prevent the Germans from taking over this role. By taking the initiative we would force them to play their other card against us and support the present régime, which would discredit them and have the most disastrous consequences for them from all points of view.

Since we did not know how to make use of the Bolsheviks by gaining an influence over them when there was still time to do so, as I would have liked us to do, let us at least profit by the policy which we have pursued and reap the benefit of having refused to recognize them.

But I am afraid that we will persist in our inaction! The real cause of this attitude is the old basic illusion we had in our country about the Russian revolution, which people have still not understood. The Russian revolution is not the revolution of the intellectual demanding freedom of thought, of the peasant wanting land, of the workman rising against the employer, of a nation whose patience is exhausted by the excesses of a régime . . . it is simply the revolution of the soldier who does not want to go on fighting. And from the start the revolutionary nucleus was formed by the *Council of Soldiers' Deputies*, which constituted the ferment of disorder and the element of dissension. The truth about the revolution and its aims was spoken during one of last year's offensives by the soldier whose answer to Kerensky's cry of "Forward for land and liberty!" was "What use are land and liberty to me if I am killed? . . . Peace comes first."

All this is basically very human, and I cannot understand people who hurl invective against the Russians and call them traitors. When Russia undertook not to make a separate peace, she undertook to carry on a war like all other wars. But the catastrophe into which Europe is plunged has nothing in common with war as it was understood at the moment when Russia signed this undertaking. All undertakings have broken down through the force of circumstances, and one cannot expect a country to perish in order to fulfil its agreements. And if the Russian people have understood the position better than the others and have not allowed mere words to hide the reality from them, can we blame them for it? After all, we had been warned a long time ago, and it is certainly our own fault that we let ourselves be taken in by Kerensky's bluster, instead of listening to the voice of the Russian people, who wanted peace and begged us to join with them in obtaining it. For it was the entire people who wanted peace, and not only the Bolsheviks, as is claimed in France. The Bolsheviks only succeeded because they fulfilled the hopes of the whole nation.

The bag arrived today via Murmansk. It brings news dating from the end of March.

Vologda, Wednesday 1st May 1918

A very quiet day. In Moscow and Vologda there have been the usual processions but no serious demonstrations against the ruling power.

At Vologda the station was decorated with red banners and festoons of fir branches framing red cloth placards bearing the usual inscriptions in large letters: "Long live the International", "Long live the brotherhood of nations", and so on. In the town, people had hung a few telegraph poles with garlands of fir branches and streamers of red paper, and in the evening some lanterns were lit.

Towards midday an aeroplane made a few loops over the town and the railway and came down as low as the station 'to greet the Allied representatives', almost touching the roofs of our carriages and putting the crows to flight! That was all: one year of revolution has sufficed for everyone to have had enough of the First of May! In fact the Patriarch had banned the celebration, which coincided this year with the Orthodox Holy Thursday, and in the evening it was a strange contrast to see crowds of the faithful coming away from the service with their candles, walking past the meagre official illuminations. The Russian soul remains faithful to tradition, and between the priests and the Bolsheviks it is the priests who have won tonight!

Vologda, Thursday 2nd May 1918

The situation is becoming more difficult. Yesterday evening the

258

orderly who went to take the Embassy telegrams to the telegraph office came back without having been able to send them off, with a note signed by a certain Lapin, which the official in charge handed to him with a very embarrassed look.

It was an order from the Soviet instructing telegraph offices to refuse all coded telegrams, including those from foreign representatives. They are only allowed to correspond in code with their governments by special authorization in each case from the People's Commissar for Foreign Affairs.

This restriction does not appear to be a consequence of the Noulens–Chicherin incident nor of the alleged counter-revolutionary conflict in the Far East, in which our Consuls are said to be involved (although as a result of this business our Consul at Irkutsk has already been prevented from telegraphing in code). It is said that this measure has been taken by way of reprisal against the fact that in France and in England Bolshevik agents cannot telegraph to Moscow in code. Be that as it may, if we do not come to some arrangement with the Soviets our position here will become very awkward: we will have to organize frequent couriers between the various Consulates to carry the telegrams to Murmansk and then transmit them from one of our battleships' wireless stations. An organization of this kind seems impossible with the railways in their present condition.

Vologda, Friday 3rd May 1918

Ludovic Naudeau has just come from Moscow and was telling me about Count Mirbach's German Mission. It occupies the Berg palace which—oh, the irony of things!—had been chosen last year to be the French Embassy. The building has been requisitioned by the Bolsheviks and put at Mirbach's disposal, but he has refused to accept the requisitioning and insists on compensating the dispossessed owner. The newspapers have made much of this gesture and compare Mirbach's tact with Commander Gallaud's stinginess: he also has been installed in a requisitioned house but it never entered his head to compensate the proprietor. The Ambassador immediately ordered our Naval Attaché to pay up too, and to get himself reimbursed by his Ministry. It has come a bit late in the day.

On the other hand the Russian newspapers seem very offended that Count Mirbach is accredited in the name of the Chancellor and that he therefore represents the German government, and not Germany and his sovereign. This shows great cunning on the part of our enemies, who can always claim that they did not send a regularly accredited diplomatic representative to the Bolsheviks. The People's Commissars, in spite of the scorn which they pretend to have for diplomatic formalities, have sensed the implications very clearly and have reciprocated by accrediting their envoy in Berlin, *tovarich* Joffe, to the German government. The Emperor William can thus dispense with having to invite him to his receptions.

On the whole Naudeau is rather pessimistic and regrets that he was not listened to this time last year, when he said that from the moment when our principal ally wished to retire from the fight, we should have tried to make peace.

He is afraid that the Germans will find enough human material among the half Russian, Esthonian, Baltic and Polish populations to balance the support which the Americans are giving us . . . and that some day they may even succeed in making the Russians fight each other! I think he exaggerates on this subject! He too is very sceptical regarding Japanese intervention and thinks that they will only act if it is to their personal advantage, and that they will be too wise to venture far from their base.

Everything is quiet in Petrograd . . . the theatres are open and they are performing *The Valkyrie* at the Mariinsky. Mirbach's arrival has at least given the Russians the chance to hear some good music and has saved them from the eternal *Tosca*. It is said that the Germans are preparing to occupy the town and that they are only waiting for an excuse to make their entry.

In fact, people are literally dying of hunger there, whereas here we are well fed: at a price, you can find everything except sugar. There is near-white bread, meat, game, milk, butter and eggs. Fish is very cheap and some of it is excellent: carp, perch, sturgeon, *lesha* (bream), salmon, *sudak* (Danubian pike-perch), *sigui* (similar to Irish pollan), small fish for frying, and so on.

Vologda, Saturday 11th May 1918

Claude Anet has come back from Petrograd, where the question of food supplies is becoming more and more difficult. One pays up to eight hundred roubles for a sack of flour and one thousand roubles for a *pouds* of sugar. This amounts to famine.

The Bolsheviks there are intolerable and Claude Anet has become acquainted with their prisons, having been arrested on the First of May, together with his pretty secretary. They searched his papers to try and find some trace of a counter-revolutionary plot but they could find nothing and, thanks to the contacts which he has in almost every circle, he was set free a few hours later.

The scene in the prison is dreadful: political prisoners and common law thieves are all penned in together, and they gather in groups of four or five to eat *kasha* out of the same bowl. While he was there they shot some hooligans in the courtyard, who had been caught red-handed looting a shop.

Terror reigned in the prison, as there was a rumour that a movement was forming in the town against the Bolsheviks, who had let it be known that at the first warning all prisoners were to be shot: preparations had been made to this effect, such as armed soldiers and machine-guns in the corners. Towards evening a cannonade could be heard in the direction of the Neva, and the unfortunate people thought that their last hour had come; but most luckily for them it was only the fleet berthed near the Nicholas Bridge, which was celebrating the First of May by letting off fireworks.

Among the prisoners were many women and some quite young children. What happens is that when the Bolsheviks are unable to arrest the man they are looking for, they shut up the whole family until he comes and surrenders. . . . Soon they will start torturing the children to force the fathers to give themselves up. . . . And less than a year ago these people could only talk of the respect which is due to the liberty of the human being!

Vologda, Tuesday 14th May 1918

Just lately we have been continually solicited by representatives of all parties, from the Right to the most advanced Social-Revolutionaries, all asking for our support against the Bolsheviks. But faced by our indecision, they are gradually turning away from us and towards the Germans, who have already restored order in Helsingfors and Kiev.

It seems that for the moment the parties of the Right have better hopes than the socialists, who are still the slaves of their revolutionary ideology. So I am sorry that we should be 'flirting' with Sakinov and that we cold-shoulder General Horvath because he is a 'reactionary'.

In various parts of the country the peasants are clamouring for "their" Tsar. But it is the religious movement in particular which seems to me an interesting symptom.

In Petrograd the Bolsheviks had forbidden the Holy Week children's processions, but they had to put up with a tremendous demonstration which took place on Sunday and which they could not prevent. An enormous crowd, said with the usual exaggeration to be two hundred thousand people, marched along the Nevsky Prospekt carrying ikons and banners, following about a hundred priests wearing their regalia.

In Moscow they had draped two of the Kremlin frescoes with red material, under the pretext of putting up decorations for the First of May. On the First of May the material was seen to be torn from top to bottom and the ikons were once more visible. This accident (if it was caused by the wind) or incident (if caused by some skilful hand) took on a miraculous character in the eyes of the people. Large crowds came on pilgrimage to the ikons, foreseeing in the torn pieces of the red banner the approaching end of the revolutionary régime. The Bolsheviks have been unable to prevent these gatherings and will probably be obliged to allow the planned expiatory procession to take place.

As well as the revival of religious feeling one must take into account the famine, which daily becomes more threatening. In Petrograd the bread ration is forty-five grammes a day—and it is bread made of straw. For three days none was issued at all, and on the fourth day it was replaced by a ration of forty-five grammes of more or less frozen potatoes. A pound (or four hundred and fifty grammes) of pork costs twenty-three roubles, and beef or horsemeat over ten! In various places there have been violent demonstrations and Red Guards have fired on workmen. There has been shedding of blood between the régime and the workers, just as there was before between the Tsar and his people.

Ill-feeling against the Bolsheviks takes a mystical and violent form at the same time. This is dangerous in Russia, and if this double force were organized nothing would be able to resist it. But some direction is needed to co-ordinate the Russian masses and support the violence with mystical inspiration: it is up to us to take the lead and prevent the Germans from doing so. But one must keep to a purely Russian formula in order to make use of these movements, which are so typical of the very spirit of Russia.

Therefore the intervention in Russia which so many people are demanding must not be in the nature of an intervention against Germany for the purpose of re-forming the Eastern front: this would be doomed to failure. It is Utopian to believe that we will ever persuade the Russians to take up arms again: peace is what they want, above all else.

But as long as the war lasts we must prevent our enemies from making use of the resources which, in spite of everything, are still considerable. In my view, our plan of action should be limited to this, without trying to foresee what will become of Russia later. . . . And indeed I do not share the fears of people who are afraid that the Germans will establish themselves for good in Russia where, they say, they will be able to found a fine colony all the more easily for not having to cross the seas, the profits from which would largely compensate for all the losses incurred elsewhere. The colonization of Russia by the Germans—or by us—seems to me impossible: it would be like trying to build something lasting on shifting sands. Therefore we should act with only the present situation in view. . . . What we ought to fear is that the Germans, by delivering the Russians from the Bolshevik yoke, will be able to take advantage of the resulting infatuation, fleeting though it may be, to obtain facilities which would be valuable to them in the present state of the country and would allow them to go on with the war, in spite of the blockade. It is therefore up to us to play the part of the liberators of Russian soil and make sure of getting the credit for it. To achieve this, the Allies will have to send the necessary few regiments to Archangel to turn the Japanese expedition into an isolated incident, so that it loses the character of a yellow invasion and comes within the category of an Allied crusade for the deliverance of the Russian people, oppressed by the Bolsheviks. It ought to be possible to spare a few thousand soldiers from our front without compromising its unity since, if one can believe the communiqués from our Transatlantic friends, there are so many Americans in France!

The necessity for *Allied* intervention is insisted on by everyone here. The Ambassador calls for it every day, while at the same time he cherishes the illusion of forming a new front against Germany. Order-loving Russians have realized the necessity for it: they accept and want this intervention. All the people whom Chevilly saw, from Krivoshein to the Patriarch Tikhon, are agreed on the urgency of achieving it. Krivoshein told him quite bluntly that if the Allies do not make up their minds, Russia will be obliged to turn to the Germans, who have acquired great prestige from the events in Finland and the Ukraine.

It is time to make up our minds, as our indecision benefits our enemies and for us, last week was disastrous.

Vologda, Wednesday 15th May 1918

The theatre of Vologda is giving a season of opera, starting with *Tosca*! Are we going to see performances of Wagner like in Petrograd, where at this moment they are giving *The Valkyrie* at the Mariinsky Theatre, and *Parsifal* at the Drame Musical?

It appears that the performances, although heavily attended, are rather mediocre; the scenery in particular is wretched, and the absence of discipline produces the same deplorable results in the orchestra as in the rest of the country. Which is saying a lot. . . .

Vologda, Thursday 23rd May 1918

The Grand Duke Nicholas Michael came to see our establishment and, after having a long talk with the Ambassador, he spoke to me about the fate of some of the members of the Imperial family.

The Emperor, the Empress, the Grand Duke Alexei and the Grand Duchesses really are at Ekaterinburg. The Russian soldiers guarding them have been replaced by former Austrian and Hungarian prisoners-of-war who had joined the Red Army. The Bolsheviks were afraid that the sensibilities and fundamental good nature of the Russian soldiers would be stirred by the contact with the Imperial family. The only original members of his suite still with the Emperor are General Tatichev and Doctor Botkin. Prince Dolgoruki, who was able to stay with him at Tobolsk, is shut up separately in Ekaterinburg prison, together with Prince Lvov, the former leader of the first revolutionary government. . . . What a lesson for him it must be, to be detained so near to the Emperor . . . he must be having bitter thoughts on the result of one year of revolution!

The relations of the Imperial family who were at Ekaterinburg before the Emperor and his own family were sent there have been moved to Alachevsky, a small industrial centre in the Urals. The Grand Duke Serge Mikhailovich is there, the Princess of Serbia, the Princess Constantin and Vladimir Paley, and the Grand Duchess Elizabeth, widow of the Grand Duke Serge who was murdered by Savinkov. The Grand Duchess was arrested in the convent in Moscow to which she had retired, supposedly, it is said, as the result of a visit from Count Mirbach.

The Queen of Greece, after some hesitation, ended by accepting the offer of a special train from the Emperor William, to go and join her son King Constantine, who is rather seriously ill. On the other hand the Dowager Empress apparently asked to be sent back to Denmark through Austria, Switzerland, France and England as she did not want to travel through German territory.

Finally, that Grand Duke Nicholas Nikolaievich is still in the Crimea where—oh, the irony of it!—he has been saved by the Germans, who treat him with great respect.

Dmitry is still in the English Legation in Teheran and there is some question of his serving in the British Army in Mesopotamia! He will be quite irresistible as a Highlander!

Vologda, Saturday 1st June 1918

News from France. Public opinion is white hot—Clemenceau is worshipped like an idol. . . . And after all, the Hindus do worship Siva who is the incarnation of evil, and Kerensky too became an idol.

Apparently it is no good saying what you think, and people are living under a régime of denunciations and postal censorship. . . . If the unfortunate people in France whose heads are being stuffed with propaganda could see what I have seen here, perhaps they would not be quite so optimistic.

In fact I persist in believing that our position is bad. In the pincer movement formed by the Franco-British front and the Russo-

Rumanian front we had a fairly good method of overcoming the enemy coalition. One of the prongs of the pincer has been broken: we can reinforce the other prong as much as we like, but it will never be a pincer again and you can't pull a well-hammered nail out with pincers which only have one jaw left . . . and God knows, that nail is well hammered in. Whatever anyone may say or do, American aid can never replace Russian aid . . . even the limited aid which Russia was able to give us. And so, what next? . . .

Regarding the business of the Emperor of Austria's letter, from here I cannot judge whether the government was right or wrong to refuse to negotiate with Vienna. Whether it was a trap laid by a very perfidious enemy, or an approach made in good faith by a chivalrous young prince whose wife is a Bourbon, I have no means of pronouncing an opinion. What I regret is that the people who rule us should once again have forgotten the traditional rules of French politeness: one does not publish letters which one has promised to keep secret. We were perhaps—but only perhaps—politically astute, but we certainly behaved like cads.

People believe now that you have deserved well of your country when you have grossly insulted the enemy. . . . In the past, people knew how to be courteous to an enemy . . . which did not prevent them from fighting him.

Even here I am struck by the way in which good manners have disappeared since the war. Everyone coming from France, whether soldiers, civilians, businessmen or journalists, appears to be either shy or arrogant, either swaggering or not knowing what to do with their hands. From looking at them, and particularly from hearing them speak, I fail to recognize the Frenchmen of other days. The officers are the ones who shock me the most. They seem to take a pride in looking dishevelled, in the manner of the '*poilu*' . . . and when by chance any of them react against this, they get themselves up with deplorably bad taste which gives them a sham and foppish look, like N.C.O.s on the spree!

Vologda, Sunday 2nd June 1918

In the Ukraine the Germans seem to be having difficulties with the inhabitants and even with the Hetman Skoropadski's government, in spite of having supported its formation.

People say too that in Finland General Mannerheim is beginning to have had enough of German tutelage and that he is thinking of sending in his resignation.

Meanwhile Poznansky, who has just been staying in Finland on his way back from Sweden, says that the country has been transformed and that the worthy Finns, who did no military service under the Tsar, have been seized with a passion for soldiering: at Helsingfors it is nothing but troops parading to the sound of German marches. I doubt if it will last for long. . . . The Finns are too intelligent to be militarists for long and they will soon regret the time when there were no soldiers in their country . . . and when there was some bread. I therefore doubt whether they will follow the Germans who, it is said, are trying to persuade them to take the Murmansk railway line, with the excuse that ethnographically that part of the country is Finnish. As a matter of fact, this is true, although it is not a convincing reason to go and get yourself bumped off if you can just as well stay at home. I do not therefore share the fears that are inspired by the Russo-Finnish treaty negotiated through the intermediary of Mirbach, which proposes giving the Murmansk region to the Finns, because I doubt whether they will go and take it, specially if it is defended by a few Allied troops. As for the Germans, I think that their French offensive is at any rate keeping them busy enough not to have any troops to spare for expeditions in the Arctic regions!

Vologda, Monday 3rd June 1918

The political situation is becoming increasingly tense. In Moscow, the Savinkov organization has been uncovered by the People's Commissars, who have arrested a number of officers, proclaimed a state of siege, and suppressed all the newspapers. He must have been betrayed by one of his own people . . . naturally!

During this time, and contrary to what I expected, the Czechs seem to be doing some good work. They are said to have occupied several important points on the Siberian railway-line and to have beaten the Red troops sent to fight against them. Apparently the peasants and the Cossacks have joined in supporting them: perhaps it is the beginning of the Bolshevik collapse.

Here in fact the Soviet, although very good-natured, is worried by emissaries from Moscow who are rousing it from its apathy, and a Red Guard is being got together to defend the town against gangs of starving peasants who are said to be marching on Vologda to overthrow Soviet rule. It is the same in all the provinces.

The government is trying to side-track by today decreeing general mobilization and calling on the entire population to arm against the bourgeois, the sharks, and the counter-revolutionaries. But this time it really does seem that the masses are rallying against the Bolsheviks. It is no longer a question of pillaging a few scared bourgeois, but of going into the countryside to snatch the small amount of flour still left to the peasants. I doubt whether they are strong enough to do this.

During this time, as in all times of trouble, the most extraordinary rumours are circulating: there was a story going round yesterday that the Imperial family had been murdered at Ekaterinburg. Fortunately today the news has been contradicted.

It is said too that on the insistence of the Soviets Austria has retracted the offer made to the Dowager Empress of free passage through Austrian territory to reach Denmark by way of Switzerland and France.

Finally, they have announced that Lenin and Trotsky will arrive in Vologda tomorrow, in order to confer with the ambassadors!

All this works wonders on the imagination of the credulous and childish Russians.

Moscow, Wednesday 12th June 1918

We arrived in Moscow five or six hours later than was planned and found the Consul M. Grenard and his assistant M. Labonne and the Military Mission, and so on, at the station. . . . We drove in a procession of cars to the Consulate, where there was a big dinner-party, after which I went to the Kharitonenko palace, where Princess Gorchakov has kindly offered me hospitality.

The journey went very well, in spite of the prodigious quantity of *tovariches*, soldiers, *moujiks*, and peasant women hanging in clusters on to the steps of our carriage, astride the buffers, clinging to the rooftops in the most uncomfortable positions, and loaded with heavy and cumbersome sacks and bundles. I admire these good people, who could see six of us comfortably installed in an immense sleeping-car, not one of whom tried to get in: they patiently relinquished their uncomfortable perch when we wanted to get out for a little air at the stations, at the risk of having their place seized by someone stronger and more agile. . . . And it is the people who are masters here! . . . How fundamentally good-natured these unhappy, perpetually resigned Russians are!

After leaving the plain which surrounds Vologda one travels through regions with rather more valleys and a much more pleasant aspect. There are fairly well cultivated fields, bright green pasture, and forests where the light green foliage of the birch trees stands out against the dark mass of the firs, and where the coverts remind one of the planting of a park. Far into the distance one can see villages with their wooden *isbas*, churches with green roofs and coloured onion domes, and windmills which here and there give the landscape an unexpected look of Holland.

The railway passes through several important towns, notably Jaroslavl with its green roofs and its churches said to be in the purest Russian style and which are reflected in the waters of the Volga.

Most of these towns have picturesque *kremlins* of which one catches glimpses, with their many-coloured walls, massive towers and bell-turrets. At Rostov the *kremlin* is on an island in the middle of a great lake, at Alexandrov it overlooks a river. At about fifty *versts* from Moscow one passes the famous *Lavra* of the Trinity of Saint Serge, one of the best-known monasteries in Russia. It is a strange and magnificent sight, this mass of towers, churches, bell-turrets and domes glittering with gold, surrounded by a crenellated outer wall of dazzling white, the corner towers painted in red and white patterns . . . which look like icing-sugar decoration! The whole thing is dominated by a bell-tower, a sort of bizarre belfry which is the work of Rastrelli and which raises a strange cut-out scaffold-like outline to the sky.

The Kharitonenko palace in which I am staying seems to me vast and sumptuous. I literally get lost in an immense room which seems all the bigger to me for having lived in a railway carriage for four months! The bathroom seems as large as a drawing-room and as high as a cathedral with its marble bath, its mirrors up to the ceiling, its porcelain tiled floor covered in soft thick carpet, its dressing-table with a pretty Dresden looking-glass, and its restful sofas. . . .

Moscow, Thursday 13th June 1918

I got up at dawn to look at the wonderful view which I can see from my window, which looks out over the Moskva Quay, just opposite the Kremlin.

The nights are less 'white' here than at Vologda, but towards two o'clock in the morning the sky takes on the iridescent colour of a rounded opal. The extraordinary jumble of churches, towers and battlements, the pink surrounding wall with its banks of spring greenery, all this strange flowering of bulbous domes, cupolas and turrets seems like a vision in this dreamlike light.

By morning I was able to make out the details: the wall was conspicuous with its bronzed and patinated pink bricks, the high towers topped with angled roofs made of bricks glazed in rich green; the white palaces; the bell-tower of Ivan Veliky with its copper bulb-shaped turrets; the cupolas, domes and onion-domes in every shade of gold from the brightest tinsel to reddish-gold and greenish-gold. It is all reflected in the calm waters of the river, making a truly fairy-tale picture. As always in Russia some of the detail is very poor, but the overall impression is thrilling.

I was able to get inside the enclosure and visit some of the churches and climb up Ivan Veliky's tower, but I could not see the famous treasure of the Patriarchs, much of which was stolen in January. Apparently the thieves have been caught, but the pieces of engraved gold and the wonderful enamels had all been melted down and all that was left of these marvellous objects was some shapeless nuggets with a few splashes of enamel. . . .

The buildings have not been much damaged, although nearly all of them show superficial marks of shells or bullets. Except for one tower of the surrounding wall whose top was blown off by a shell, and an ikon which was torn off the Holy Gate, the damage is negligible. And anyhow most of it is easily repaired, and it is the general effect which is so particularly beautiful: seen in detail, the individual monuments are nothing special, except for the famous church of Vassily Blagennyi in the Red Square in front of the Kremlin.

It is the most fantastic building I have ever seen. The exterior of the church provided the inspiration for the Cathedral of the

Resurrection in Petrograd; but the Moscow model remains unique, and in putting out the eyes of the architect who conceived this extraordinary building, Ivan the Terrible achieved his object—it remains the only one of its kind.

Each part of the building is in a different design and colour, with variegated, primitive flower patterns, the details of which are charming. The domes which surmount the church are in a great variety of shapes: in spiral twists, in the shape of fir-cones, of pineapples, cabochon or faceted, and in all the strangest colours. The interior is even more bizarre. There is no nave, but as many chapels as there are towers: the ceiling of each chapel is high up in the dome above it, in the top of which there is a painting, so cleverly lit that it is as though it were seen through a pair of enormous opera-glasses. The walls are frescoed in fantastic arabesques and flowers surrounding stiff, gilded saints, and you feel as though you were inside an immense wax candle. Each of the chapels is of course divided in two by a richly carved iconostasis covered with ikons, as in all Orthodox churches. All the chapels, of which there are at least a dozen, are connected by winding corridors of unexpected shapes, in which the walls and vaulting are decorated with brightly coloured frescoes representing imaginary flowers and fruit, with wildly flowing arabesques alongside naïve and rustic pots of flowers.

In the Red Square near the church is the stone platform where the Streltsy, who had been condemned to death by Peter the Great, spent their last night. Opposite, the Saviour's Gate with its denticulations and bell-turrets has something Gothic about it. Unfortunately it was grazed by shells which did some damage, but it resisted the attacks of the Bolsheviks just as it survived those of Napoleon's soldiers, who had mined it before leaving Moscow. (It was only by a miracle that the Cossacks were able to put out the fuses.) Decidedly, men are all the same when their instincts are let loose by war: whether they be Germans, Russians, or . . . Frenchmen, they pillage everything without having any plausible military reason for doing so.

The 'heroes' of the revolution are buried near the Holy Gate, and their dilapidated graves are covered with the remains of red flags and wreaths, which are turning into manure worthy of the men who are buried there. Let us hope that soon nothing will survive of these little mounds full of cracks . . . nor of the follies of the *tovariches* who are rotting inside them.

271

The rest of the town provides nothing of interest, except for the picturesque churches you find round every corner, but which are crowded out by the mass of hideous modern houses.

I lunched with the Gorchakovs and some of the other guests in the palace. In fact this enormous house is practically full: the Gorchakovs, the Olives, the American Military Mission, the Italian Military Attaché Ruggieri, Mme Polotsov, Kossikovsky, Obolensky, Captain Sadoul, and so on—about sixty people.

The house consists of a main building with balustraded balconies, and two pavilions with a big courtyard on one side and a garden on the other which is French in style. It is in the most beautiful position in Moscow, opposite the Kremlin which rises up on the other side of the river. The sumptuous interior is full of antique furniture, marbles and tapestries, and valuable paintings by Poussin, Corot, Troyon, Ziem and Diaz. When one realizes that on two occasions gangs of anarchists camped inside the house, forcing the owners to take refuge in a hotel, one must give them credit for the fact that nothing was damaged, and that the only things they took were Sadoul's tooth-brush and a machine-gun belonging to the Red Guard whom Trotsky had ordered to defend the building against the anarchists, and who had wisely made himself scarce as soon as they appeared.

We talked politics, and all the Russians who were there think that the Allies will have to act quickly if they are not to be supplanted by the Germans. The Germans have certainly restored order in the Ukraine: the factories are working again, the land has been given back to its owners, and the people who had appropriated it have even had to pay damages with interest. In spite of the sympathy which our hosts feel towards the Allies, one feels that they admire the Germans and are grateful to them, which after all is only natural when one considers that they were reduced to abject poverty and that thanks to our enemies they have been restored to their former position. They would certainly have much preferred to owe this gratitude to the Allies . . . but can one expect them to resent the Germans?

The Ambassador and his family are living in the house of a rich bourgeois, which is luxurious but in the most abominable taste, and belongs to a certain Berg. He is the brother of the man whose house was destined by Tereschenko to be our Embassy and which now, under the rule of Trotsky, harbours Count Mirbach and his mission.

The resulting confusion is quite funny. It seems indeed that a mischievous God is having fun creating confrontations of this kind, as our fiery General Lavergne is under the same roof as the Herr Consul of Germany!

Moscow, Friday 14th June 1918

My day was partly spent in doing a bit of shopping for all the people left behind in Vologda. It seems that the town was formerly very commercial, and there are some beautiful shops of which the most thriving are in covered galleries near the Red Square. Unfortunately they have got practically nothing left and the shopkeepers are reluctant to part with what little remains, as they cannot replenish their stocks. Prices are exorbitant: there isn't a tie under twenty roubles, and postcards cost a rouble each.

In the restaurants things are even more expensive. I dined with Joseph Noulens in a sort of music-hall beer-saloon, the Empire, where you eat your meal while watching a few dance 'turns'. The entrance fee is ten roubles, and we had to pay one hundred and twenty roubles for one portion of garnished veal, some stewed fruit and a bottle of mineral water. *À la carte*, there was no course under twenty roubles, and it was just radishes, sardines or cucumbers—meat dishes cost twenty-five to fifty roubles. In spite of this, the enormous room was full of every kind of people, from soldiers and *tovariches* to Germans. One and all seemed to deny themselves nothing: caviare, *zakouskis*, and fresh vegetables.

I cannot understand where all these people get the money to live on. They have never spent so much, and they pay out Kerensky notes of forty roubles as freely as ten-kopek pieces before. The *izvozchiks* charge ten roubles for a few hundred yards, and for a slightly longer drive it is fifty roubles.

But alongside all this, what poverty there is! The former aristocrats and the bourgeois are dying of hunger, and when I was doing the street where all the antique dealers are, I happened on a shop kept by Poliakov and other former officials from the Ministry of Foreign Affairs. There in fact they are selling, at fantastic prices, all those things which the former rich have had to part with in order to have enough to eat: silver, jewellery, china, knick-knacks, and even family portraits.

At present, even though both towns are dead, one is struck by the contrast between Moscow and Petrograd. . . . Even without the shopkeepers, Moscow still remains the capital of '*kupietz*',[1] and Petrograd, although without a tsar and without a court, still looks 'residential'.

But what impresses me too is the purely Russian side of Moscow in relation to the western aspect of Petrograd . . . especially its religious and mystical character. Here, it really is *Holy Russia*, from the Saviour's Gate which one could only pass through with un-covered head and in front of which everyone stops to cross themselves even though it is closed, to the Chapel of the Virgin of Iberia, where queues of kneeling worshippers overflow into the street. One continually meets venerable landaus drawn by four horses harnessed four abreast in Russian fashion, containing an ikon which is being taken to a house to heal some invalid or to ward off some calamity.

In spite of the Bolsheviks, the Russia which at first sight seems only to exist on the lacquered *kustaris* boxes is less far removed than one thinks: it is the Russia of painted *isbas* and golden ikons, of *troikas* travelling at the full speed of the trotting horse in the middle with a galloper on either side and pursued by a pack of wolves . . . and in spite of the war and the revolution, in spite of Lenin and Trotsky, one can find it if one takes the trouble to open one's eyes.

I spent the latter part of the evening at the Gorchakovs', where I stayed until dawn listening to Count Apraxin reading his memoirs: he was on the personal staff of the Empress, and he wrote his memoirs day by day during the tragic times which he spent at her side at Tsarskoye Selo. It was very interesting.

Moscow, Saturday 15th June 1918

A very full day, but a very interesting one. I spent the whole morning at the Tretyakov Gallery with Princess Gorchakov and Lazarev.

The collection of pictures of the modern Russian school, so alive and colourful, greatly interested me: luminous landscapes by Guiorgi, the interiors of forests by Chichkin, which so truly convey

[1] Merchant or tradesman.

the brilliant green of Russian woods in spring, scenes of Russian life by Perov, Schwarz, Korzukin, Maximov and Klodt, which by their movement and the realism of the detail remind one of the minor Dutch masters, and paintings of historical events, with figures dressed in the picturesque clothes of the *boyars*, by Surikov and Flavitsky and so on.

Several rooms are devoted to the works of Repin, which are masterpieces of their kind: Ivan III embracing the corpse of his son, the Empress Sophia in prison after the revolt of the Streltsy.... Among the contemporaries: Lanceret, Benois, Syrov, and Somov (the Lady in Blue).

What pleases me with the Russian painters is the way they try to keep away from banality. In this context, I noticed the Scenes from the Gospels by Gary, in particular a portrayal of Christ before Pilate. In it one can sense all the arrogance and disdainful condescension of the Roman Governor, who is seen from the back in his short toga and with his hair cropped in a straight line across the back of his neck, so sure of himself in the superiority which his position and a Roman education have given him. In front of him stands the poor devil of an Asiatic with the face of a visionary, with shining eyes, a tousled beard and unkempt hair, lost in his own dream and unable to answer the Governor's question: "*Quid est veritas?*"

I was also most interested in some very stylized cartoons for some church frescoes by Voznezov, and by the fantastic decorative paintings of Syrov.

The eighteenth century is represented by a series of remarkable portraits of which the best are by Levitsky, who is the equal of our great portrait painters, and by some views of Petrograd and Moscow, certain of which have some of the charm of Canaletto.

The collection of Verestchagins is astonishing. I don't like his rather uninspired style of painting, but his drawing is excellent and forms an incredibly valuable accumulation of the documentation of his epoch: there are views of India and Turkestan, and scenes from the Russo-Turkish war, seven or eight rooms full of them. Here is the famous picture of 'The Apotheosis of War', showing a pyramid of skulls with a flock of vultures: a reproduction of it should be hung on the wall of every school in the world.

After a luncheon at the Consulate at which the most extraordinary wines were served, from some of the best French vineyards

275

and of the most highly thought-of vintages, I went with the Ambassador for the classic drive to the Sparrow Hills. It is from here that *La Grande Armée* had its first fantastic view of Moscow. I must admit I was a little disappointed. Apart from the Convent of the Virgins in the foreground, which is very characteristic, the meanderings of the River Moskva and the wooded hillsides do not make up a typical Russian landscape: you could easily be at St. Germain or St. Cloud. As for the forest of spires, domes and gold crosses which so amazed Napoleon's soldiers, all this has disappeared behind modern houses and factory chimneys, and you can only just see the Kremlin. It is a pity, because the seven hundred churches of Moscow must have presented a fairylike scene, thrusting their golden spires above the dark mass of low *isbas*.

I spent the evening at the *Chauve-Souris* cabaret, where there is a varied programme of singing and dancing and so on. Amongst other things, they sang Fortunio's song by Offenbach with great spirit. The audience was elegant, and the women were pretty and well dressed.

I went afterwards to have supper with the Ambassador, who told me that a Red Guard had shot at his car in the afternoon. . . . Luckily no one was hurt and it seems to have been accidental rather than a deliberate attempt.

Vologda, Monday 1st July 1918

The Bolsheviks have seemed worried during the last few days. In Soviet circles they say that the Japanese are preparing to advance on the Trans-Siberian railway and that Allied fleets have attacked both Murmansk and Archangel . . . that railway lines have been destroyed and bridges blown up, but that the Red Guards are holding out with the strength of despair. This last piece of news is the most surprising, and shows that the Russian imagination is still as freakish as ever and is not defeated by any unforeseen emergency. In truth, the whole thing boils down to a police action at Murmansk, which ought not to be enough to justify Soviet alarm.

What appears to be much more serious is the news of fresh Czech successes and the possibility of a general railway strike. Whatever may come of it, the Bolsheviks are cleverly exploiting all these reports in order to take repressive measures and stifle in advance any movement against their régime. They have arrested several important figures, notably Count Kokovtzov.

In Vologda itself, on the orders of Commissar Uritsky of Petrograd, they have arrested the Grand Duke Nicholas Michael, as well as the Grand Dukes George Michael and Dmitry Constantinovich, and have put them in prison.

The Ambassador has protested to Moscow through our Consul against the imprisonment of the Grand Duke Michael who, in his capacity as a member of the French Institute, is our protégé, and he has asked Scavenius to intervene in our name in Petrograd. This gesture does honour to M. Noulens: up till now our government have behaved like cads regarding the Imperial family, in front of whom our politicians crawled flat on their faces when the Tsar was on the throne.

At the same time the Bolsheviks try to intimidate their adversaries by making a parade of their preparations for resistance. Numerous detachments of the Red Army pass through the station: they have cut up their old green army jackets into points and in their dilapidation they present a particularly repulsive feminine appearance. Sailors sit comfortably installed in first-class carriages with their tarts, vases of flowers on the little tables and machine-guns in the corridors. They are clearly going to go on the spree rather than defend 'the conquests of the revolution'. Large metal goods vans, once intended for the transport of coal, have been transformed with loopholes and armed with machine-guns, and lined with wooden beams filled in between with padding made of sand. Other open trucks are loaded with guns, boxes of ammunition, cars, aeroplanes and war material of every kind.

A special watch is kept on all travellers, and for those who are going in the direction of Archangel or Murmansk they insist on special authorization from the Soviet. None of this is particularly worrying in this delightful country where the more a thing is forbidden, the easier it is to do it. You start by asking for a 'bumaga'[1] from some authority or other, and you end by making one out for yourself, allowing yourself the most extravagant privileges. . . . It works like a charm, provided it carries enough impressive seals.

It seems, however, that we are on the eve of happenings, or at least of incidents . . . although in Russia one can never make

[1] A document, or paper.

prophecies. The real situation seems to be summed up in the statement made to one of my colleagues by a railway mechanic, who said to him: "We are all Bolsheviks when there is no bread. . . . When there is bread, we don't give a damn for them."

Vologda, Tuesday 2nd July 1918

As a result of the threatened railwaymen's strike, the peddling of goods has once more been allowed, and the station is filled with crowds of peasants and women burdened like mules, bowed down under the weight of enormous sacks full of flour and potatoes. All these people with their birch-bark shoes and linen bands round their legs, the women with coloured handkerchiefs on their heads, crawl about between the carriages and camp on the ground among mountains of parcels and bundles, drinking tea out of metal cups or just sleeping on the ground. Near the hot water urn—the *kipitok* —people wait in long lines, carrying their teapots made of blue enamel or patinated red copper.

With Pingaud I wandered for some time in the midst of this jumble, stepping over stretched out bodies and stopping to chat a little and get some impressions of popular feelings about the situation.

An old peasant with a great white beard and hair down to his shoulders pointed out to us an armoured railway truck with its machine-guns: "And to think that we are at peace—peace without annexations or contributions!"

When he realized that we were French, he poured out his heart and vented his hatred of the régime "which is starving Russia", and entreated the '*soyuzniki*' (the Allies) to come and help the peasants to get rid of it. Very soon a circle formed around us and all these good people were talking on the same lines. Decidedly, the Bolsheviks no longer have the support of 'the masses'. Some Red Guards came up and having risked a few remarks against "Imperialist Allies" they got a jolly good dressing-down. As for ourselves, we were afraid of provoking an incident, and therefore made ourselves scarce, but not before saying a few words of thanks and encouragement to these worthy *moujiks*, who are so attractive in spite of everything.

278

Vologda, Wednesday 3rd July 1918

I was able to get some news of the Grand Dukes who are incarcerated in the town gaol, where they are being relatively well treated. They are allowed to walk in the little garden and to see each other; and the prison governor, who seems to be a nice man, shuts his eyes as much as he can to visits from outside. They each have a room and can have their meals brought in. The Grand Duke Nicholas Michael's morale is excellent and he has no complaints, except for the smell of the W.C.s.

He is in fact most courageous and bears his misfortune like a true gentleman. I heard that some time ago, when he was still at liberty, he went for two days without bread. . . . It must be hard, if you think that a few months ago he was a Grand Duke!

Vologda, Saturday 20th July 1918

The Emperor has been executed at Ekaterinburg. The news which we did not want to believe seems certain this time, as we heard it from a reliable agent in the telegraphic communications system, through which the Soviet of Ekaterinburg informed the Commissars' Council of Moscow that "in order to prevent his being removed by the counter-revolutionaries, they had had Nicholas Romanov executed." The Commissars approved, but recommended that "above all it must not be known".

In spite of this precaution the news has spread like wildfire and everyone is prostrated: the people, however apathetic they may usually be, have been stunned by the audacity of their masters of one day, who have dared to kill their tsar.

The fact that the local assembly of a provincial town, consisting of a few peasant revolutionaries and hooligans, has been allowed to take such a grave decision shows to what depths of weakness the power of Moscow has sunk, which before was so jealous of its authority. It has weakly accepted as an accomplished fact this act which could have the most serious consequences, with the sole proviso that "it must not be known", in order to escape the anger of Russia and the censure of the civilized world.

I fear that we are entering an age of Terror. Since the execution of Admiral Chastny, the assassination of Mirbach and the crime of Ekaterinburg, the beast of the people has smelt blood . . . and it will not forget it in a hurry!

Vologda, Sunday 21st July 1918

The horrible business of Ekaterinburg seems to have let panic loose among the Bolsheviks. On an order from Commissar Uritsky of Petrograd, the Grand Dukes were today transferred from their prison in Vologda to Petrograd.

I was able to get into the siding where their carriage had been taken by an escort of Red Guards and I was able to shake the Grand Duke Nicholas by the hand. His courage is wonderful, but his time in prison has greatly aged him and he looked very tired. I was only able to stay for a moment as the Commissar accompanying the Grand Dukes moved everyone away who had gone up to the carriage. This man, dressed in a smoking-jacket with a big black tie was ostentatiously smoking on the doorstep of the carriage, and is one of the most unsympathetic people I have ever met . . . and if we ever return here as masters, it will afford me great pleasure to give him a few nasty moments. . . .

Moreover, when the carriage was connected to the ordinary Petrograd train, he changed his attitude, as the crowd visibly sympathized with the prisoners. He became obsequious and felt it was a good thing to say to me: "I have a French name, I am called Condé. . . ." I answered: "It is the name only, sir, luckily for France. . . ." He pretended not to understand me and allowed me to go near again and talk freely to the Grand Dukes. I was able to tell them that the Ambassador would do everything he could for them, and I undertook to deliver messages for them. Gentil and Armour who arrived at that moment were also able to talk to them. The Grand Duke Nicholas Michael asked us to keep his friend Frédéric Masson informed. He spoke to us of the assassination of the Emperor, which came as a terrible blow to him. . . . He remains very calm and envisages his fate with serenity, but he has few illusions.

The Grand Duke George, in a grey suit and a travelling cap, is the same as ever. He asked us to break the news to the Grand Duchess, who is at present in London.

As for the Grand Duke Dmitry Constantinovich, with his smooth but ill-shaven face, dressed in a suit made of soldiers' cloth and wearing a shabby cap, he looked impecunious but still had the grand air and the majestic bearing of this generation of Romanovs. He recommended his niece, Princess Bagration, to my care: she was there with her two young children, poorly clad in an ugly worn-out dress and a wretched old hat. I busied myself trying to book sleepers for her in my name, but at the last moment Commissar Condé allowed her to make the journey in the carriage with the Grand Dukes.

General Bruner, aide-de-camp to the Grand Duke Nicholas Michael was there with some servants, including the faithful French chauffeur Renhold, who has remained with him all the time and who could not keep back his tears.

We all had heavy hearts. . . . What is going to become of them? The death of the Tsar gives rise to the gravest anxiety.

Vologda, Monday 22nd July 1918

As far as our limited wardrobe allows, we have all gone into mourning for the Emperor, as indeed have all the bourgeois and people in society.

The Bolsheviks have turned savage and have certainly changed during the last fortnight. I am afraid that the Russian revolution, which up to now has hardly shed any blood, has entered a period of Terror.

An officer who was captured at Jaroslavl by the Reds, and who managed to escape from Petrograd where they had taken him and who is now in hiding here, told me that the Bolsheviks are now executing all their prisoners: they take them out of their cells at night and shoot them without any kind of trial. At Jaroslavl, the Whites are still holding out in spite of their munitions and supplies being exhausted and are waiting for help from the Allies which, alas, will arrive too late: the Reds are behaving in the most abominable way, massacring everywhere and even going so far as to bury alive any Whites who fall into their hands. . . . Revolutionaries of every country are all the same, and the Reds of this country are like our own 'Blues', who in the past used to bury the *Chouans* up to their necks and play bowls in this living skittle alley.

In Petrograd, the situation is still very bad. Although the cholera epidemic is dying down there are still numerous victims, some of them in the French colony. The Soviet has decided to mobilize the bourgeois of between eighteen and forty years of age into the Highways Department, in order to bury the cholera victims. They have taken a new census of all apartments in order to house *tovariches* and Red Guards, at the cost of "putting the bourgeois in the cellars", as one of the town councillors has said. The poor bourgeois! One wonders how there can still be any of them left. This is the food ration, copied from an official document, which was allowed them for the first week of July—a theoretical ration as most of them cannot even draw it:—*Ration for two days:* one eighth of a pound of bread (fifty grammes) and five herrings. Red Guards receive in addition half a pound of bread, two eggs and one pound of 'fresh'(?) fish, without counting what they steal.

According to the news from Moscow, the Commissars are refusing to give in to the conditions imposed by Germany, who is insisting on the occupation of the town by a battalion. A little more of this and certain people will be talking about the possibility of an accord between the Allies and the Bolsheviks. Luckily, the Ambassador will be quite unshakeable on this point: inasmuch as we could have recognized the Bolsheviks last October—since we did in fact recognize Milyukov and Kerensky—so now it would be criminal to recognize them at this moment, especially after the assassination at Ekaterinburg, for which they have been outlawed by civilization.

Besides, their attitude has made all reconciliation impossible, because they have suddenly become threatening towards us. The Soviet has sent a note to all the heads of missions ordering that everyone coming to our Embassy must be previously provided with an authorization from the Soviet. This means that all Embassy activities are impossible and that we are to be treated like prisoners. But what can we do? Where can we go? They will never let us go to Archangel, and if the Ambassadors return to the train they are at the mercy of the Bolsheviks, who only need connect it to an engine to send them wherever they please.

We have envisaged the possibility of reaching Archangel by boat on the Vologda and Dvina rivers, and this morning I went to the Navigation company on orders from the Ambassador. But here too there are great difficulties, especially as the water level has gone down considerably and the boats can hardly get as far up as this. And anyhow, would they let us leave?

Vologda, Tuesday 23rd July 1918

A very agitated day, which could have ended badly.

On my arrival at the Embassy, at a little after eight o'clock this morning, I found a note from M. Noulens asking me to join him at the American Embassy, to which he had been bidden by our *doyen* along with the other heads of missions.

The *doyen* had received a telegram from Chicherin saying that in the event of a battle in the town the Soviet authorities could not guarantee the safety of the Embassies any more than that of any of the other houses, and that in consequence the Allied representatives could not stay "a day longer in Vologda" without danger.

Without anyone knowing for certain what imminent battle is referred to in Chicherin's telegram, the heads of missions decided to leave . . . not for Moscow, as Chicherin was counting on a feeling of fear which is habitual with Russians and unfortunately with diplomats too . . . but for Archangel.

I was asked whether it was possible to make up a single convoy with the trains of the various missions, because above all it is necessary to stay together, and whether this convoy could leave that same evening. I answered that at first sight it seemed impossible, as we had seven carriages of the *Compagnie Internationale* for the French, the Serbs and the Italians, four carriages for the Americans and the Japanese, and one for the English, without counting the luggage vans, service cars, etc. . . . But in Russia, where everything is difficult, nothing is impossible and at the station I was assured that everything would be ready for tonight, and that we could leave towards ten o'clock . . . if the Soviets authorized it.

The whole day was occupied in packing, moving house, and so on. The arrival of Gallaud, back from his expedition to Archangel where he went to take the air for two days, has produced even greater panic. He declared that it was absolutely impossible to go there and that things will end badly if we do.

Francis, deeply shaken by these views, already regretted his hastiness of this morning. But M. Noulens held firm, saying that we must make certain of our position and find out if the Allied representatives really are free to move or if they are prisoners of the Bolsheviks. . . . "If they don't let us go," he added, "we can return to our Embassies and the protest will have been made."

The experiment to my mind seemed hazardous, because if the Bolsheviks want to take us to Moscow or anywhere else, all they have to do is to attach an engine to our train and we are trapped.

However, at ten o'clock everyone was installed in the carriages, except for Francis who had definitely cooled off the idea and had stayed quietly dining at home and playing poker, saying that he would come to the station when everything was ready.

And in fact nothing was done at all, and at eleven o'clock our train and the American train were still in their respective sidings and there was no sign of an engine.

After spending the evening in the restaurant-car there was nothing left to do but to go to bed and to say goodbye—or rather "*A demain*"—to Pingaud, who has to stay in Vologda to guard the Embassy. But the worthy Pingaud had no sooner left the carriage than he returned precipitately, saying that the train was surrounded by Red Guards and that nobody was allowed to get off it. I go with him to the doorway and we try arguing with the *tovarich* . . . but it is no good. Pingaud gets angry and sends for their chief, who arrives on the scene. We announce our identity and ask him what right he has to take such steps against us. He replies that he is carrying out the orders of the revolutionary tribunal. Pingaud then orders him to prove his authority. He refuses. Matters worsen somewhat, everyone shouts in turn, and Pingaud tries to get away and go to the Embassy. The exasperated *tovarich* warns us that he will have to shoot if we insist, and he has Pingaud arrested. When I protest at this, he gives the order to arrest me too and two men seize hold of me on the doorstep of the carriage. As they were ready to shoot I could do nothing, and they took me away without even allowing me to get my coat.

It was a tragi-comedy. . . . Pingaud and I, surrounded by soldiers with fixed bayonets, the whole diplomatic corps looking out of the windows, the Ambassador repeating, "And to think that all this time Francis is playing poker . . .", Mlle Fayssat in a dressing-gown with her hair down, our panic-stricken maid shouting "*Gospadin* the Count!" and Spalaikovich furious, tearing his hair out with both hands!

They took us, Pingaud and me, as well as Fradel who had been able to follow us, to the railway station where they shut us up in a room with a sentry on the door. . . . After what really did seem to me rather a long while the Soviet Commissar arrived and naturally gave the order for us to return to the train. Pingaud took advantage of it to hurry back to the Embassy and as for myself, the Red Guards once again took me to task for wanting to stop at the American train on the way: there were only the Chancellery employees there, as Francis and his secretaries were still playing poker in the Embassy. I had to get angry again, but this time I took the initiative and insisted on one of the *tovariches* taking me back to the Commissar.

I had the good luck this time to find Citizen Lapin, with whom I had already had dealings over the arrest of the Swedish consular representative. I protested against the treatment we were getting and insisted on his giving us authorization to circulate freely between the two trains . . . unless the members of the missions were under arrest, in which case I requested to be informed . . . with due warning to think carefully about the consequences this measure could have.

He appeared to be very surprised, whereas in fact the cunning fellow knew exactly what was going on. He told me there had been a mistake and that the men had been posted all round the train to ensure our safety, and not in any way to prevent our free movement. I fully realized that the whole business was engineered in Russian fashion to still further annoy the Allied representatives, but of course I pretended to believe what he told me and thanked him. The station-master arrived to make his excuses for his part in the affair, and we marked our reconciliation with a hearty handshake.

Then I asked Citizen Lapin to come with me to give fresh orders to his sentries. On our arrival at the train we had to submit to a pantomime homily from Spalaikovich who stood framed in the doorway of the Serbian carriage, but this was nothing compared to the scolding Lapin got from Commandant Tartarin-Gallaud, who had at last emerged from his compartment now that all danger had passed. I succeeded in calming his tempestuous complaints, and all ended well. . . . And in fact as it started to pour with rain the whole of the Red Guard vanished as if by magic, which proved that they had finished acting their part and that the little comedy was now over.

Vologda, Wednesday 24th July 1918

The day was spent in long conferences between the heads of missions, as a result of which several telegrams were sent to Chicherin confirming their intention of leaving for Archangel. The People's Commissar answered that they were free to move, but that he all the more regretted their refusal to settle in Moscow because, as it would probably be impossible for them to remain in Archangel, the missions would doubtless be obliged to leave Russian territory.

However, he did not succeed in making the heads of missions decide to move into the suburbs of Moscow, into the beautiful villas which had been appropriated for this purpose. Confident in the knowledge that consent had been given for their departure, the heads of missions finished making their preparations.

The train was finally made up during the evening: it forms a big convoy, to which has been added a further carriage of Red Guards "to protect us", and a carriage which has just arrived from Odessa in which are our Consul Vautier and his colleagues, who have been expelled from there by the Germans. I measured four hundred paces from the head of the train to the tail, and it weighs at least four hundred and fifty tons. . . .

Tovarich Lapin accompanies us as far as Archangel in his capacity as Commissar of the Soviet, with an escort of Red Guards.

As is always the case here, it took a good deal of time to get everything done: first it was the Commissar who was not ready, then it was the Guard who had to get their rations, and then the Commissar went off again to fetch money! At last, at about one o'clock in the morning, we took off with great difficulty. . . . Leaving Vologda means something to me, in spite of everything: the outline of the churches shows up against the wan night sky, which is already growing paler. . . . As we passed by it, I greeted the monastery with its many-coloured towers mirrored in the tranquil waters of the Vologda, while the moon went down behind the cupolas of the church . . . and we set out towards a new adventure.

Archangel, 4th September 1918

Today we learnt of the splendid success of the French battalion which broke up the Bolshevik lines along the railway-line and seized the station at Obozerskaya. Unfortunately this minor victory was not carried off without loss, and a captain and several men were killed.

This success allows of renewed hope, and it should be possible to make the most of it since the famous American reinforcements at last arrived today, brought here in three magnificent transport ships. This amounts to nearly five thousand men who will provide our battalions with valuable support, because, whatever Mr. Wilson's government may think, these reinforcements will be used against the Bolsheviks. As a matter of fact the Americans have sent these troops, not to fight against our enemies, but "to protect the stocks of war material belonging to the Allies". As the Bolsheviks have laid hands on this material and carried it off . . . the only way to 'safeguard' it is to get it back again. The Americans will therefore be able to fight the thieves without thereby 'attacking the rights of peoples' and without 'intervening in the internal affairs of Russia'. . . . They have brought with them two orchestras, or 'bands' as they rightly call them, for one cannot qualify by any other name the bands of evil-doers made up by these ragtime players. The 'band' of sailors from the *Olympia*, which is rampaging round since our arrival in Archangel is going to constitute a danger to our ear-drums.

These sailors' music in fact gives me great pleasure . . . from far off, let it be clearly understood. There is nothing more comical than to see them in their little white straw clown's hats struggling with their big drums and their cymbals, while the slide-trombones are manœuvred by athletic arms into letting out deep bellowings! The favourite tune *Teasing the Cat* (I read the name on a paper over the shoulder of one of the musicians during a lull) is a sort of solo on the big drums, accompanied by the slide-trombones, which could 'tease' not just a 'cat', but a hippopotamus!

Well, perhaps we have good reasons for denying ourselves German music—but the Germans have certainly got better ones for renouncing American ragtime. They will have less difficulty in sticking to their decision than we will.

Archangel, Thursday 5th September 1918

The success at Obozerskaya has been confirmed. The Bolsheviks have retreated about twenty kilometres to the South. But fighting is very severe: there is point-blank shooting in thick cover and in almost impenetrable marshes. The attack on the enemy has also to be made point-blank, as they are entrenched behind mountains of tree-trunks amply furnished with machine-guns. In fact there are not enough men to be able to overthrow these positions and make a good haul: and it is practically impossible to move away for more than a hundred yards on either side of the road, as it is an impenetrable jungle in which one runs the risk of being shot like a rabbit. All the men I have talked to—and they are splendid fellows—are somewhat put off by this very special kind of war, and although they all asked to be sent to Russia they almost regret having left the French front. They say that the Bolsheviks fight courageously; so do the Russian volunteers who are on our side, but it is a savage and merciless fight. The arrival of American reinforcements will, I hope, alter the situation. As always in Russia, the collapse will happen all at once, and when one thinks the Bolsheviks are winning will be the moment when they take flight. The news from the Far East is reassuring: the vice has got a grip, and although its jaws are not very strong, they are starting to come nearer together.

And the taking of Obozerskaya in particular has had a considerable moral effect on the population, and has contributed to the prestige which the German withdrawal in France has added to the Allied cause.

Archangel, Friday 6th September 1918

I went this morning to watch the parade which has been organized in front of the palace of the government for the arrival of the Americans, and on the way I met Lindley with a long face, who told me that all the members of the government were arrested last night and put on to a boat which is now cruising through the White Sea on its way to Solovietzky.

288

The coup was carried off with great cunning by the only two Russians here who are worth anything and whom I believe to have more sincere feelings towards us than any of the others: Captain Chaplin, who was in command of government troops, and M. Startsev of the Kadet party, government Commissar for food supplies.

The heads of diplomatic missions whom I saw at the palace are furious, but I really cannot see why they should have any feelings for this government of social revolutionaries which has caused us nothing but bother. . . . The military on the contrary, and in particular General Poole and his headquarters staff, had radiant faces . . . and even if they took no part in last night's little operation, they cannot have done much to prevent it.

The attitude of the Ambassadors is all the more incomprehensible to me as all this had been more or less foreseen during the last few days and they must have guessed about it from half-hints. . . . Their vague and embarrassed answers could have been taken for tacit agreement by men who had decided to act.

I cannot therefore help feeling that the departure of Tchaikovsky and his gang is a good riddance. They had been getting more and more insufferable and had gone so far as to protest in their newspaper against the "pretension of the Allies" in choosing a town governor from among the officers. Let them stay in the monastery at Solovietsky, where Tchaikovsky will find plenty of ideas for the next religion he wishes to proclaim, and let them leave the Allies to manage things here.

The bulk of the people seems profoundly indifferent. Only a few enthusiasts have protested and have sent a delegation to Mr. Francis, threatening to start a general strike if the Allies do not immediately arrest the organizers of the *coup d'état* and bring back Tchaikovsky's puppets. . . . The poor American Ambassador tried to make these people talk sense. I have never so much regretted not being able to take his place, because I would have invited the gentlemen of the delegation to clear out of their office and thank Heaven to be able to get away scot free, and I would have reminded them that if they take any action there are plenty of prison walls in Archangel which, though they are made of wood, would do the job perfectly well. It is a serious mistake to argue with Russians—one must make a show of strength, as it is the only form of argument they have recognized for centuries.

M. Noulens realizes this . . . but he finds my method repugnant, although it would be the most efficient one. He feels that we ought to make our authority felt by both of the two present parties and to this effect we should get back Tchaikovsky's lot, in order to show the leaders of the *coup d'état* that we do not count what they have done, because it was undertaken without our knowledge. Then a new government would be formed, chosen by the Allies, in which it would no doubt be possible to unite both the arresters and the arrested and bend them equally to our will.

This reasoning seems to me too subtle to be understood by Russians. Tchaikovsky and the people who are demanding his return will pretend that we have given in to them, and the Allies will thus appear to have submitted to the will of the revolutionary delegates. In order that M. Noulens' plan should be accessible to Russian intelligences, we would have to start by locking up the delegates who have been threatening us!

This little *coup d'état* has occupied everybody's minds and there were very few people at the funeral of the unfortunate captain who was killed at Obozerskaya. . . . I went to await the arrival of his body at the landing-stage, to which it was brought by a small steamer. . . . He was a robust, colourful *bon vivant*, whom I had seen a week ago when he was enthusiastic about the idea of getting up a bear-hunt . . . and as I followed the wretched coffin made of badly squared-up boards I thought, with a heavy heart, that it was he who a few days ago was in command of the guard of honour in other similar circumstances. What a horrible thing war is, and what victory could ever make one forget so many deaths? . . .

Archangel, Saturday 7th September 1918

Today there is a certain amount of movement in the town. It all started yesterday evening with an attempt at an electricity strike, but sending a few Allied troops was enough to get the trams going again. The overhead lamps, so dear to the Gallaud family, are once more shedding their unbearably crude light on the heads of the Gallauds' guests, but for half an hour they had been replaced by the much more attractive light of candles.

Unfortunately the Allies did not persist in their determination and had the incredible weakness to tolerate the posting-up of a declaration this morning, signed by two of Tchaikovsky's ministers who had escaped from yesterday's net, in which they call for a general strike. As any appeal to stop working is never addressed in vain to Russians, they listened.

The heads of missions then wanted themselves to put up a notice but, incredible as it may seem, they could find no one to print it. . . . How can one tolerate such defiance in a town where we have our own troops, and where a whole Allied squadron is anchored . . . and what a contradiction it is to send Frenchmen to get killed sixty miles from here by the Bolsheviks and not properly to reprimand the people here for their behaviour!

We have had news from Petrograd: the Bolsheviks have invaded the British Embassy and the Naval Attaché, Commander Cromie, who tried to defend it, has been killed but not before striking down a certain number of his assailants.

I hope that the English will avenge his memory and that they will show themselves to be stronger here, where they have every means of applying force.

Archangel, Sunday 8th September 1918

The heads of missions have had the weakness to give in, in appearance at least, and we are awaiting the return this evening of the men who escaped from the phalanstery, and to whom power will be restored . . . they will be given a little lecture by Francis.

The Bolsheviks have in fact been spreading a rumour that we have got the Grand Duke Michael to come here, that the *coup d'état* was organized for his benefit, and that the Allies were getting ready to re-establish him on the throne. . . . Our heads of missions were afraid of seeming not sufficiently democratic, and they decided in favour of Tchaikovsky and his socialists. It was a clever manœuvre on his part.

As for myself, I feel furious when I think of the weakness of those same people who so violently accused the various Russian governments of lack of strength, and who in Petrograd were always saying: "Oh, if only we had had a few battalions here, it would never have happened!" . . . With four cruisers in the roads here and the town bursting with troops, we give in just like the poor Emperor did. We are just as contemptible as Kerensky himself; and to think that this very day we celebrated the anniversary of the victory of the Marne!

To commemorate this event, a very successful party was given on board the *Amiral Aube*. The buffet was spread out among the guns which were decorated with pennants of many colours and between which was festooned a garland of many-coloured electric lights. In the corners, branches of green leaves were placed in the shining copper cases of the shells which the Bolsheviks had fired against the Allied ships when they entered the mouth of the Dvina. The contrast between all this war material and the ballroom decorations was strange: the immense shafts of the funnels striding across the ship like the pillars of a crypt are surrounded by circular gun-racks, in which the well-kept arms shine out from the mass of greenery and stand out against the brilliant background of flags. An exotic note was provided by the Archimandrite, who was accompanied by a priest with a huge beard and an Armenian colonel who was dressed in an impressive Caucasian uniform.

The staff of the ship were very good hosts, and there are some very agreeable officers among them. One of them, M. Belin, is an excellent violinist and we made a plan to get up a concert of French music in order to raise funds for a monument over the grave of the French soldiers killed by the Bolsheviks.

Archangel, Monday 9th September 1918

I had a happy moment today when I saw the whole of Tchaikovsky's gang disembark from the ship which brought them back from Solovietsky, wandering through the streets, looking crestfallen and shamefaced. As a matter of fact M. Noulens took the precaution of putting a guard on the government palace to prevent them from resuming their functions before coming to the heads of missions for a sort of investiture.

Unfortunately, under the influence of the disastrous Francis, the Ambassadors, instead of treating these people as they deserve, allowed themselves to be taken in by their lies and believed in their good faith.

The result was hardly unexpected. A few hours later the strike committee put up notices thanking the workers for having by their attitude ensured the return of the government, adding that it counted on their renewed help should the government be threatened by "anyone else".

I tore down a number of these notices and I went to the police to demand the removal of the others, and to ask that anyone putting up new ones should be arrested: I only just managed not to get reprimanded for taking this initiative.

Lubersac agrees with me and is very discouraged and predicts that it will all end badly. If our Ambassador were acting on his own I think he would do what is necessary, but his forcefulness has become dulled in too long conferences with Francis and the members of the government. They are people with whom one ought never to have any discussions . . . because when one argues with a Russian one is always in the wrong.

Archangel, Tuesday 10th September 1918

A Czech officer who has come from Ekaterinburg and managed to cross the frontier has given us details about the end of the Imperial family.

After their removal from Tobolsk to Ekaterinburg, the Emperor and his family were kept in a house (the Ipatien house) which was surrounded by a wooden palisade up to the tops of the windows and which allowed no light to penetrate into the rooms in which they lived. They were subjected to every kind of vexation and their last kopek had been taken from them. Count Apraxin was at first able to stay with them: they had taken away his money too, and finally he was separated from them and locked up in the ordinary prison.

It is a fact that it was during the night of the 16th to 17th July that the Emperor was shot by a certain Goloshkin, a Jewish dentist who came from Switzerland in the sealed train which took Lenin through Germany. This man, who called himself a Commissar, had two others with him, called Safarov and Bieloborodov.

According to our informant, the fate of the Empress and the Grand Duchesses seems to have been even more horrible than that of the Tsar. After the entry of the Czechs into Ekaterinburg on the 25th July, a detachment which had been sent to lay hands on a gang of pillaging Bolsheviks who were terrorizing the neighbourhood found the following things near the mine-shaft of Vernissetinsk, about ten kilometres from the town: in a pile of ashes were discovered the remains of a belt and several corsets, a shoe-buckle, a little Maltese cross made of platinum and enamel, some stones from the Urals, a key and various other objects. Count Apraxin was shown these things and apparently formally identified them as having belonged to the Empress and the Grand Duchesses. The belt was the one which the Empress habitually wore, and the little cross was like the ones which it was usual to give to each Grand Duchess at birth. As for the Ural stones, they were those which the Grand Duchesses had bought in his presence to make necklaces, when their pearls and their valuable jewels were taken away from them. Finally, the little key was one which belonged to Apraxin himself, which he remembered having left behind when he was separated from the Imperial family and taken to prison.

It is assumed that the Empress and the Grand Duchesses were murdered by the Bolsheviks in this remote place, and their bodies burned or thrown into the mine-shaft: it was full of water, which was being pumped out in order to carry out a search when our informant left Ekaterinburg. The murderers must have been disturbed while carrying out their crime or else while trying to cover up its traces, doubtless by the arrival of an advance guard of Czech troops.

A glimmer of hope remains, which is that we may be faced with an act which is being staged in order to put people off the scent or to cover up an escape. The objects which were found, of whose authenticity there can be no doubt whatever, may have been put there to give a false scent. . . . But this glimmer is a very faint one.

Archangel, Wednesday 11th September 1918

We are still showing the most incomprehensible weakness and are making every allowance for this government, which is composed of revolutionary socialists as cunning and cruel as the murderers of Ekaterinburg! . . . and purely because they say they are the enemies of Germany! . . .

The government of that old scoundrel of a Tchaikovsky has had all its powers restored to it and we palaver with this gang for hours, arguing whether it can 'legally'(!!??) do or not do a certain thing, put or not put a certain word in its notices. And while the Ambassadors are weighing up each sentence of the government's next proclamation with these people, this rabble have in spite of their solemn promise issued a quite different proclamation and had it posted up in defiance of all of us. And we tolerate it!

The Assembly of the '*zemstvos*' met today and welcomed the heads of missions, accompanied by Tchaikovsky and his gang. This represents a very relative success, if you know Russia. . . . This nation of children cannot refrain from applauding anyone who is the success of the moment, whether it be the Emperor, the Allies, Belgium, Kchessinskaya or Kerensky. But the fate of all these favourites of a day's duration shows how ephemeral Russian cheers can be.

Military operations have once more been halted and the Allies continue to suffer losses. On Monday two Frenchmen and an American were buried, and today I saw nine American coffins go past.

On the other hand, the news from the Far East allows of a certain amount of hope. General Janin is in command out there, and he is a subtle and intelligent man who knows the Russians well. He is one of the only ones who could see straight about Russia and the revolution when he was in charge of the Military Mission, and that is clearly why he has been recalled.

Archangel, Friday 13th September 1918

In Russia there will always be these bizarre arrangements and situations which would be incomprehensible anywhere else.

In this way, we have just been informed by Moscow that we may enter into wireless communication with the Czechs at Samara![1]

The story of the Samara wireless station is itself one of those truly Russian episodes. It was the Bolshevik radio service itself which sent two railway carriage-loads of wireless material to the Czechs. Our agents got them to their destination, although the Czechs are at war with the people in Moscow. . . . One must have lived in Russia to be able to visualize what this odyssey represents in the way of disorganization, compromises, false or genuine documents and seals, treachery and . . . bribery.

Autumn in Russia, like spring too in this country, has the intense charm of things which only last a short time. And in the same way as the green of springtime, the golds and reds of autumn have an

[1] Now Kuibishev.

extraordinary primitive brilliance which I have never seen anywhere else. The yellow of the leaves, the black and white zebra stripes of the birch trunks, and the grass which is like the green in a child's paintbox, form a picture of violent clashing contrasts, just as the Russian soul itself does. When contemplating them one can understand the opposing colours and the bold stylization of the painters of ballet scenery, which one would otherwise be tempted to regard as the product of an overheated imagination, whereas really these people have merely kept their eyes open and reproduced what they have seen around them. How far removed the autumn of Archangel is from the scale of golds and reds of the autumns of Versailles, which are so delicately and subtly harmonious! This is a picture of two civilizations!

But as it stands in its wild and exaggerated simplicity, how beautiful it is! Almost in front of our Embassy, round a bad municipal statue, there is a large circle of small trees which I had never noticed in the ordinary way, but which has now taken on the splendours of a great mass of orange-red azaleas. . . . It is as though these poor little trees were trying to make up for their usual mediocrity by this firework display of colour, which is almost as ephemeral as a burst of rockets, and that before hiding themselves under the great white cloak they want to leave us the memory of this sparkling vision of springtime vegetation in a land of sunshine.

Archangel, Sunday 15th September 1918

Rumour has it that Tchaikovsky's government is going to resign at the beginning of the week. . . . The applause of a few shaggy *moujiks* who went by the name of '*zemstvos*' and met last Thursday will allow it to say that it is leaving after scoring a success!

In reality the mess is complete. . . . Tchaikovsky and his people have no authority, and the conflict with the English General Staff is getting worse in spite of the lectures addressed to both parties by the Ambassadors. . . . During the last few days the government, fearing a new journey up the White Sea, has been asking for a guard to watch over the palace. . . . The Ambassadors, wanting to be conciliatory, ask General Poole every day to give the order. . . . Every day Poole confirms by letter and by telephone that the necessary has been done . . . and still there is no guard watching over the portals of the Ministry . . . I was going to say, the phalanstery.

It has occasioned great anger among the Ambassadors, who do not want people to laugh at their beloved Tchaikovsky, but who can do nothing about it themselves. . . . They vituperate about the lack of discipline of Poole and the military in general, and are talking about applying sanctions. But the interested parties are not a bit worried, as they know that the only sanction will be a lunch-party the next day . . . the least nasty to be had in Archangel.

Archangel, Monday 16th September 1918

Rumours about the departure of the 'supreme government' are being confirmed. It will apparently be replaced by a Russian governor who it is supposed would have to take orders from the government which has just been formed in Samara.

The Ambassadors would like to keep their Tchaikovsky as the representative of the Constituent Assembly. Even though he may have no effectual power this might work, because he is rather decorative with his hoary beard, his white curls, his long frock-coat and his little skull-cap of purple silk. This dud Ribot[1] does quite well for ceremonial occasions and if the part he plays is restricted to this, it could be all right. But I think he is too cunning for that. Under his senile appearance he is an old fox, false and crafty, and as much of a dissimulator as all Russian revolutionaries who are used to living in secret and telling lies.

He gave further proof of this roguery when it was a question of arresting the leaders of the strike committee, an arrest which had been decided on in agreement with his government. They looked for them all over the place and couldn't find them anywhere . . . for the simple reason that they were in Tchaikovsky's own house.

Archangel, Tuesday 17th September 1918

Sanitary conditions are mediocre, and everyone is rather worried

[1] Presumably a reference to Alexandre Ribot, a French politician who was Minister of Finance, 1914–17; succeeded Briand as Prime Minister in March 1917; and was Foreign Minister from March to October 1917. He brought about a treaty of alliance with Russia in 1895.

by a sudden epidemic which the doctors have called "Spanish flu":
they are no better at naming an illness than at curing it, and it is
making serious ravages, particularly among the recently arrived
Americans.

From the Chancellery every day I hear the roll of drums beating
time for the march of a guard of honour and announcing a grim
ceremony, and I can see the procession approaching from behind a
group of trees clad in their autumnal gold: three or four lorries, each
carrying several coffins draped with a flag. . . . In this way, about
forty men have been buried during the last three days.

Archangel, Wednesday 18th September 1918

The government continues to announce every day that it is going
to resign, but it is careful not to do so.

Nevertheless it has communicated a plan to the Ambassadors
whereby a declaration explaining its departure is to be issued to
the people, together with a projected network of decrees with the
purpose of 'detaching' from the 'supreme government' all the
administrative organizations: they would then be placed under
the authority of the governor, who is supposed to wield power in
the name of the government of Samara. This is a Byzantine form of
red tape which is in true Russian tradition . . . the *chinovniks*[1] have
not changed.

What is to be feared is that all these rogues, who are revolutionaries
and Bolsheviks at heart, will divert us with their red tape in order
to gain time and stir up a popular movement whereby they will
seize the excuse to remain in power. Then they will claim that the
will of the Russian people has triumphed over the Allies.

Archangel, Thursday 19th September 1918

The officers of the English cruiser *Attentive* invited me on board
today. Their ward-room is very comfortably arranged: big leather
armchairs, a fireplace in the corner with a cheerful log fire, a leather-
covered bench round the hearth, and a table covered with books and
magazines—you would think you were in a cottage in old England.

[1] Functionary, clerk, or bureaucrat.

The ship's mascot is a bear cub, which has already grown quite powerful and drinks whisky by raising the bottle to its mouth with its two front paws, and then climbs about the rigging with the loutish look of a drunken sailor!

The English officers are always charming to us whenever we see them, but this does not prevent their General Staff from defending "with asperity" what it believes to be "the interests of Great Britain". Admiral Kemp seems particularly selfish: in the last ten days the English and French have been quarrelling over a rather beautiful ice-breaker, the *Svietigor*. . . . The British General Staff had at first allocated it to the French Navy, and landed them with all the bother of cleaning it and getting it back into good condition . . . now that this has been done, they are trying to re-appropriate it. . . . It's typically English.

When I got home I learnt of the death of Viscount Molono, who always saw things surprisingly clearly: I will always remember the dinner-party at the Japanese Embassy on the 1st January 1916, when he gauged the strength of Germany and the weakness of Russia so well, at a time when all the other people who were there were so gravely mistaken!

Archangel, Friday 20th September 1918

Tchaikovsky's government is recovering its hold and is becoming a real danger to the Allies.

In the most insulting way it has sacked the only man on whom we could rely, Admiral Ivanov, on the grounds that he was a friend of Major Chaplin, the organiser of the *coup d'état*. Now they claim to have replaced him with a certain Colonel Durov, who is looked on as an adventurer and a suspect person by all the people who are familiar with Russian military circles. The assistant to this undesirable person is said to be General Samarin, who is known to have betrayed Kornilov and has been ignored since then. I cannot understand how the Allies can give their assent to such appointments. As a result there is a great deal of discontent among the Russian officers, and it is being said tonight that two hundred of them have sent in their resignation.

The heads of missions are most indignant, and are talking of applying to these good people all those measures which they took good care not to use against the strike instigators of last week, saying that officers should above all obey the government. . . . It would be easy enough to answer that in that case they have only to obey the Bolsheviks of Moscow, because I fail to see how Tchaikovsky's government is more legitimate or has more claim to their obedience than that of Lenin. The big mistake which these officers made was precisely in submitting too fully and in obeying the régime of the revolution and of Kerensky. If they had kept their oath to the Emperor and fought fiercely from the start they would have made a clean sweep of the rabble and rallied all the decent people, and Russia would not be in the state she is in now. Moreover, one cannot entirely blame the Archangel officers, as most of them want to follow up this gesture by joining up as private soldiers in the French Legion. They thereby show that they are faithful to the Allies but refuse to serve under this hateful social-revolutionary party which has already brought Russia to the edge of the abyss. . . . After all, one cannot reproach an honest man for refusing to serve once again under more Kerenskys!

Archangel, Saturday 21st September 1918

The gusts of wind during these last days have swept away most of the leaves whose autumn tints I admired so much, and the birch trees raise their now completely white branches to a grey sky which is full of moisture. The blue mist which rose from the Dvina during the fine weather has changed into frozen rain which makes the pavements of loose boards very slippery. . . . Winter is drawing near, and its approach makes the situation most worrying. We cannot now hope to join up with the Czechs, in spite of the effort they are making along the Perm-Viatka line, where they seem to be concentrating their whole action, at the cost of losing ground in the South. . . . This at least is how our officers explain the abandoning of Kazan, the capture of which has been triumphantly announced in the Bolshevik communiqués.

Archangel, Sunday 22nd September 1918

Thiébaut has sent news from Stockholm of the imminent arrival of Commander Archen, who has managed to escape from Petrograd and from whom we will hear details of the situation in Russia.

In fact we only get news from Russians who manage to cross the lines by risking their lives and at the cost of terrible hardship. Everything they report is terrifying . . . the Bolsheviks have gone mad. Everywhere there are mass shootings of officers and great slaughter of bourgeois. One must no doubt make allowances for the Russian imagination, because on the other side they tell just as many stories about what happens here: the other day a worthy fellow arrived on foot from Petrograd to look for his family, because over there he had been told that the Allies had reduced Archangel to ashes and put the population to the sword. . . . Pray Heaven that the news from Petrograd will bear as little relation to the truth; but I am very much afraid that everything we hear is true, because the Bolsheviks have had a fright, and whether they be Russians or Jews . . . or both together . . . when these people are frightened they are terrible.

Archangel, Monday 23rd September 1918

The manœuvres of Tchaikovsky and his gang are taking shape just as I had foreseen. He now claims that as the Samara government has not got the Pan-Russian character he believed it had when he spoke of resigning, his decision to relinquish power is no longer relevant to the facts, and he resumes his duties. His government has taken advantage of this to play a still more socialist and Bol-shevizing game, to the extent that Durov, who was in fact chosen in place of Ivanov because of his left-wing opinions, is already in complete opposition to the people who called him to power. There is talk of his resignation. Much as his appointment was undesirable, so his departure would be regrettable, because all these changes create an impression of weakness and disastrous muddle.

Luckily we feel comforted by the latest news from France. The situation on the French front and particularly the successes in Macedonia and in Palestine allow one to hope that, in spite of everything, this accursed war will actually come to an end one day!

Archangel, Tuesday 24th September 1918

A charming dinner-party at the Steigers', who somehow discovered

the means of serving fresh tomatoes and slices of celery by way of
hors d'œuvres, which is prodigious in Archangel!

In the afternoon I went to buy some furs, which are still good
value although we are far removed from the prices which were being
asked a few years ago, when one paid from ten to twenty-five roubles
for a wolverine skin and from twenty-five to thirty roubles for a
beautiful white fox. Ermines from Pechora are worth twelve roubles
each, but they are very beautiful. White bear is very expensive:
the best examples sell for two thousand five hundred to three
thousand roubles, that is to say a little over two thousand francs.
They showed me one absolutely outstanding lot of ten sables for
which they are asking twenty thousand roubles, which it appears is
a bargain.

As a result of endless conferences, the heads of missions seem
to have come to an agreement with Tchaikovsky about the new
organization of the government.

Power will be exercised by a 'directory', instead of deriving from
a 'government'!! . . .

Tchaikovsky will be President and Durov who, after having been
considered undesirable by the Allies and having fallen out with
Tchaikovsky, is now judged by everyone to be indispensable and
will equally be part of the government. The other members are
chosen from the world of commerce or finance, and are men with
technical knowledge rather than politicians. In this there is at least
the appearance of an attempted agreement which will perhaps produce some results . . . if Tchaikovsky is acting in good faith; but I
cannot help feeling that this old man, in spite of his seeming to be
a worthy old gentleman, surpasses them all in roguery. He is a real
Slav, and our Ambassadors will always be swindled by him.

He has just done it again quite recently. . . . There was so much
talk of the Grand Duke Michael's presence in the outskirts of
Archangel that the Allies themselves ended by believing it. From all
sides our information services were receiving indications, confirma-
tory details, and cross-checkings which seemed most unforeseen and
confirming what we had heard from other sources. All this was so
cleverly done that it seemed practically certain that the Grand
Duke had been able to go into hiding somewhere quite near
Archangel. The Ambassadors who had been alerted carried the
affair to its limits in order to get the Grand Duke to go abroad, as
much to set people's minds at rest as for his own safety. Up against

a brick wall, Tchaikovsky was forced to explain. He produced a disgraceful police report, which was as badly drawn up by his officials as the first-hand accounts were cleverly presented by his spies. . . . The report proved that the whole thing was a thoroughly put-up affair, and when pressed by M. Noulens Tchaikovsky ended by admitting it himself! This is a typically Russian business, which shows that the genius for police intrigue is as strong in this sub-prefecture as it was before in the capital of the Tsars.

Archangel, Thursday 26th September 1918

I made an expedition to the monastery of Saint Michael, up the river at the entrance to the town, which is rather amusing with its stone outer wall and its little squat corner towers which are pink and surmounted by flame-coloured capstones and look like big mushrooms.

The church has a certain air of distinction with its five bulbous domes and its detached bell-tower surmounted by a spire. An archway below this tower forms the entrance to the convent. The whole effect is amusing, but it hasn't got the character of the Vologda churches.

There is a religious museum where they have collected together some ikons, objects made of walrus ivory, gold vessels, and some church ornaments. The best things there are the ancient textiles representing saints in the Byzantine style, embroidered in gold on a wine-coloured ground, with inscriptions in Slavonic characters.

Archangel, Friday 27th September 1918

The French battalion which had come here for a rest after its success at Obozerskaya has left again for the front lines, where the Americans have done nothing during its absence. It would seem therefore that our men will be expected to make a fresh effort.

It is certainly time to act, because winter is approaching. . . . On the other hand it does seem that the Czech retreat is not purely strategic as one had hoped: they have been waiting for help for such a long time that they must be getting bored—and after all, they too are Slavs!

But one must realize that they have to deal with adversaries who have been more or less organized by the Germans, and who have nothing in common with the red hordes of three months ago. We are now feeling the full impact of the mistake which the Allies made in not hurrying. Where before a battalion would have sufficed, today a regiment would have difficulty in succeeding. The Bolsheviks have got used to the idea of fighting against Allied soldiers and they resist, whereas in the beginning they were seized with panic and could only think of abandoning everything. In this land of fantasy, one must appeal to the imagination before anything else. Intervention as I visualized it should have been sudden and irresistible: it would have had incalculable results and would have cost practically nothing. Expeditions in small doses constitute a campaign just like any other one, since we are facing the soft Russian mass which takes the blows without being broken. It was not a Russian campaign like this which I had in mind when I hoped the Allies would come to Archangel.

Archangel, Saturday 28th September 1918

Tchaikovsky's swindling continues. The Ambassadors had come to an agreement with him yesterday evening on the plan for organizing the governing power at Archangel; but he came today to tell them that he had *forgotten*(?!) to mention the existence of a 'legislative council' as well as an 'executive directory'. This is naturally composed of all the former ministers whom we wanted to get rid of. Everything has got to be gone through again; but the patience of the Allies is limitless, and they think that "the thing will work".

Durov, the future Governor, on the other hand seems wiser: in order to get General Samarin accepted (whose past record has made him hated in military circles), he has chosen as his assistant a certain M. de Bockhart, a former magistrate who appears to be an intelligent and honest man. Lubersac and the English, who are otherwise very hostile towards Durov, approve of this choice.

Archangel, Sunday 29th September 1918

The good news of the last few days makes me hope that in spite of everything, the end is in sight. If Bulgaria makes peace a collapse will follow, as it certainly seems that on the French front German resistance has been broken.

Because of this, the evening organized for the benefit of the Slavo-British Legion was very gay . . . in fact too gay, as the English officers made too free with the whisky. . . .

The honours were done by a certain Baroness Accurti: she is a sister of the Koraly who married the Duke of Leuchtenberg, and here she plays the Egeria to General Poole. This far too much publicized affair is the subject of a great deal of gossip. 'Poupoule' is in fact very faded, but she must have the fiery temperament of Polish Jewesses and has awakened the somewhat extinguished ardours of the good General, who cannot have been used to such peppery fare in respectable Albion.

Archangel, Monday 30th September 1918

The communiqués from the Polar front, following the example of those from more important theatres of operation, are favourable. . . . The French and the Americans yesterday attacked the Bolshevik lines along the railway and advanced about forty *versts*. We have no details and I only hope that this success will not have cost too dear.

Archangel, Tuesday 1st October 1918

Several naval officers have arrived in the last few days, having come from Petrograd on foot. They are in a state of utter destitution and give terrifying accounts of what is happening there. The Bolsheviks had refused them the right to work and had removed from them any chance they had of not dying of hunger by driving them out of the docks, where they were trying to get work as stevedores. They were even forbidden to sell newspapers in the streets. Russia is always the same, and the plight of these unfortunate people reminds one of that of the 'outlaws' in the time of Paul I, to whom exile in Siberia seemed like Paradise!

Archangel, Wednesday 2nd October 1918

The armistice with Bulgaria is the beginning of the end. Turkey, having been beaten in Palestine, will not be long in following the movement, the more so as many Turks were only dragged into the war unwillingly. This time I am beginning to believe in victory.

I hope that the Allies will realize the interest we have in encouraging the satellites of Germany to leave her orbit, by imposing just and moderate peace conditions. The triumph of force should only serve to impose justice; that is really the most striking condemnation of war, because one comes back to the point of departure and, although being in a position to exert force, one must nevertheless act according to justice.

Unfortunately the victors are always intoxicated and lose all idea of what is fair and sensible. In this way Spalaikovich caused a real scandal in the Ambassador's house, where he went in a fit of furious temper because Saint-Sauveur, when congratulating him on the victory—achieved by the French army of course—added: "It's a good thing, Bulgaria will have gone to war and got nothing out of it." . . . As for Spalaikovich, he wanted to annihilate the whole of the Bulgarian race: to him, victory means pillaging everything, violating everything, and burning everything; and this old *comitadji* was tearing his hair out at not being able to join in the party. If I can judge by their representative, the Serbs are no longer thinking of the rights of peoples, which they previously advocated so loudly. The rights of peoples are good enough for reclaiming the so-called Serbian territories which are under other sovereignty; they are not good enough when it is a question of preventing Serbia from dividing Bulgaria up at her convenience.

I hope that the Great Powers will not listen to these agitators and will establish peace once and for all in this Balkan hornet's nest, and take advantage of the fact that Russia will not be there to muddle everything up.

The armistice conditions of General Franchet d'Esperey make me feel fairly hopeful in this regard. He has been hard—harder than the Germans at Bucharest—because he insists on the departure from Bulgaria of the German diplomatic missions, whereas Sainte-

306

Aulaire is still in Rumania. But he does not impose on the Bulgarian nation humiliations which a people cannot forgive, and if we are reasonable it will be possible to forget it all in a few years.

At last an Embassy bag has arrived. . . . I had had no news since the last one on the 16th August, as the one which arrived on the 25th August only brought some letters which had been soaked in sea water. . . . They really are abandoning us too completely, and it is inadmissible that no courier should reach us, given the amount of ships which come here.

Archangel, Thursday 3rd October 1918

The situation here is still the same, and it is impossible to follow the ups and downs of Tchaikovsky's gang. What is more serious is that from the point of view of operations against the Bolsheviks anything decisive is still a long way off . . . but winter is closing in. Colonel Donop, with whom I talked at length, doubts whether we will be able to reach Vologda before the bad weather begins: he fears the disastrous effects of the so-called democratic policy which the Americans have imposed on us here.

It has reached the point where our troops have been deprived of food supplies during the last few days because the stokers of the ships on the Dvina have gone on strike. When efforts were made to force them to return to work they complained to Tchaikovsky and Francis, who excused them in the name of the principle of freedom of labour. . . . This would be permissible in peace-time, but at a time of war it goes beyond the limits.

In the same way, the Allies have not as yet established their right to requisition. The peasants are piling up their products and refusing to sell, while waiting for prices to rise still further. I quite understand that it is repugnant to us to use the same methods as the Bolsheviks who, by shooting a few *moujiks*, were able at a moment's notice to collect together processions of heavily laden carts in every village. But there is a big difference between this and letting ourselves be cheated by the Russian peasant, who is the most crafty and grasping of all peasants, and we too often forget that there is a war! But as long as we continue to make concessions to the *guilty Bolsheviks* who constitute the *social-revolutionaries*, we shall be obliged to tolerate everything.

Major Archen, who managed to escape from Petrograd through Finland, arrived today from Stockholm.

What he has to tell is beyond all imagination. At the time of their rise to power the Bolsheviks were Utopians, humanitarians, and generous-minded visionaries: today they are raving madmen. Their criminal folly first manifested itself towards the beginning of July at the time of the execution of Admiral Chastny in Moscow. It reached its full violence after the murder of Mirbach and the monstrous crime of Ekaterinburg. Alas, the epidemic shows no sign of weakening, and everything is to be feared for our unfortunate companions who have remained in Russia with the same confidence which I would have felt myself.

Over one hundred and fifty French people have been shut up in Peter-and-Paul, where they have been for four days without food and subjected to the worst treatment. Every night, below the windows of the dungeon into which they were crammed, the Bolsheviks shot some unfortunate officers who were accused of being counter-revolutionaries, and the sinister sounds of the shooting could be heard from the Embassy itself.

Things are even more atrocious at Kronstadt. They had deported a convoy of about three thousand arrested officers to the island: the sailors immediately started shooting them down without any form of trial. Tovarich Posern, the Assistant to the War Commissariat, although a true Bolshevik, did at least go there to try and prevent the massacre when warned by telephone. Someone who saw him on his return told Archen that he was pale and unnerved, and he admitted that he could never have imagined any sight so ghastly as the one he had just seen.

All the former officers have been obliged to come and give themselves up, and were at once arrested. There are said to be nearly forty thousand of them. Would they not have done better to defend themselves?

Mass arrests are taking place, and at a moment's notice the streets are blockaded at both ends by squads of Red Guards. All passers-by who happen to be between the blockades are apprehended, searched and interrogated, and immediately incarcerated if they can be suspected of being counter-revolutionaries, or if they are of French or English nationality. Darcy, who had been arrested at the beginning of the Terror and then released, was re-arrested during one of these hauls when he was on his way to dine with the Scaveniuses. He was shut up in the Fortress: from there he was transferred to Moscow, where he has been accused of fomenting a plot against the revolution with the aid of some French officers, several of whom are also in prison.

Major Archen cannot praise the Scaveniuses too highly. Scavenius' determination is wonderful, and as for Mme Scavenius, he can only speak of her with emotion. She was able to obtain permission to go and visit our compatriots in the prisons and she does not hesitate to go there almost every day, in spite of the horror of what she sees. The French colony, which is hard to please, really worships her. The Ambassador has requested the Cross of the Legion of Honour for her, and it gave me real pleasure to send this telegram myself. I thought of the time when I was looked at with disapproval as being one of the frequenters of the Danish Legation, and when some people went so far as to use the word "Boches" when speaking of the Scaveniuses, simply because they were sensible and tried to show us the true situation as it really was at that moment.

The Ambassador has made the same request for Armand de Saint-Sauveur, who has shown himself to be courageous, active and resourceful. He keeps up communications between the various French elements by means of his motorcar, which he has only managed to keep by a prodigious effort. He has been arrested several times but has always succeeded in getting out of it.

The Embassy is guarded on the outside by the Bolsheviks, but thanks to Scavenius' determination and the protection of the Danish flag, they have not dared to break into it up to now. Nevertheless, they decided to make a raid on it just like they did at the English Embassy; but the French officers who occupied it were determined to defend themselves to the end, and not to let themselves be taken alive on French territory. On the night when the raid was due to take place, Saint-Sauveur went to join them to take part in the fight and share their fate. The Bolsheviks were warned by Scavenius of the decision of the French, and they did not dare to make the raid which they had planned; they even let our officers go to the burial of Commander Cromie, who was killed defending the English Embassy, without daring to stop them.

This proves how regrettable it is that nobody dared to stand up to the Bolsheviks. After the murder of the English naval attaché they were in great fear that England would retaliate strongly. . . . One of them said to Scavenius, when he mentioned this possibility: "Whether it is the Allies or the Germans who are the winners, we know that in any case we will be shot."

But since the beginning of the revolution all the forces of order have remained passive . . . the terrorized bourgeois submit to all the demands of their tyrants. In order to ensure their obedience the Bolsheviks have drawn up lists of hostages, who are to be put to death in the case of any attempt against the leaders. Alas, the Grand Dukes are first on the list: Uritsky, who has since been killed, told Princess Paley this in the most brutal terms when she went to beg him to set the Grand Duke Paul free.

The disorder in the town is indescribable, and the streets are not kept clean. The Bolsheviks have authorized one day of pillage every week, when everyone has the right to go into the houses of the bourgeois and take what they please.

In Moscow the situation is just as bad. The Consul and General Lavergne are still in the American Consulate, into which they only just had time to rush before being arrested. But the house is surrounded and the Bolshevik Peters, the probable successor to Chicherin, talks of nothing less than smoking them out. They have only a little food left and there is the greatest difficulty in getting anything to them.

Everywhere, the Bolsheviks are all the fiercer for having been frightened. From their secret telegrams which we have been able to decipher, one feels that they considered themselves lost at the time of the Allied Landing at Archangel and the Czech advance . . . their gangs were fleeing everywhere and their position was desperate. It was panic, to the extent that everyone in Petrograd was expecting deliverance from one day to the next, and that a newspaper was able without any difficulty to ask for the list of Bolsheviks to be shot by the Allies on the day of their entry into the capital.

Major Archen travelled through Finland to get to Stockholm, making part of the journey on foot and there, on the other hand, things are going fairly well. There are hardly any Germans left, and the Finns do not allow those who remain to impose on them. General Mannerheim himself, whom he saw in Stockholm, does not hide his real feelings: he says that he only worked with the

Germans because the first thing to be done for his country was to get rid of the Reds, and there was no one else to whom he could turn for help.

At the present time I am convinced that something could be done in this direction and that in his country, among his compatriots and among many Scandinavians, we would find substantial help in our fight against the Bolsheviks . . . those scourges of humanity.

Archangel, Saturday 5th October 1918

I have given up bothering to know whether we have a government here or not. . . . In any case, it does not much matter.

Sanitary conditions are worrying. The epidemic of 'Spanish flu' is still spreading, but fortunately as the cases increase, so apparently does their seriousness diminish. In four days, two hundred men on board the *Amiral Aube* fell ill. Nursing is made difficult by the lack of medicine, alcohol being the only remaining one which is in fact effective. I searched in vain in the chemist shops for permangamate or phenic acid for gargling, which has been advised as a preventive. There is also a great deal of scurvy, which is not surprising as neither fresh vegetables nor fruit are to be found.

Clément Simon has returned from a short trip of about a week on the Dvina. I meant to go with him, but there was too much work and I had to give up my plan, and I regret having missed such a unique chance of seeing country to which I hope never to return.

He is very pessimistic about the conduct of military operations and has the impression that the English are not up to the situation. If they had known how to tackle it, we would have been at Kotlas long ago. For the moment, the General Staff seems to have given up the idea, and Clément Simon came back in one of the gun-boats which the English have sent back here on the pretext that the Dvina might freeze up and that it is definitely too late to do anything. Needless to say this retreat has had a deplorable effect, as they have the tactlessness to do it in a very apparent manner, by bringing the four gun-boats back all at the same time and parading them in broad daylight in front of the riverbank population, who are panic-stricken at the thought that the Allies are leaving and the Bolsheviks going to come back.

Archangel, Tuesday 26th November 1918

The situation here is always the same. And yet Admiral Kolchak's *coup d'état* in Siberia has rather disturbed people, and old Tchaikovsky said to me: "It is disgraceful that at the hour of the victory of justice, it should be force which triumphs in Russia." He forgets that if we had only had justice without force, we would not be celebrating victory today.

Besides, he will certainly have to resign himself to seeing order restored by a *"coup d'état"*. Russia does not proceed in any other way, and what else are the February revolution and that of the Bolsheviks if they are not *"coups d'état"*, or more exactly "attacks by force"?

Admiral Kolchak is by way of being a strong man. It is he who, when the sailors tried to disarm him, threw his sword of honour which he had received during the war against Japan into the sea from the top of the bridge, telling them to go and fetch it.

I hope that he will be able to retain his power and administer the knout which will be so healthy for all these fanatics: the nature of the Russians is such that they will be delighted.

Archangel, Wednesday 27th November 1918

I am alarmed by all the news which is reaching us from France. It seems that we are trying to impose useless humiliations on Germany. The wish to do so is perhaps understandable, but it is very dangerous for the future. Napoleon's shameful conduct towards the Queen of Prussia cost us Waterloo, and perhaps Sedan. A real gentleman strikes down his adversary, but he salutes him once he is down.

What surprises me most is that the English should do the same as us, because it is so uncharacteristic of them. The ceremonial with which they surrounded the surrender of the German fleet is hardly worthy of them: one may take ships, but one does not humiliate officers and crews who have fought courageously.

But what is still more ridiculous is the resolution passed by the French parliament proclaiming that "President Wilson and the Allied heads of state have deserved well of humanity". . . . In what way are our members of parliament qualified to speak in the name of humanity? It is quite bad enough that they speak in the name of France. I could have understood if the French parliament had passed a resolution that the heads of state in question had deserved well of France, but it is ridiculous for it to answer for humanity. . . . What do the negroes of the Congo think of it? . . . or even my neighbours the Samoyedes of Novaya Zemblya? Not to mention the Germans, Austrians, Turks, etc., who also form part of this same humanity, and who have good reason not to share the opinion of our parliamentarians on the heads of state who have beaten them.

All these emphatic declarations run the risk of calling forth too facile answers, and I laughed a good deal today when I read a paragraph by Lenin in *Pravda*, on the triumph of the "President of the Dollar Republic, the Republic of the electric chair and Stock Exchange swindles". . . .

Archangel, Sunday 8th December 1918

This morning we received a telegram from Paris, worded thus: "It would be advisable to attach M. de Robien to Clément Simon's mission to Prague, with the temporary rank of official agent. Will you ask M. de Robien to come to Paris as soon as possible?"

The telegram arrived a bit too late for me to leave in the *Stephen*. The Ambassador therefore replied that he would take me with him, but he asked if he could keep me to advise him on Russian affairs.

I must admit that I was very flattered at having been chosen for the first mission to enemy country. There will be useful work to be done in Prague in curbing the ambitions of the Czechs, because if we let these *nouveaux riches* have their way, we will be sowing the seeds of a new war in this part of Europe.

Paris, Saturday 11th January 1919

The grey quays of Boulogne . . . Englishmen, and Chinese. German prisoners are at work, guarded by Territorials. My first sight of France after such a long time is a disillusionment to me.

Departure at eleven o'clock in a special carriage put at the disposal of the Ambassador.

On the way—English camps. On the outskirts of Amiens there are traces of bombardments, trenches and barbed wire entanglements.

Arrival in Paris at six o'clock. At the Gare du Nord I am struck by the lack of order . . . and yet I have come from Russia. There are no taxis, but I have no difficulty in bribing a military lorry which is on the prowl and which, in return for a good tip, loads up my luggage and packing-cases!

INDEX

Lenin, Vladimir Ilyich, 36, 40, 65, 76, 79, 87, 88, 91, 134, 145, 148, 165, 173, 174, 178, 191, 192, 194, 195, 198, 199, 252, 274, 293, 300, 313

Lindley, Sir Francis, 240, 288

Lubersac, Marquis de, 73, 148, 254, 293, 304

Lvov, President of the Holy Synod, 107, 110

Lvov, Prince, 20, 88, 264

Marchand, René, 255

Maria Pavlovna, Grand Duchess, 37, 43

Maria Pavlovna II, Grand Duchess, 81, 82, 115

Mariinsky Palace, 50, 82

Mariinsky Theatre, 219, 260, 264

Mensheviks, 147, 227

Michael, Grand Duke, 20, 104

Milyukov, P. N., 20, 35, 36, 40, 44, 47, 50, 58, 177, 242, 282

Mirbach, Count, 204, 218, 245, 251, 252, 259, 260, 267, 272, 280, 308

Moutet, 33, 58

Municipal Council, 115, 134; of Petrograd, 145

Muraviev, 34, 38, 144

Nationalization of banks, 183

Nicholas II, Tsar, 15, 18, 19, 21–25, 28, 35, 41, 60, 74, 79, 94, 95, 121, 131, 134, 144, 158, 164, 171, 173, 177, 191, 195, 216, 235, 249, 256, 262, 267, 277, 291; abdication of, 20, 35, 125; assassination of, 279, 280, 281, 293

Nicholas Michael, Grand Duke, 34, 35, 37, 54, 116, 253, 254, 264, 277, 279–281

Nicholas Nikolaievich, Grand Duke, 46, 179, 226, 265

Niessel, General, 148, 170, 190, 210, 217, 232, 236

Nihilists, 22, 36

Nostitz, Countess, 43, 46, 78, 238; General, 57

Noulens, Joseph, 64, 82, 83, 107, 117, 170–172, 186, 193, 194, 202, 211, 217, 223, 240, 248, 251–253, 256, 259, 264, 273, 276, 277, 280, 283, 284, 290, 292, 303, 313

Novya Jizn, 147

Novye Vremya, 84, 109

Obolensky, Princess, 36, 218

Officers, submission of, 18

Olga, Grand Duchess, 19, 101

Orthodox Church, 220, 258, 271

Paléologue, Maurice, 15, 20, 26, 33, 35, 36, 39, 41, 46, 54, 57, 90, 100, 209, 242, 243

Paley, Irene, 81

Paley, Nathalie, 81

Paley, Princess, 81, 104, 142, 153, 216, 225, 254, 310

Paley, Vladimir, 43, 81, 82, 104, 225, 226, 254, 265

Paul, Grand Duke, 74, 81, 104, 115, 142, 153, 154, 173, 225, 253, 254, 310

'personal labour corps', 218

Peter-and-Paul Fortress, 17, 18, 21, 33, 76, 88, 102, 116, 132, 133, 134, 136, 152, 153, 159, 160, 173, 190, 192, 193, 308, 309

Petrograd, evacuation of, 103, 104, 105

Petrov, 239, 240

Pingaud, 39, 169, 182, 196, 202, 278, 284, 285

Plekhanov, 33, 36

Pogroms, 214

Poincaré, 241, 242, 243, 247